Turning
on the System

TURNING
ON
THE SYSTEM

War in the Philadelphia
Public Schools

BY *Henry S. Resnik*

PANTHEON BOOKS

A DIVISION OF RANDOM HOUSE, NEW YORK

Library of Congress Catalog Card Number: 69-20186

Manufactured in the United States of America by
The Haddon Craftsmen, Inc., Scranton, Pa.

2 4 6 8 9 7 5 3

FIRST PRINTING

This book is dedicated to three teachers
who made learning possible:
Ivan Feidel, Richard Tyre, and Oscar Sachs.

Acknowledgments

I WISH to thank all those generous souls in Philadelphia who welcomed me to their schools, classrooms, conference rooms, offices, and homes while I was collecting information for this book. They are too numerous to name, but for a year and a half they helped me to feel that Philadelphia was my second home.

My research was supported by grants from the Thomas Skelton Harrison Foundation and the Rockefeller Foundation. I am grateful to Mr. Peter Hearn for his help in obtaining the former of these.

Thanks also to Tom Rivers and Jon Eisen for their broad editorial insights, and to Mel Rosenthal and Rebecca, my love, for their meticulous attention to the finer points.

Contents

Introduction

I WENT to Philadelphia in the fall of 1967 intending to write a magazine article about the newly opened Pennsylvania Advancement School, an independent curriculum laboratory set up by the Philadelphia public school system that was already being heralded as a radical departure from traditional education and a model for progressive change. While visiting the Advancement School, however, I discovered that the city's entire public school system was then in the middle of what some authorities were calling an educational revolution. I wanted to see what this revolution was all about, and I spent the next one and a half years observing it. The subject of this book is what I learned in that time.

Philadelphia was special because it seemed to be well on the way, more than any other American city, to coping successfully with the failures of urban education. The movement for educational reform held enormous promise, and at the beginning the so-called revolutionaries leading it talked of completely "humanizing" the system. Alienation and *anomie* would be supplanted by involvement and creativity. Everyone in the system, fulfilled by new roles and attitudes, would be "turned on." It was a magnificent dream.

Educational innovators had already had a go at reforming American schools during the "progressive" era of the 1930's; but now, it seemed, these earlier efforts would be a mere warm-up. The structure of American society was weaker than it had been even then—the system was collapsing, the country seemed ready for different answers. And the time had come for a renaissance of truly "human" values.

I never expected that these values would flourish without opposition, but the strife I encountered in Philadelphia was so much greater than anything I anticipated that for a while it dazed me. Moreover, though I was convinced at the outset that I was on the side of justice—I was for the humanists and libertarians, of course—my vision later began to blur. I saw too much violence committed in the name of humanity to believe that the word really meant anything.

Readers of this book will find no clear answers to the tragedy of our country and its schools; I realized early in my period of observation that I would find none. I latched on to people who struck me as courageous dreamers and dedicated humanitarians whenever I found them, then stayed around to watch and hope— and even, at times, to join them in their fight. But I found no magic solutions.

I have not tried to draw a comprehensive picture of Philadelphia's innovative programs, having failed to mention scores of programs that would deserve attention in a more thorough study. Nor can I claim to have presented a totally "objective" account either of the programs I did see or of what happened in Philadelphia during the time of my observation. Although I strove to be well informed about what was going on in the public schools, I undertook the project with certain biases. In fact, the real subject of this book, as I have already said, is what I have learned —about education, about social change, about humanity, and about urban life, during a critical period in history.

I. *Battle Plan*

THIS IS A BOOK about a year or so of civil war in the city of Philadelphia at a time when most American cities were disintegrating, a time—the mid-1960's—when America had run out of dreams. America is a nation that tends to scoff at dreams; but the country had actually been dreaming far too long. The great vision of opportunity and wealth for all, the magnificent ideal of freedom —these dreams could no longer hold America together. The romance was over; the lies behind the dreams were beginning to glare in the ever-present media floodlights. War was inevitable.

The war was only occasionally violent, though there were at times deaths and casualties. Guns were rarely used; contracts, salaries, threats, strikes, votes, and sit-ins were the customary weapons, and most of the major battles took place in the relative calm of public meetings, official conferences, courtrooms, and voting booths. But it was war nevertheless. There were many fronts and leaders, a kaleidoscope of shifting alliances, loyalties, and ideologies. They fought the war on most of the campuses and in all the big cities of America, the same loose confederations kept alive by the miracle of modern communications, surviving on air waves and printer's ink. All sides wanted power, freedom, and justice; all had some idea of what was right.

As might have been expected, the schools were the scene of epic battles. It was so easy to say in the mid-1960's that the schools were "not doing their job" and to believe that one knew what their job was supposed to be.

At one time—in the "prewar" period, the years of growing discontent—the Philadelphia public school system was among the worst in the country (though the same could have been said of almost any large urban school system). It was the usual story of neglect and corruption, unresponsiveness and top-heavy bureaucracy, racism and oppression. Philadelphia's dropout rate was the highest of the nation's ten largest cities; nearly a quarter of the buildings were antiquated firetraps; two thousand teachers out of a total of twelve thousand were permanent substitutes without full accreditation; segregation and inequality were widespread; pupil achievement was far below national norms. And the school bureaucracy was probably even more rigid than most. It was dominated by one man, a semi-legendary figure named Add Anderson, whose main goals for the system seemed to be efficiency and economy. In the eyes of Philadelphia's social revolutionaries, Add Anderson was the wicked czar who had to be overthrown before "meaningful" change could take place.

As a growing interest in schools brought the iniquities of the Anderson administration to light, a groundswell of educational reform, inspired by extensive changes in the city government (during the late fifties and early sixties, Philadelphia had gained a reputation as one of the most reform-minded cities in America), began to rise in protest. Finally, in 1965, a citizens' coalition succeeded in overthrowing the incumbent school administration by pushing through a home rule charter that gave greater fiscal control to the Board of Education—which had been fiscally dependent on the state legislature—and established a smaller Board (nine, instead of fifteen members) selected by more equitable methods than before. While the new structure was certainly an improvement on the old, the real achievement of the coalition was a new Board eager for change. Richardson Dilworth, the city's crusading mayor from 1955 to 1962, became president of the Board, and he was chiefly responsible for the Board's success in initiating a complete revitalization of the school system. A silver-haired, seventy-year-old aristocrat, Dilworth had a penchant for bluntness that alienated many people and charmed others, but his admirers saw him as a paragon of humanity, grace, intelligence, and political skill. Long after others had fallen in battle, he remained one of the great fighters.

The new Board took office in December 1965, and at the end of a year it had ample grounds to boast, in a widely circulated report, that "probably no large school system has ever moved so far, so fast, in so many ways as has Philadelphia during the past twelve months." This was supported in the fall of 1967 by a federally funded study which claimed that Philadelphia was in the midst of "the most dramatic reform in urban education since World War II." Some of the most important advances were: a six-year capital program that would eventually renovate or replace all the city's school buildings; the beginning of conversion to a K-4-4-4 system (kindergarten–four years elementary–four years intermediate–four years high school); kindergarten for all the city's school children, as opposed to the seventy percent of 1964–65; a rise in the operating budget from $152 million in 1965 to $208 million in 1967–68, with new sources of revenue to support it; and a long list of innovative programs. Less measurable, but equally significant, were the televising of board meetings, a manifestation of openness to public concern, and the recruitment of noneducators for key school positions—city planners for a newly created office of planning, and a leading accountant from Price, Waterhouse for the budget office—which Dilworth saw as desperately needed infusions of new blood.

Philadelphia's superintendent of schools, who had taken office in 1964, bridged the old and new Boards of Education, and while his administration was responsible for numerous reforms, he was not, in the words of one of the new team, "the visionary leader we wanted." In September 1966 he reached an amicable agreement with the Board not to continue in office—the manner of his departure was so genteel, in fact, that he was kept on as a paid consultant for twenty-nine months. The door was now open for a superintendent more closely attuned to the Board's purposes and style, and after much searching, Dilworth decided that Mark R. Shedd, then superintendent of schools in Englewood, New Jersey, was the best man for the job. While the vote was not unanimous, the Board agreed. Shedd was hired in November 1966, his appointment to be effective September 1, 1967.

The news was greeted by considerable skepticism. Englewood, the critics argued (they were not yet actual enemies), had 28,000 people, 4,000 school children, and 6 schools; Philadelphia had

2,000,000 people, 275,000 school children, and 280 schools; Shedd was only forty years old, and he had been superintendent in Englewood for less than three years. It all added up to an alarming lack of experience.

Board members defended the new superintendent, however, citing his ability to handle difficult problems in a school system that was virtually a miniature Philadelphia. He had integrated the Englewood system, they pointed out, and he had also established ungraded primary schools. Dilworth called him "a young man with the kind of energy and drive who can move our school system ahead the way it must be moved." Another Board member described him as a "cool young tiger." But the doubts persisted. "It's a little bit like picking Colonel Eisenhower to head the invasion forces in Africa," commented one observer. "Who the hell had ever heard of him?"

According to many observers, Shedd began to rally his forces long before he took office, even though his predecessor's term did not end officially until August 1967. Working as a consultant to the Board two or three days a week until the conclusion of his own term in Englewood, Shedd visited Philadelphia schools, talked with teachers and principals, got to know the system thoroughly, and recommended changes as he went along. He advised a wide-ranging reorganization of administrative staff—was instrumental, for example, in moving a successful black principal to an all-white high school and putting several young men into district offices. He established ties with various community leaders who he hoped would become key figures in the movement for change. In cooperation with a group of parents, he helped to direct the renovation of a dead-end school in West Philadelphia. He spent several evenings each week at meetings of community groups from which the top school administrators had once been imperially distant. He hired a neighborhood corporation, formerly a street gang, to direct orientation programs for incoming teachers. He invited the experimental North Carolina Advancement School to make its new home in Philadelphia, hoping that it, too, would be a major agent of change in the school system. He planned the first moves toward decentralization.

Shedd was a persuasive speech-maker as well, and he seemed

to relish meeting touchy situations head-on. Addressing a group of teachers, he quoted the rebellious lyrics of folk-rock songs. "Something is happening," he repeated from a song by Bob Dylan, "and you don't know what it is, do you, Mr. Jones?" They were all the Mr. Joneses Bob Dylan was talking about, he said. They must all find out what *was* happening and do something about it. At a workshop on human relations, he prodded the chairmen of school human relations committees by suggesting that, rather than smooth over racial tensions, they act as catalysts in bringing those situations into the open, that rather than ignore them, they create a climate for dealing with them, honestly. Wherever he went, he attacked the breakdowns of bureaucracy and the evils of the system.

"Responsiveness" and "relevance" were the key terms Shedd used to describe what he wanted in his administration; "humanization" and "revolution" were almost as familiar. "Meaningful dialogues" were encouraged; "gut issues" were to be faced. One of Shedd's favorite phrases was "turned on"—most frequently used to describe what kids in school ought to be but weren't.

At the conclusion of a two-day conference of teachers early in September 1967—just after he had formally assumed office—Shedd spoke to the assembled staff and offered the most complete statement of his goals to date. Underlining the failures of public education, he urged the teachers to look for a change in attitudes, particularly in terms of what they expected of themselves and their students. More specific, however, was his program for decentralization and community control, by then among the issues of widest concern in the battle of the schools. The recommendations included: a "talent pool" from which principals could select new teachers, rather than arbitrary placement of teachers by a central office; decentralization of the budget; discretionary funds for principals that would make possible the rapid acquisition of special supplies and materials; a semi-autonomous model school district that would encourage community participation in planning and operations; a fund from which principals could draw in order to institute special projects in their schools, with grants as high as $12,000 or $15,000; and a special fund for teachers that would grant up to $300 for individual projects.

All these proposals were in line with Shedd's desire to cast the central administration more in the role of a foundation than of a military headquarters, and, with the exception of the model school district, all were realized, if only to a limited extent, within a year. The teacher grant program, certainly an immediate and effective symbol of Shedd's sincerity, had distributed a total of $15,000 to more than seventy teachers by the end of November 1967.

The other major aspect of Shedd's proposed campaign was the "affective"—contrasted with purely "cognitive"—curriculum, in which the emphasis would be on social dynamics and the cultivation of self-awareness and sensitivity, with broader use of the humanities, art, music, dance, and drama as a means of developing a sense of human potential and identity. Shedd had already created a central office of affective development. During the summer there had been several workshops in sensitivity-training for administrative staff, and these frequently jarring confrontations were fast becoming one of the most controversial innovations of the new regime.

Indeed, "affective curriculum" was merely another term for one of the major ideological beachheads of the urban war. Part of the trouble with America, according to an ever-increasing group of insurrectionists, was the "dehumanization" that was the inevitable product of all the country's major institutions. Men were mere numbers in the great IBM machine of a supertechnological society. Huge governments, huge corporations, and huge educational systems seemed to be involved in a conspiracy to rob man of his individuality. The affective-curriculum wing of the Shedd campaign was similar, in fact, to the human-potential movement that gathered under such banners as Esalen, Daytop, and Encounter throughout the country.

Finally, Shedd called for a new professionalism that would make teaching a meaningful activity in itself, rather than a rung on the ladder to an administrative career. The new professionalism would develop creativity and individual initiative; it would bring an end to the traditional teacher's role of isolated supervisor, closed off from the world both intellectually and physically by four confining walls. Shedd admitted that his plan resembled Utopia, but

he emphasized the process of change as the important factor—
and the time had come for that process to begin.

This, then, was Shedd's program for what he often referred to
as an educational revolution, and at the beginning no one
doubted that he would fight hard to bring it about. To the old
guard and the conservatives of all ages, he was more than a
young tiger—he was a fire-breathing dragon. But while Shedd's
eloquent statements of his goals already had polarized those
urban elements who had an interest in the schools, the battle
had only just begun. It was one thing to talk revolution, quite
another to make it happen. And the urban warfare of the 1960's
required of its leaders unlimited tactical inventiveness—the only
factor one could count on in a battle was chaos.

At the start, Shedd seemed to be winning. The scuttle-butt
from the school administration building at 21st Street and Benjamin Franklin Parkway offered a wealth of scandal. It was common knowledge, for example, that Shedd's emphasis on responsiveness was chiefly directed towards the needs of the city's
blacks—virtually unheard of in a system that had been dominated for generations by whites. In addition, Shedd had recruited
a team of talented assistants—many from Harvard, where he had
taken his doctorate—who amounted to a full-scale youth movement. Bright, pretty girls and young men who knew their facts
now inhabited the second floor at 21st Street, where gray, middle-
aged faces had been the rule only a few years earlier. Shedd was
building, in effect, a second, highly personalized administration
and quietly kicking nonteam players upstairs into innocuous,
though frequently high-salaried, positions. Pressure was accumu-
lating for an explosion. (Shedd, the divorced father of four children, remarried after a year in office. His bride was not, however, as some had predicted, an attractive young radio news-
caster who happened to be black.)

Shedd seemed to be making so much progress that there was
system-wide speculation about how long he could last. His ideas,
his programs, and his style constituted a full-fledged assault on
the old guard. It could only be a matter of time, some said, before
his enemies found ways to strike back, possibly to oust him. But

with few exceptions, he had the enthusiastic support of Dilworth, whose personal power was immense. He had also been reasonably lucky with the Board as a whole, though at least two of its members soon began to voice regular opposition. Perhaps most important, the public supported him. In a popular referendum in April 1968 a $90 million bond issue was passed by the largest majority since the advent of the new Board, and the Shedd team took this as a sign of overwhelming public confidence.

A little over a year later, however, the Board's next bond issue, its fourth, was turned down. Some observers said that the voters had been provoked by the Board's renewal of Shedd's contract shortly before the elections in which the bond issue was a key question; but, while Shedd had certainly alienated large portions of the city during the preceding year, he was not enough of a monster in anyone's eyes to account for the defeat. Indeed, after a few lively sparks, principally in the early speeches, Shedd had demonstrated a genius for blandness. He was unquestionably a liberal, but the very fact that his contract had been renewed was testimony to his caution.

Snapshot: *An Articulate Foe*

One had to admire such seasoned fighters as Celia Pincus, the former president and perennial spokesman of the Philadelphia Federation of Teachers. Miss Pincus conveyed the impression of being an old maid schoolmarm with unshakable convictions, but she could summon up waves of appreciative laughter while roasting her enemies. Never mind that the PFT, a formidable power in the school system, had been forced by shifting alliances into a position of extreme rigidity; Celia Pincus knew where her loyalties lay. And there was often truth in her barbs. Addressing a group of parents in the spring of 1969, Miss Pincus declared:

> My greatest quarrel with Dr. Shedd is that he came into Philadelphia with a feeling that he was going to lead the children of this terrible city out of their darkness into a land of hope and glory, and he was going to do it in his own way. . . . To assure himself of success, he has surrounded himself with a youthful group of subordinates. I like young ideas . . . but I will

not accept the new language. Everything is "a hangup" or it is
"innovative" or "You have got to be flexible." Like if you pull
your spine out, you become flexible. . . .

Hunger is not new. Torn pants are not new. They are not
innovative. Therefore, there are no funds for that kind of
problem.*

The "young tiger" image of the early days would probably
endure even after Shedd left Philadelphia. At first, however,
opposition came not from the terrified administrative staff—
Shedd's most predictable enemies, the ones who were most committed to business-as-usual—but from those whom the superintendent at first counted on as his allies. During the 1967–68
school year, for example, the most important single event was a
mass school walkout of about 3,500 black high school students
in order to attend a demonstration at the central administration
building on November 17. The purpose of the demonstration was
to protest the quality of education in the high schools generally
and to present a list of specific demands—among them courses
in Afro-American history and permission to wear African garb
in school. Although the demonstration had been carefully organized (with the help of leading militants from predominantly
black North Philadelphia), the school administrators, even the
black ones who were in contact with the community, had only a
day's notice.

Shedd's response was to invite a delegation into the board
room on the first floor of the building to discuss the issues.
Several Board members and administrators were also present.
While the discussion was in progress the demonstrators outside
became increasingly excited and restless. Plainclothes police circulating in the crowd grew nervous. One or two or fifteen demonstrators (later no one could be certain how many) began to
walk on the roofs of cars parked in front of the building (some
witnesses said that this was untrue, that the demonstrators were
wholly innocent), two busloads of uniformed policemen stationed
nearby moved in—and the "riot" was on. Within an hour the
police had dispersed the crowd, using what many observers later

* "Teacher Raps Shedd, Calls Schools 'Mess,'" *The Evening Bulletin*, Vol.
122, No. 362 (April 10, 1969), p. 6.

asserted were excessively brutal methods. Fifty-seven persons, forty-two of them juveniles, were arrested and charged on a number of counts, including riot and interfering with policemen; twenty-two persons were seriously injured.

The battle of November 17 remained front-page news for several weeks. At first there were demands for the resignation of Police Commissioner Frank L. Rizzo, who had personally directed the maneuvers outside the administration building and whom civil rights activists called a blatant racist. Then, from the other side, came demands that Shedd and Dilworth resign. Rizzo's supporters claimed that the students had been given permission to leave school for the demonstration, that the schools had failed to do their job (no irony intended), that Dilworth was the "pied piper of anarchy." Dilworth and Shedd, the principal spokesmen for the school system, claimed that the police were mainly responsible for the disturbance. "You just can't cap a volcano," Dilworth said. "The easiest thing in the world we could have done was to call Rizzo and his riot squad and say, 'You handle this.' We'd have been inviting riot and disorder such as this city has never seen."

But the strong position taken by Shedd and Dilworth at the beginning of the dispute weakened as time went on. Within a week after the demonstration several Board members had expressed disapproval of Shedd's handling of the incident, and two had publicly given their support to Rizzo. Then, as the tempest abated, Shedd and Dilworth took precautionary steps that appeased some of their critics: They announced that they would seek injunctions against outsiders in the schools (there had been a series of "incidents" earlier in the year) and curb demonstrations that might cause disruption of classes. As if to satisfy both sides at once, they reaffirmed their recently established policy of allowing students to wear ethnic dress in school; announced that they were setting up training programs in black history for several hundred teachers (this had begun prior to November 17); predicted that the subject would be an elective in the coming school year; and formed an ad hoc committee of students and community leaders for system-wide planning and curriculum development. But the pendulum seemed to swing back again on

December 1, when, after a two-hour private conference with Mayor James H. J. Tate, Dilworth proclaimed a "new era of good relationship between city and school officials." Tate had been in Florida on November 17 and had telephoned his support for Rizzo.

The demands and needs of the black community became an inflammatory issue on several different occasions in the following months; questions of power and politics grew increasingly obtrusive. In January 1968 there was a flareup over eleven field workers whom the Board's Office of Integration and Intergroup Education wanted to hire. Two of the candidates were among the school system's most outspoken black militants, and Dilworth insisted that the Board vote on the candidates singly, apparently believing that the white community would never tolerate the hiring of the entire group. One of the militants was eliminated, amidst cries from blacks in the audience of "Racists! Nazis!"

An even more corrosive incident arose during a series of sensitivity-training "retreats" that Shedd had set up in order to cool the system and the community in the wake of November 17. The three weekends, sponsored by an anonymous foundation which paid the participants, gathered students, community leaders, and school staff for open-ended—occasionally all-night—workshops in telling it like it was. The meetings and the names of the participants were top secret, but news quickly leaked out that a main theme of the discussions was white racism, with agonized school staff doing most of the listening. Finally, early one morning during the third weekend, a tired T-group leader, who happened to be white, told it a bit too much like it was, using the work "fuck" for emphasis. School administrators exited in a huff, the Board was reprimanded in a series of outraged letters and telephone calls, and the retreats were brought to an end.

Shedd wanted to continue the retreats, but the Board, assaulted by conservative forces in the school district and community (at one point several city councilmen threatened an investigation), refused to appropriate any more money. After the dispute had calmed somewhat, the Board agreed to more retreats—following a different basic plan that was designed to avoid "confrontations" —during the 1968–69 school year. But Shedd had learned the hard way that his policy of openness and honesty was bound to encounter resistance.

Snapshot: *Spies*

"Paranoia" was a familiar word among liberal and left-wing leaders active in the urban war. With widespread bugging and investigators in all sorts of bizarre disguises a commonplace, the foes of the establishment had cause for their anxiety. But Philadelphia's Police Commissioner Rizzo would not be associated with such deviousness. When it was discovered that the Police Department had compiled a thorough report on one of the sensitivity-training retreats, which were supposed to be top secret, Rizzo countered that his investigator had prepared the report simply because he had "stumbled onto" the information while trying to find a high school principal who happened to be a participant. "We have reports on lots of meetings," Rizzo told an *Inquirer* reporter, "but I don't consider this spying. It's part of police planning."

Specific problems of racial conflict continued to be explosive, but at the beginning, at least, the closely related question of community "control" merely simmered. The new Board had pledged itself to wide community involvement even before Shedd's arrival; one of its best known innovations was a group of experimental "community schools" which remained open well into the evenings, offered courses for adults, functioned as centers for various social and health needs, and were advised by community boards. After November 17, community-student-faculty advisory boards for planning and curriculum were established in most of the black high schools. Whenever members of a community expressed interest in either a new or existing school, an advisory body was immediately created. One school was being planned as an integral part of a federally sponsored community corporation. The Board even went so far as to give a group of community planners $127,000 (most of it a grant from the Rockefeller Foundation) toward establishing a community-run minischool, which opened in the fall of 1968 in one of the poorest sections of West Philadelphia.

Despite Shedd's stated commitment to community involvement, however, the struggle for local control was potentially as abrasive in Philadelphia as it had been in New York—where it was bringing the largest school system in the country to a halt and intensifying the usual conflicts of the urban war to incredible extremes. The conflict in Philadelphia began to take shape in May 1968, after several months of negotiations, letters, and discussions between the Board's office of planning and a group of active citizens in Germantown, one of the most heterogeneous and politically aware sections of the city. The group had formed almost spontaneously in order to have a role in the planning and operation of a Germantown middle school scheduled to open in 1970. At the beginning, they asked for a role in choosing the principal, lower-level administrators, and staff, with the power of annual review and dismissal of at least the principal. But the demands of the "ad hoc committee" varied with news of technicalities and legal barriers, generously provided by 21st Street.

After the final skirmish, the group found itself with virtually no power over the school whatever. Shedd's major concession— other than establishment of the usual community advisory board which no well-informed citizen regarded as affording genuine community control—was permitting the community board to share with the district superintendent the power to review the principal's performance. Guidelines must be established for the system as a whole, Shedd told the perplexed and somewhat intimidated citizens' group at a special meeting, and he would consider using the new school as a model in future discussions of the issue. In October 1968 he set up a commission to study the entire question. But, as one disillusioned member of the new team pointed out, he had already been talking about it for a year and a half.

As for decentralization (the shifting of administrative power to the field), the record was only slightly more promising. Various grant programs were expanded during the 1967–68 school year, but they did nothing to change the basic structure of the system —mainly they provided quick rewards for individual initiative, frequently side-stepping red tape. The Model School District, on which a task force of school and community people worked for several months, finally collapsed—for a number of reasons, perhaps the most important of which was a general distrust of the school system in the community. "The community may be defrauded if it expects too much of the MSD," reported a summary prepared by the North City Congress, an independent citizens' group. "So long as the community believes that it can actually control the educational process in and through the MSD, and that revolutionary improvement can be made in and through the MSD, its hopes are well above the limits of reality."

Having written off this failure as at least a means of sensitizing the community to possibilities, the Shedd team went ahead with plans for several school clusters and an entirely new district consisting of an integrated high school and its feeder schools. In addition, district superintendents, once the silent minions of central office, were given expanded staffs and greater budgetary powers.

But war strategists in the cities of America, like the American naval captains who accidentally sank allied submarines in World War II, were all too often the victims of crippling paradoxes. Shedd's talented central staff continued to make the big decisions, and with so much creative thinking going on in the top administration, the system was in some ways more centralized than before. Frequently "decentralization" was simply a matter of more efficient management and dissemination of new policies and programs to the field. As the education director of the Urban League—hardly an alienated militant—put it in a memorandum written in the summer of 1968, the Board of Education "does not inform the community of programs until after decisions are reached. Even groups that are supposed to be working with the Board aren't informed until it's too late for them to be involved."

Snapshot: *Entente Cordiale*

She is one of the leading black community organizers in the city, and, entering the administration building at 21st Street through the regal front entrance, with its landscaped courtyard and bronze doors, she looks as if she has earned a place among the powerful. Middle-aged, of medium

height, elegant in a tailored suit, she smiles a greeting that
conveys radiant health and total delight with what she is
doing.

"There's no end to it," she says. "I've just come from a
news conference in West Philadelphia—they say at the
University of Pennsylvania that they want to admit our
children, but they go right ahead demanding those high
scores. Well, we really *told* them; they have to change their
entire policy. We're not giving up on this one. And then
there's the Model Cities Program—I'm working with the
communications network for North Philadelphia. I'm late
for a meeting right now."

She continues as we wait for the elevator. "The big thing,
of course, is we want them to change the name of Benjamin
Franklin High School—*we* want it to be called Malcolm X.
The kids have to have something like this; they have to
know who they are, what their identity is. We were all
ready with a hundred boys to show up at the board meeting
last night and really show them we meant business, but
we decided at the last minute to hold off."

Why?

Her voice drops. "No confrontations right now," she confides. "We talked with some people upstairs, and we agreed
to wait until after May 20—that's the day for voting on the
new bond issue, and naturally we want it to pass. *Then*
we'll give it to them."

The Shedd administration had become more rapidly and
deeply involved in the general disintegration of American society
than anyone could have predicted, but Philadelphia had a unique
battle of its own: a growing political struggle between City Hall
and the Board of Education. For most of a year the target of
Mayor Tate's attacks was not so much the school system, however, as Richardson Dilworth. Overtones of personal animosity
and professional jealousy—Dilworth had been one of the city's
most beloved mayors; Tate was a humdrum, though capable,
politician—rang clear throughout the controversy. Often the
battle seemed to be little more than Tate's senseless vendetta

against a man who had, as one observer put it, "more class than he could ever know."

The conflict began in earnest with Tate's re-election in November 1967, a victory which seemed to release an overwhelming confidence in the city administration to grab power from the school system. Power, in this case, consisted mainly of the half-billion-dollar capital program and a large number of high-paying jobs (education was never a serious issue). In February 1968, just as the tensions generated by the events of November 17 were beginning to wear off, Dilworth and City Council President Paul D'Ortona clashed over the site of a proposed expansion for Gratz High School, one of the poorest in the city. Then Tate started to alternate his periodic avowals of cooperation with the school system with declarations that City Hall should eventually have control over such matters as personnel shared by both systems, other overlapping services—and the school system's budget.

The real blowup occurred in the spring of 1968, when it became clear that the Philadelphia school system would not be able to avoid a major budget crisis. One scarcely needed a mastery of new math to understand the problem: The Board had to raise $242 million in order to maintain minimal operations for the 1968–69 school year, and it was roughly $33 million short. Dilworth's first move was to seek aid from the state legislature; but even the tactic of inviting key legislators to visit the Philadelphia schools to see how bad they were raised only $5 million. Finally, Dilworth's only recourse was to his old friends in City Hall. Threats and counterthreats ensued, but the dispute amounted in the long run to a furnace full of hot air. By early summer, City Hall had reluctantly agreed to a one per cent rise in the wage tax, but quickly retracted the promise in the face of citizen protest. Then Dilworth moved to eliminate personalities from the controversy by stepping down as the Board's principal negotiator and assigning the job to a panel of three other Board members.

Throughout the spring, Dilworth had been repeating the scary prediction that unless the additional money was forthcoming, the schools would be forced to close in March or April 1969. And the budget, he warned, had already been pared "to the bone."

By late summer, however, the negotiations for a new contract
with the Philadelphia Federation of Teachers indicated that
there was a chance the schools might not even open on schedule.
Since one of the teachers' demands was for a huge jump in salaries, the contract negotiations were directly connected with the
budget crisis, and a strike could be ugly—community leaders
were planning to take over the schools in the event of a strike and
not leave when it ended. Finally, less than a week before the
scheduled opening of school on September 6, Tate capitulated
by offering $30 million, which would be part of a new tax pack-
age that the city itself desperately needed. School board negotia-
tors, fighting down to the wire (the contract was settled at 5:30
P.M. September 5), also capitulated, offering the union a settle-
ment that most of the teachers saw as a major triumph and those
friendly to the Shedd team considered a sellout.

While Shedd was only indirectly involved in what was, for the
most part, a battle of public relations—the Dilworth-Tate debate
was conducted almost entirely through headlines—it formed the
background for two of the most dramatic skirmishes of the 1967–
68 school year. The first came when Shedd and his advisers
realized that, faced with the genuine necessity of "trimming
fat," they had a perfect chance to unload some of the administrators who had been kicked upstairs at 21st Street. Thus, in
mid-May, they announced the elimination of 381 administrative
positions—representing almost one-fifth of the central staff with
salaries amounting to roughly $3 million. The people involved had
tenure and, technically, could not be fired. With their positions
eliminated, they had the choice of taking other administrative
jobs, usually at substantial pay cuts; returning to the schools,
whence most of them had come; or resigning. The move had
every appearance of a desperate measure in a time of crisis, but
actually a large number of those affected were being paid to do
nothing. Rarely during the urban war, in Philadelphia or anywhere else, had an army succeeded in such an all-out massacre
as the firing of the 381. It was the kind of move that most reformers would never have dared, and for several weeks afterwards it made headlines in educational journals throughout the
country.

Even members of the new team reacted with horror; the

firings were brutal, people said, downright inhuman. The Board had voted to make the cuts without seeing the names of the administrators involved, but later one Board member, usually friendly to the Shedd team, declared in a tone of pain and guilt, "These people were all needed." Not merely horrified, a group of four hundred administrators, including most of the establishment that Shedd was doing his best to rock, raised over $20,000, hired two prominent lawyers, and launched a court fight. Shedd had succeeded in terms of his immediate objective—eliminating deadwood—but he had inadvertently dealt a great blow to the morale of the entire school system.

The other incident, of largely symbolic importance, occurred when the Board member who had become Shedd's most predictable adversary read aloud at a Board meeting a memo he had somehow obtained a copy of, but which was clearly not intended for public consumption. Written by one of Shedd's closest assistants, a twenty-eight-year-old Harvard graduate and former *Bulletin* reporter, the memo suggested that the Board create a "climate of crisis" in order to arouse public interest in budgetary needs, use "Madison Avenue techniques" in communicating with civic groups, and generally "sex up" the budget in order to make it more appealing and acceptable. The memo had been sent to four of Shedd's other advisers, and while its author protested that it was merely a suggestion which had not been acted on, there was enough similarity between Dilworth's drumbeating for money and the memo's proposals to cause widespread suspicion and distrust. Tate and D'Ortona promptly blasted the memo, of course, with their customary headlines, and Dilworth rebuked the administrative assistant, calling him a brash young man. But the damage had been done. The memo could be—and was—construed as promoting a cynical exploitation of public concern.

Snapshot: *The Other Side*

Jack Bookbinder, a slight, graying man in his mid-fifties, is the head of the Administrators' Alliance, which came into being at a Monday night meeting late in May 1968 in the auditorium of the Moore College of Art, one of the institutions that line Benjamin Franklin Parkway not far from the office of the Board of Education. The group was able to use the Moore auditorium because of Bookbinder's own connections with the college—he is the Board's director of Art Education, he has worked for the school system for twenty-two years, and he has contacts. Now he has been called upon to lead the fight against the firing of the 381 administrators that has shaken the Philadelphia public school system to its foundations. Nine of the administrators were in his own department, but he himself was not affected. The group has already raised $14,000 for anticipated lawyers' fees.

"I'll be here next year," he says, "but my colleagues chose me to be the leader. I can hold an audience—they don't fall asleep. I was interviewed on TV last night, and I told them, You don't dispossess a man, you simply burn his house down; you don't starve a man, you simply withhold his food—they caught that on TV. I wish I had thought then of saying, This will be your epitaph if you work for the Board of Education: 'I am not dead, they have merely eliminated my position.' We're going to fight this, though; we contend that they acted illegally. But it's not just a legal issue—it's a moral one.

"The meeting was beautiful—there was a lot of emotion, but none of it spilling over. I didn't sermonize, I just told a story. It was about a kid of ten who came to this country with his family. He didn't remember his father at all—his father had to stay behind in the old country. But one day the boy was sitting waiting in an office on Ellis Island, waiting for the great man whom he hadn't seen for eight years. And suddenly a man comes in, removes his hat, gropes for his papers—no doubt special papers from Washington, the boy thinks. The man stands before the desk behind which is a man named Authority; the man stands there awkwardly. He can't handle the papers because of the hat he's holding. He doesn't know what to do—he starts to put the hat on the desk, then stops and bends down and puts it on the floor. But there was room on the desk."

He pauses, and when he speaks again, his voice is trembling: "*I* was that boy, and I swore then that *I would never put my hat on the floor for anybody!*"

The greatest obstacle to change, Shedd himself often commented in the early days of his administration, was the system's pathological commitment to the status quo. Administrators, principals, and teachers who had been in the system for years (and, they believed, would remain long after Shedd had departed), could be formidable, and possibly devastating, enemies. The most vivid illustration of this followed Shedd's announcement of a proposed merit-pay system for principals; a few days after the announcement, two hundred principals walked out just as he was about to address them at a luncheon. A compromise, more favorable to the principals than to Shedd, was quickly reached.

Another hindrance to real change, although not quite as important as the rigidity of the system, was the atmosphere of continual crisis in which the Shedd administration had to operate. Some critics of the Shedd team suggested that the new superintendent created these crises, but clearly Shedd and his assistants were victims of forces beyond their control. The new team had come to Philadelphia with the hope that enough of the "right" people working for change at the top could really have an effect on the entire school system, that they would be able to counteract not only the inertia resulting from decades of neglect but the fragmentation of the city as well. Even by the end of Shedd's first year in office, however, all the talk of revolution seemed like naïve pipe dreams. Shedd and his assistants, many of whom began to look for other jobs, were apparently no better at working miracles than anyone else who had promised to end (or win) the urban war.

After almost two years of Mark Shedd and a full three years of the new Board, the Philadelphia public school system remained essentially the same institution that it had been before the battle began. The tone was somewhat different, and there was still substance to the claim of the Board's recruiting office that Philadelphia was "where the action is." But the faults that Philadelphia shared with other urban school systems were far from being eliminated. What, then, were the achievements, if any, of three years of concentrated, purposeful reform?

There is a certain irony in the fact that one of the new Board's major successes was in helping the school system "catch up" to what it should have been accomplishing during the years of neglect. Indeed, the Board's constant requests for additional money caused an ongoing controversy that would continue long after Mayor Tate's reluctantly granted tax rise—the days of "economy" were over, and all the cities of America faced a perpetual budget crisis. But important as material advances were, new buildings, annexes, and renovations had very little to do with new approaches to education. The same deadening teaching methods could survive even in a magnificent new school complete with flexible classrooms and well-equipped instructional materials centers. Apparently aware of this, the Board had adopted educational innovation as one of its principal goals.

"Innovation" could mean all things to all men, but the word was at least a signal to the far-flung advocates of change throughout the Philadelphia school system. While a coherent program of innovation never actually took shape in the atmosphere of uninterrupted crisis, the Shedd administration did all it could to encourage those teachers and administrators who wanted to break out of conventional educational formats. During the 1967–68 school year, when the level of experimentation was at its peak, the budget for such programs was buoyed up by nearly $29 million in federal funds—the largest amount of federal aid to a single school system in the country.

The innovative programs were so numerous and varied that no summary can do them justice; even a cursory description, prepared for the Board's Office of Innovative Programs, fills a small book. They included the largest program for computer assisted and individually prescribed instruction in the country; team teaching on a system-wide basis in all middle and upper summer schools; and dozens of projects for developing new classroom and school structures. There were several laboratory schools which had total autonomy to develop new learning environments and curriculum. Many of the innovative programs were designed to supply at upper grade levels the basic skills that so many students had failed to learn in the lower grades. But the real thrust of

the Shedd administration's efforts at educational change—true to
the ideals of the early speeches and the concept of affective
development that Shedd had stressed from the beginning—came
from those projects that reflected a commitment to individual
growth.

These were the programs that attempted to realize the time-
honored dream of a genuinely humanistic education. The
dreamers included the young in spirit throughout the school
system, the "radicals" of all breeds, and even the ones who had
few answers but were looking for alternatives to what had always
been. Shedd and the Board had attracted a huge influx of young
teachers, in addition to the youth movement in the central office—
the average age, for example, of the Advancement School staff
when the school opened in Philadelphia was twenty-six. Hundreds of college students, recent college graduates, and returning
Peace Corpsmen had been recruited through a variety of programs. The leaders of the movement were the true innovators:
the director of the Parkway Program, in which the curriculum
was designed by students and teachers working together; the
founder of the Learning Centers Project, a system-wide network
of discovery-oriented classrooms whose main lesson was freedom;
and several men at 21st Street whom Shedd had hired to engineer
his revolution. The dream of a humanistic education, being also
a dream of genuine human community, inspired such grass-roots
efforts as the Mantua-Powelton Minischool, run entirely by community residents, and a long list of attempts at community organization from the top. Teachers in one school could be completely
ignorant of an "exciting" project in another school a few blocks
away—communications in large school systems are never good,
least of all during wartime—but the movement often seemed to
thrive on apathy and resistance. It survived the resistance, and it
continued to grow even after Shedd's forces suffered crippling
defeats.

But, like the vast, confused New Left to which it had so many
ideological ties, the movement for humanistic education was
never actually "together." As innovation became a cliché instead
of a goal, a rivalry for newness turned many program leaders
into prima donnas of change. A widespread agreement on values
was not enough to unify the movement's thousands of adherents

scattered over the nation's fourth-largest city. At best, Shedd and his assistants could do no more than lend their support when it was needed; the confusion of war—and the defeats—precluded the kind of leadership they had hoped to offer.

Above everything else, and on a level where ideology no longer mattered, the urban war was a struggle for power. By the late 1960's the predictions of George Orwell and Aldous Huxley were coming true in ways even more horrible than those visionaries had imagined. There were too many people in the world; too much power was in the hands of a few; and modern communications had eclipsed even the illusion of innocence. "Humanism" seemed a ludicrously old-fashioned term in an age of instant obsolescence, but one of the most unavoidable facts of life in the sixties was that the chances of a truly humane society were less favorable than they had ever been. If history is viewed as a struggle of humanity against inhumanity, good against evil, and freedom against oppression, it now seemed that some malevolent force had robbed mankind of the ability to choose. Power and freedom were irrevocably opposed to each other, yet on all fronts of the urban war they had become virtually equated. Force and humanity were opposites as well, but it was a time when the humanists themselves were compelled to bear arms. Often it seemed that a commitment to humanism was merely another trick, a subtle mask covering a lust for power.

And the only certainty was that it would all accelerate. It would all go clattering and screaming on until somebody put a stop to it.

II. *Years of Discontent*

The Concerned
Power Structure

AT FIRST, the reformers remember with a certain irony, nobody paid much attention to the schools. They discovered later that the schools were in bad shape, but by the end of World War II the city itself was on the brink of ruin. Decades before "the crisis of the cities," Philadelphia jokes were almost a national pastime. According to one of the perennial favorites, a radio giveaway show was offering as first prize a week in Philadelphia. Second prize: two weeks in Philadelphia. "I went to visit Philadelphia," stand-up comics used to say, "but it was closed." And W. C. Fields is supposed to have exclaimed in the midst of a dire emergency, "Better here than in Philadelphia."

Beneath the jokes lay a harsh reality. After more than sixty years of corrupt Republican machine politics, Philadelphia's indignities included foul drinking water, a garbage dump that burned eternally within a mile of the business district, and huge slums, one of which surrounded the wreck of the city's principal tourist attraction, Independence Hall. By the late 1940's the exodus to the suburbs, just beginning in most cities, was virtually complete in Philadelphia. Other cities had been victimized by political machines, but the situation in Philadelphia was unique. In New York and Chicago, the politicians exploited the city while maintaining a bare minimum of services; in Philadelphia, they merely exploited.

Reform-minded Philadelphians had been grumbling about the city's decline for years, but no one really tried to change the situation until 1948. That was the year when Harry A. Batten, one of Philadelphia's leading businessmen, expanded a watchdog group called the Committee of Fifteen to include almost every important business and professional leader in town and renamed it the Greater Philadelphia Movement. The sole objective of GPM was civic reform, and the coalition set out immediately to rebuild the city. They obtained a home rule charter from the state legislature; though traditionally Republican themselves, they toppled the local machine and backed a group of fighting Democrats—Joseph Clark and Richardson Dilworth, who made the office of mayor a symbol of progressivism for the decade beginning in 1952, were the political leaders of the movement; and they embarked on one of the most ambitious urban renewal programs in the nation.

By the early 1960's central Philadelphia had undergone a transformation. Independence Hall, beautifully restored, surmounted an elegant mall; the garbage dump had been replaced by an ultramodern food-distribution center; historic Society Hill, which had been a slum, was now one of the most fashionable residential neighborhoods; and the head of the city planning commission was widely regarded as a genius. But the job was far from over. The ghettoes, mainly in North and West Philadelphia, were growing at a rapid pace; almost thirty per cent of the population was black. A restored Independence Hall might be pretty, but it could do nothing to save Philadelphia from the pressure-cooker syndrome that was plaguing every major American city.

The pressure was bound to affect the schools. The black community cried for justice on all fronts; many saw the schools as the key to social progress. But the residents of the "inner city" were not alone in their indignation. For several years, pressure had been building at the top as well.

Despite her New York childhood, Annette Temin had the salty appearance and tenacity of an old-time Yankee. She also had a social conscience that bordered on radicalism. She knew, however, that she would need certain tools if she were to be an effective reformer and as soon as she and her husband, a Washington lawyer, moved to Philadelphia in 1930, she enrolled for a master's degree in education at the University of Pennsylvania. Between 1930 and 1950 Mrs. Temin focused a good deal of her volunteer work on the Jewish community in Philadelphia's Germantown section. For many years she was president of the Hebrew Sunday school and chairman of the Germantown Jewish Center education committee. She was also president of a neighborhood home and school association (the school system's version of the PTA). But in 1950 her service to Philadelphia education began to broaden considerably. That was the year she became chairman of the education committee of a local chapter of the League of Women Voters and, in her attempts to get reforms in the public school system, realized that "we weren't going to have any impact."

Nobody then knew the full extent of the system's problems; the most recent general survey had been completed in 1938. But Annette Temin had good reason to question the locally popular notion that Philadelphia had the best schools in the country. She had worked closely with the system through the Home and School Association, and she had seen how difficult it was to change established patterns. Moreover, she knew as well as anyone else that the system had been virtually tyrannized for almost twenty years by a single man. Though she had never met him, she had a formidable enemy in Add B. Anderson, secretary and business manager to the Board of Education.

"I was fighting Anderson on the budget," recalls Elizabeth Greenfield, the politically active widow of one of the city's wealthiest businessmen, who became a member of the Board of Education in 1957. "He would always pad it so that he'd end up with a surplus. I argued that this gave the public a false impression. Once when I was fighting him on this issue, he telephoned me at home one night. He said he was doing what seemed right from his point of view. He had lived through the Depression, a time when the school board hadn't been able to pay its bills. And once while we were having this fight, he said, 'I hope you're not angry with me. We have two different points of view— you might say that you're the New Deal and I'm the conservative.' I said, Yes, I thought this was right and that we were both going to continue fighting for what we believed in. I didn't know about his reputation when I went on the Board, but I must have been one of the few people in the city who didn't."

Anderson did more than pad the budget, however. "Anderson owned the school board," says William Wilcox, the executive director of GPM and for several years one of Anderson's most outspoken opponents. "He deliberately chose weak superintendents so he could dominate them." There was a period of several years, after the battle started, when Anderson refused to speak to Wilcox at all.

And, as director of the Citizens Committee on Public Education in Philadelphia, which finally launched a full-scale assault on the Anderson administration, Robert Blackburn had a number of skirmishes with Anderson over a period of years. One of them, for example, involved a proposed all-black school at 46th and Market Streets. "Citizens Committee" wanted the location changed so that the school would be integrated. Later in the fight, when Anderson had begun to weaken, Blackburn repeated his frequent inquiries about the new school at a meeting with Anderson and the superintendent of schools. "I don't know of any plans for a school at 46th and Market," said the superintendent. Anderson refreshed his memory with "You know, Allan, that colored school we're going to build there."

Occasionally the very absurdity of the situation gave rise to a bitter sort of humor. "Normally when the committee approached the board for a role in planning a school," says Blackburn, "they were told it was too early. We used to say there was a golden moment, a half hour one afternoon, and then it was too late."

Anderson died in the summer of 1962 after an illness of many years. According to one Philadelphian who had been campaigning for better public schools since the late thirties, "If Add had lived, the reform movement would never have succeeded."

But Add Anderson was not the only thing wrong with the Philadelphia school system. For as long as anyone could recall, membership on the school board had been a strictly gratuitous status symbol doled out to prominent citizens who had the favor of the reigning politicos. Board members were chosen by a supposedly impartial committee of judges, but the solid-gold names gave many citizens pause. Renewal of membership was virtually automatic—many board members were in their seventies, and they were commonly known as "The House of Lords." The ten-story, granite-and-marble administration building, one of the many symbols of power and prestige that line Benjamin Franklin Parkway within walking distance of City Hall, was called "The Palace on the Parkway."

On the one hand, the Board of Education was a genteel group of prominent Philadelphians who represented all that seemed sensible, secure, and good. As one reform leader put it: "At least the Board wasn't *crooked*. They may have been senile and ineffective, but they seemed honest." On the other hand, their reluctance to do the hard work of running the school system, combined with Anderson's absolute rule, amounted to the most severe and deliberate repression. The Board had a practice, for example, of never answering questions or criticisms on the few occasions when they were compelled by law to hold public hearings. And, according to a highly critical report issued by GPM as late as 1962: "In the one recent instance where controversy occurred in a public meeting of the Board, all reference to the dispute was expunged from the published minutes."

Other American cities had recalcitrant boards of education, and even the concept of dual control—two chief officers, a superintendent and a business manager—was not unique to Philadelphia. In no American city, however, had this kind of institutionalized atrophy, as in the city administration before it, led to the all-powerful dominance of an Add Anderson. While the entire central school administration could be described collectively, in the words of one critic, as "an arthritic turtle," Anderson, ever vigilant, did his job remarkably well.

This was the system that Annette Temin decided to take on in 1950.

Her first move was to seek help from the Greater Philadelphia Movement, which had already made a name for itself in overthrowing the ancient city machine. The executive director at this time (Wilcox did not join the organization until 1954) discouraged her, explaining that GPM did not set up ongoing committees, but preferred to attack specific problems on an ad hoc basis.

In the following year, however, GPM published a report on the school system; the principal focus was on finances, and generally the tone was mild, even approving. Mrs. Temin despaired of getting any substantial help from GPM.

The inspiration for her next move came from a group of prominent businessmen and professionals across the country—they included columnist Walter Lippman and Roy Larsen, president of Time, Inc.—who had established a National Citizens Commission for the Public Schools. The main purpose of the organization was to stimulate the formation of local committees, partly as a reaction to the McCarthyite witch-hunting that began to prey on the nation's public school systems around this time. In May 1952, Mrs. Temin convinced the League of Women Voters to establish a citizens' committee on education as part of its program; the League was nowhere near as powerful as GPM, but at least it was a base for action.

"There were ten on the education committee," she recalls, "but it became something that the whole League was interested in. The main question was, How do you go about setting up a citizens' committee? We had booklets from the national council, and one suggestion was to join the home and school association. Home and school associations are exactly what they say they are—joint school people and parents looking at particular schools and very much dominated by the principal. And we couldn't get to first base with the Home and School Council, the administrative group in the school system. We couldn't get anything on the agenda." After a fruitless year, Mrs. Temin realized that working within the school system was a dead end.

The first big break for the reformers came when the Philadelphia *Bulletin* sponsored a forum on education with Roy Larsen, president of the National Citizens Commission, as the main speaker of the day. Mrs. Temin and her team of assistants waited outside the Academy of Music, where the forum was being held, and, as the audience, well primed by the Larsen speech, left the building, the volunteers distributed leaflets announcing an organizational meeting for their citizens' school committee. About fifty people showed up at Gimbels' Clubwomen's Center a week later, and the first phase of the campaign was on its way.

The founders of the newly formed Citizens Committee on Public Education in Philadelphia included representatives of several diverse organizations throughout the city—political groups like ADA, churches, unions, the Chamber of Commerce, the NAACP, and the universities. All of them were eager to support the schools, and the air was filled with talk of good deeds, both intended and realized. But those who knew about Add Anderson were prepared to go much further than mere support. Annette Temin would continue to be a driving force, and it was here that John Patterson and Jane Freedman joined her in the fight.

Tall, clear-eyed, and red-haired, John Patterson—known to most of his confreres as "Pat"—had a quality of directness and gentle humor that had endeared him to at least two generations of the city's educational reformers. His genial informality belied the fact that for several decades he had provided the major intellectual thrust of Philadelphia school reform. With degrees from Philadelphia's Normal School and the University of Pennsylvania, Patterson had aimed at a career in teaching, for which he felt "a vocational call." After teaching for several years, he became director of the Public Education and Child Labor Association (PEA), a state-wide, tax-free agency that watched over the public interest in school matters and smoothed the way for relevant legislation. The agency was supported by what was then the Community Chest (now the United Fund), and Patterson recalls that he had to play down some of his zeal for reform because of the organization's tax-free status: "In those days I was a stormy petrel, trying to get some money for the teachers. Finally the agency was kicked out of the Fund for excessive legislative activity, though the official reason was that we engaged in activities 'out of line with the Fund's goals.'" In addition to higher salaries for teachers, Patterson was fighting at that time for an increase in the mandatory age for school attendance; PEA finally convinced the state legislature to raise the age from sixteen to seventeen.

While serving as director of PEA, Patterson continued working toward a degree in educational administration. His contacts with Philadelphia's school system, in which he conducted most of his research (his master's thesis was entitled "Education in Slum

Neighborhoods vs. Privileged Neighborhoods"), gave him first-hand knowledge of the system's inadequacies. Thus, in the mid-1930's, Patterson's agency became one of a small number of civic groups that began to demand a complete survey of the system. The last general survey had been done in 1921.

Two of Patterson's teachers at Penn were also on the board of PEA, and in 1937, when the Philadelphia school board finally decided to heed the rising cry for a survey, all three of them were hired to help with the year-long job. Among the problems the survey found, dual administration, with its attendant ambiguities of power distribution, was one of the worst; in addition, Add Anderson's predecessor as secretary and business manager was trying to run the system too cheaply (though he did find money to begin construction of the Palace on the Parkway). The system needed fiscal home rule; there was no department of personnel; the method of appointing Board members needed revision; and there existed great inequalities between white and black schools. But even though the survey was made public, it elicited almost no citizen action. "It was obvious," Patterson says, "that only the squeaking wheel gets the grease. The quiescent communities got what was left. Philadelphia was twelve per cent Negro then, but the problems were the same as they are now." Discouraged about the chances for school reform, Patterson spent the next several years in private business and in New Deal activism.

After World War II, Patterson joined Dilworth, Clark, and other returning veterans in their big push for change in Philadelphia. "The war was a key thing," says Dilworth. "So many of the young men got out for the first time. They went all over the country and saw things. When the younger people got back they realized something had to be done." Dilworth himself had belonged to a group that called themselves "the Warriors"—they were mainly lawyers and businessmen—and their purpose, even before the war, had been to dislodge the city and state political machines. In addition to working with the Dilworth-Clark team, Patterson revived the PEA, which was now devoted exclusively to the Philadelphia schools. But civic reform in those early days of the movement focused entirely on city planning, water supply, highways, and similar matters. During these years, PEA kept beating the drum without getting anywhere. "You couldn't get five minutes at a meeting of your political compatriots," Patterson says, "to talk about schools."

John Patterson was an old friend of Abraham Freedman, a prominent lawyer, and his wife, Jane. Patterson had also known Elizabeth Greenfield for more than ten years. The Greenfields were old friends of Dick Dilworth and Joe Clark. Albert M. Greenfield happened to be one of the richest men in the country, and Philadelphia was the nation's fourth-largest city, but in some respects, it was still very much a small town, whose most powerful leaders and prime movers were "just folks." Thus, it was perfectly natural that Patterson should join Jane Freedman and the others when the League of Women Voters began to round up support for the fight against Add Anderson and the school board.

Jane Freedman and her husband had previously worked closely with the civil rights and public housing movements; he had written the redevelopment law that provided the basic guidelines for rebuilding the city. Like most of the active reformers after the war, however, they paid little attention to the public schools. Their own children attended the Miquon School, a small private day school that stressed innovation and parent involvement. The parents actually helped run the school, in fact —for reasons of economy as well as community—and this experience provided an added push when the League of Women Voters, of which Jane Freedman was a member, began to form their Citizens Committee.

At first, Mrs. Freedman was not a particularly active member of the newly formed committee, but she possessed certain assets that later proved invaluable. The "concerned power structure," as she liked to think of her friends in Philadelphia, may have been more intimate than similar groups in other large American cities, but it was no less exclusive than the usual apathetic power structure. She was a Sunstein; the Sunstein family, like the Gimbels, the Levys, and the Rosenwalds, was part of a close-knit Jewish establishment which had ties to the less conservative members of the close-knit WASP establishment. Jane Freedman was one of the few reformers who could communicate with the empyrean, and as time went on, she communicated with increasing effectiveness.

Even though Citizens Committee had several other influential members from the beginning, the obstacles to success were almost overwhelming. At one of the first meetings, for example, a deputy of Anderson's tried to block the formation of the committee altogether, threatening a boycott from the Home and School Council. The Committee survived this threat, but it was still far from being an effective instrument for change. "We made ourselves a nuisance," says Jane Freedman. "What else could we do without money and a staff? We kept making statements and asking questions. Education wasn't news at the time; we couldn't even get mention in the press. We went on for several years as a few people putting out a newsletter, and we had a little office. At one point we were about to dissolve, it was so frustrating."

Although the committee's activities seemed to make no dent on Anderson at first, they did eventually begin to have an effect on public opinion. By the late 1950's, Citizens Committee was running an annual "Town Meeting," in which representatives of more than forty community organizations gathered to attend lectures and seminars on various topics ranging from finances to teacher shortages. The committee also included, by this time, several members of GPM. When Anderson could no longer ignore the constant complaining, he made a practice of addressing the group periodically. Later, he deferred to it even more by granting a monthly conference between Citizens Committee representatives, himself, and the superintendent of schools. But the struggle had scarcely begun; members of the Board of Education continued to refer to the group rather patronizingly as "Mrs. Temin's committee."

Most of the old-time warriors in the battle of the Philadelphia schools agree that despite all the years of reformist activity, the first important move toward change was initiated by Elizabeth Greenfield, who joined the Board of Education in 1957. Mrs. Greenfield had had occasional contact with the city's public schools before, but not until she became part of their future did she realize how sick they were. And she soon learned that she and

Add Anderson were diametrically opposed on almost every detail. "I was absolutely appalled," she recalls. "I was not really aware of the depth of need. I wanted to have a citizens' committee appointed to study the situation, particularly to improve teachers' salaries." But Anderson would not brook opposition from Board members. At one meeting, after Mrs. Greenfield had been making her objections known for more than a month, he shook a finger at her and said, "Just keep quiet! You listen to *me*."

But she refused to keep quiet. Finally, Anderson compromised by allowing her and a committee of Board members—many of whom were glad to join their dissenting colleague—to prepare a study of the school system. Published in December 1958, the Greenfield Report pointed out that, among other deficiencies, Philadelphia had the lowest teacher salaries of the nation's largest cities; that there were 738 permanent teaching vacancies, most of which had been filled by unqualified substitutes; and that there was no accurate way of evaluating the achievement of the city's school children in relation to those of other cities because the system refused to administer nationally standardized tests.

The Greenfield Report was the first public criticism within memory to come from the Board of Education itself. The Board adopted its findings unanimously, and they formed the basis for the largest school tax increase in Pennsylvania since the turn of the century. In addition to her activity as a Board member, Mrs. Greenfield began to spread the word among her husband's many friends throughout the city—the heads of Wanamaker's, the Pennsylvania Railroad, and Bell Telephone; Mayor Dilworth; and others of similar stature—that the time had come to fight for change in the schools.

Citizens Committee rejoiced over the report, and the tax increase strengthened their drive for more extensive community involvement. The schools were beginning to be a hot issue. The Greenfield Report was partly responsible, but the growing civil rights movement and the hysteria that followed Sputnik were also important factors. In the winter of 1959–60, one of the committee members discovered that a women's civic club was dissolving and that the club had a substantial amount of money to be dispensed to worthy organizations through court hearings. Citizens Committee managed to convince the court that they deserved $12,000. This, combined with an office lent by a member of GPM and small sums of money raised by Mrs. Freedman and other members, gave the Committee sufficient capital to hire an executive director and get to work on a city-wide campaign.

The choice of a full-time director was one of the most important steps in the Committee's history. The "concerned power structure" wanted a man who could communicate effectively with "top management"—the bankers and professionals whose support was vital to the success of the venture—but he had to be equally at home with the leaders of grass-roots community groups, many of whom were near the other end of the social ladder. He should have experience in the field of human relations, yet he should also be fairly young. His job would be, in essence, to win the confidence of as many powerful Philadelphians on all levels as he could. As Jane Freedman later explained, he had to be a master at "relating."

Bob Blackburn was the son of an airline pilot; he had grown up in "numberless suburbs" all over the country, gone to Oberlin College, where he majored in sociology, and spent his junior year at the Hampton Institute, in Hampton, Virginia, where he was the only white student among 1,500 blacks. When Blackburn graduated from Oberlin in 1957, he took a job with the Philadelphia division of the National Conference of Christians and Jews. But as time went on, he found the NCCJ's national office too conservative, and after a series of run-ins he began to look for another job. He had already had dealings with the Philadelphia school system, which by that time had an Office of Intergroup Education (several years later he became its director), and in the summer of 1960, when Blackburn was twenty-five, an official of Citizens Committee invited him to meet with some of the Committee's top leadership. "He was obviously bright, interested, and attractive," says Jane Freedman. "He was a person interested in reform—not just in one field, but in the whole spectrum. He was a sincere, committed person, and he had a great sense of humor." The Committee had interviewed several other candidates, but Blackburn got the job.

Bill Wilcox, who had been executive director of GPM for six years, was also a sincere, committed person, and an ardent reformer skilled in community relations—and he had a great

sense of humor. Although he had virtually no experience with
schools, he shared Blackburn's interest in the broad spectrum of
reform. "Wilcox's own style is to lead his organization where
there is a readiness for change," observes Blackburn. "He found
that when he pressed on the school system, he could feel it give;
underneath, it was rotten." Through her husband's membership
in GPM, Jane Freedman had known Wilcox for years, and she
lost no time in introducing him to the new director of Citizens
Committee.

The Wilcox-Blackburn friendship took on almost legendary
proportions within the school reform movement, for the two
men became the principal organizers of the network of power
and pressure needed to topple the Anderson administration.
Blackburn soon proved that he was the right choice for the job
with Citizens Committee; Wilcox was already widely regarded
as the mastermind of GPM. In addition to their many other common interests, the two men discovered that they were both avid
hikers and mountain-climbers. They talked on the telephone frequently, had regular meetings with mutual associates, went on
camping and hiking trips—and, in short, their partnership
became a minor obsession.

Blackburn's main role in Citizens Committee at the beginning
was to enlist the cooperation of local community groups, and his
work with GPM was only one part of his job. During the fall and
winter of 1960 he went to an unending series of meetings, sometimes several a day, lecturing, conferring, informing, listening—
and "needling," of course, with increasing effectiveness. Citizens
Committee succeeded in forcing the school board to include a
library in the plans of a new building, then helped to block the
construction of the notorious "colored" school at 46th and Market.

One of the committee's main objectives at this time was a new
survey of the school system—the last had been the 1938 survey
in which John Patterson assisted. Although the Board rejected
a provision for citizen participation—which the committee had
specifically urged—it finally commissioned a team of researchers
from Stanford University to do the job. The survey was not
completed until February 1965, but it managed to shake up some
of the Board's sacred traditions even while it was still in progress.

The reform movement had begun to snowball so fast in the

early 1960's that the Board finally felt compelled to take a serious
look at the problems of widespread de facto segregation, and
this time citizen participation was actually invited. The report
of the Special Committee on Nondiscrimination was not officially
completed until July 1964, but, like the survey, its findings influ-
enced Board decisions long before then. As a result of the report,
for example, the principle of "absolute equality" was abandoned
in favor of strong compensatory programs in the ghetto schools.

When the two reports were finally published in their entirety,
no one who knew the school system was really surprised—
although in some cases the results were shocking. The dismal
picture included extensive overcrowding; the highest dropout
rate of the nation's ten largest cities; pupil performance in
elementary and junior high schools well below the national average; an inadequate kindergarten program; and a large number
of obsolete school buildings in deplorable condition—62 of the
city's 252 schools had been built before 1907. Segregation greatly
intensified all the other problems; the black population in the
schools was fifty-three per cent, and more than half of the schools
had an enrollment of ninety per cent or more of one race. As in
most American cities, the (white) middle class continued its
exodus to the suburbs, abandoning the inner city to the (not
entirely black) poor. And, like most American cities, Philadelphia
had begun its reforms too late.

"The system was dramatically bad," says Blackburn. "The call
for change built to a crescendo. Finally, it almost didn't matter
what the mechanism was." But a mechanism had to be found;
the upheaval in Philadelphia by the early sixties was so great that
nothing short of rebuilding the system with active citizen participation would satisfy the discontented. Add Anderson's death in
August 1962 did nothing to diminish the urgency of the call for
action; the inertia of his administration would take many years
to overcome.

Bill Wilcox had been studying the school system with a view
to changing it since his arrival at GPM. In 1959 he had submitted
a memorandum strongly urging that the group move to eliminate
the system's dual administration and the unsatisfactory procedures for selecting Board members. In 1960, this time with
Blackburn's support, Wilcox began to compile a thorough report

which he intended as the basis for a full-scale attack. He hired
a vice-principal from a school in New England—"We have a
view that you can't turn these things completely over to 'experts'"
—to collect data, and then, working with Blackburn, Patterson,
and several young lawyers, spent almost a year sharpening the
report to a fine point. Its recommendations included fiscal home
rule, an end to dual administration, a new method for selecting
Board members, and stronger school-community relations. There
were also extensive recommendations dealing with conditions in
the schools, particularly the teaching staff; but Patterson urged
GPM to publish the administrative section first in order to get
action as quickly as possible.

The first part of the GPM report appeared on May 17, 1962,
and within two weeks the reformers had pulled enough strings
in the state capital to set up an Educational Home Rule Assembly
under the leadership of one of GPM's most powerful members.
Essentially the Assembly was a lobby for school legislation; but
it also created a program to bring the story of the city's schools
"to every corner of Philadelphia and, where necessary, carry the
message throughout Pennsylvania." The membership included
Jane Freedman, Blackburn, several members of GPM, and heads
of various community organizations, most of whom were also on
Citizens Committee.

The specific mechanism of change was yet to be found, however, and finally Wilcox, a part-time amateur lawyer, "had the
nutty idea one afternoon that we could use the home rule law to
set up a home rule commission for the Philadelphia schools. I
knew that the school system could be changed by taking a section
of the state constitution providing for home rule for cities and
boroughs." This approach had succeeded for the city government
a decade earlier, and Wilcox immediately got in touch with his
friends in Harrisburg to test the idea. "I remember walking into
the state legislature one day," Wilcox recalls, "and Austin Lee
[a leading Democratic senator from Philadelphia] said to me,
'The governor [William Scranton, a liberal Republican] wants
to see you.' I went into the governor's office; there was great
tension in the air, and the governor said, 'What's this idea about
educational home rule?' And then later, downstairs, there was a
crowd of reporters."

The governor approved, but the legislature did not begin to consider a fiscal home rule bill until February 1963. The bill was made into law in August, and at that time the legislature established a commission whose main purpose was to create a constitution for governing the restructured school system.

Up to this point, the reform movement had possessed an almost romantic urgency, but the work of the commission was strictly business: settling legal matters, haggling over details, and hearing testimony from just about any citizen who had an opinion. Minor conflicts occasionally erupted—there was a dispute about the selection of new Board members, for example—but the reformers who had initiated the movement could do little but wait. They waited for two years. Finally, in April 1965, the charter was ready; even then, there was disagreement among the reformers about whether to put the charter up for a vote, since it would have to be either adopted intact or rejected. Bickering and politicking had taken so much steam from the movement by this time that when the special election was finally held on May 18, 1965, the charter was passed by the narrow margin of twenty thousand in a rather apathetic turnout. The drama that had characterized the movement for so many years was missing in the victory.

Actually, there had been a series of victories over the years. The main provision of the new charter—a smaller Board of Education selected by a citizens' nominating panel and the mayor—was crucial, but some of the worst problems had already been dealt with. Citizen involvement had been the key factor throughout the campaign, and the schools would no longer be the exclusive property of "educators." The new Board was emphatically a symbol of more responsive leadership. In the years to come, the same complaints would be heard about the new Board that were made about the old—"too conservative," "stuffy," "bigoted"—but in 1965 it seemed that the way was open for a completely rebuilt system. This was the goal, at any rate, of the Board's new president, Richardson Dilworth, who had helped to rebuild the city itself two decades earlier—a goal whose attainment Dilworth intended to guarantee by hiring Mark Shedd as superintendent.

After the battle was over, the members of the coalition, who had worked so hard together for years, gradually returned to normal business. GPM had several projects in addition to the schools. Citizens Committee resumed its school visits and periodic colloquiums. Bob Blackburn entered the Peace Corps and spent two years in Nigeria. Most of the reformers adopted a wait-and-see attitude. But the period of relative peace could only be short-lived in a time of such turbulent social change as the 1960's.

By the beginning of 1968 the progress of the school system was again so seriously threatened that Citizens Committee decided the time had come for another mobilization. The immediate cause was the third bond issue that the voters would be called upon to pass in order to support the new Board's $490 million capital program. Ever since the local elections in November 1967, Mayor Tate had been talking about a consolidation of city and school board powers, among them the making of the school system's budget. Many of the system's sympathizers shared Dilworth's oft-repeated fear that this was a threat to take over the system and its vast resources for purposes of political patronage. The mild hysteria engendered rumors that Tate and his ward leaders were secretly fighting the bond issue, hoping that a defeat would deliver the school system into their hands.

Thus, for the second time within a decade, Citizens Committee convened a meeting of community leaders from all over the city. The proposed topic for the evening was a discussion of the relationship of the city and the school system, but the committee's leaders fully expected a strong move to support the bond issue and a show of power similar to that which had pushed through the home rule charter two and a half years earlier. The meeting was held on a balmy evening in March in the thirty-second-floor board room of one of the city's leading banks, in the heart of the fashionable business district.

With its massive oval conference table, paneled walls, and elegant portraits of dead directors, the room was an appropriate setting for a coalition of power. There were no windows, but the hall outside offered an impressive view of the city that suggested unchallenged dominion over all one surveyed. To the members of "the concerned power structure" the room could not have meant a great deal, but other visitors—many of whom came from the city's poverty areas—had trouble concealing their awe. Some eighty community leaders attended the meeting; about twenty were black.

The president of Citizens Committee opened the meeting with a brief explanation of its purpose. There was serious concern, he said, about racial tensions within the school system; the relation of the city and the schools was also a problem; and, in short, the Committee was interested in discussing anything that "threatened the work we did to establish an independent home rule school district" since the charter was adopted.

Everyone in the room was interested in the future of the schools, but the reform leaders who expected a quick rally in support of the bond issue were soon disappointed. Although one member of the "concerned power structure" suggested fairly early in the meeting that the group's immediate purpose should be to support the bond issue, his suggestion was lost in a growing storm of criticism, mainly of the attitude of the school board toward the black community. "We think it's important that the coalition be reactivated again," said one black leader, "in terms of those organizations which are in the mainstream of education in Philadelphia *today in 1968!*" Many speakers, black and white, criticized the Board for slighting the black community by failing to support some of Shedd's policies. "This brings the meeting into focus," said one of the black speakers. "Now, in effect, what does the black community get in return for its support?"

The anger of those who supported the blacks' demands increased as the evening went on, and finally one of the most outspoken of the black leaders articulated the feelings that seemed to have sparked the conflict in the first place: "What we're all saying is that we're not speaking the truth to each other. Citizens Committee is a p.r. extension of the *Board*."

Had the portraits on the walls been alive, they would probably have turned their backs on the whole discussion. But they would never have allowed such a gathering in the first place. Here, in this most unlikely setting, another vital "dialogue" had begun. Nothing was resolved at the meeting, but there could be no question in the minds of the "concerned power structure" that in two short years their numbers had increased more than they would have ever thought possible.

George Hutt

GEORGE HUTT's *battle began in the days when people could still say "quality integrated education" without embarrassment—he joined the Board of Education in 1965, but his pursuit of positive school reform gradually became one of routine plugging for the closest thing to justice within the limits of reality. His other black colleague on the Board, Reverend Henry Nichols, was generally a more cautious and conservative man, often a strong opponent of Shedd, and there were times when Hutt seemed militant by comparison. But Hutt was torn between the growing intensity of the pressure for change and his allegiance to the Board he served; he seemed at times to be running hard just to stay in the same place.*

In 1966, at the age of thirty-seven, Hutt took on a job closely related to his duties as a Board member: the directorship of the newly formed College Bound Corporation, a federally sponsored "lobby," as he called it, to get kids into college who otherwise wouldn't make it (seventy-five per cent of the students served by College Bound were black). Both jobs—he devoted as much as twenty hours a week to his nonpaying Board position—reflected his commitment to the future of black people within the existing structure of American society. To the most militant blacks, it seemed that George Hutt, working for the establishment in well-tailored business suits, had been thoroughly "co-opted."

But he remained a fighter. It was he who exploded from the administration building on November 17 and confronted Police Commissioner Frank Rizzo with the accusation that the demonstrators were innocent, that the cops had started the riot. It was

*he who promised to take the teachers' union to court when they
won (from the majority of the Board) the right to refuse transfer
to black schools. And it was he who had the trust and respect of
many blacks who had almost given up on the system altogether.*

I started out just as a curious parent. That was when I realized,
in '62, after having lived in this town for seventeen years, that I
had a daughter old enough to go to school in kindergarten. I'd
come to Philly in '45 from a little town in South Jersey to go to
college, but I only had enough money for one year at Temple. I
dropped out, then took jobs as a sales clerk and a jazz shop
operator. I got married in '50, decided to go back to school, and
went to Drexel [Institute of Technology] for engineering for nine
years at night. I'd gotten my degree in '63, and I had a job as an
electrical engineer.

But I didn't really know the city, didn't know anything at all
about the school system. I had to ask the next-door neighbor
where the nearest school was. I found it—the Heston School, an
all-black school in West Philadelphia— and went to register my
daughter early, in May of 1962. When I went to register her, they
said, We're sorry, no room, you can put your name on the waiting
list, but there probably won't be room later on. This was a shock
to me—it was the first real contact I'd had with the inner workings of the city—I'm a country boy, and in the country everything's great in the city. But this was a real letdown.

I pondered on it for a while, then started looking at schools in
general. I looked for the next nearest school—got a Bulletin
Almanac, they listed the schools' locations. I'd even decided to
buy a car for my wife so that she could drive the kid back and
forth. So I found an integrated school—the Cassidy School, at
62nd and Lansdowne—and they accepted the application. But
then I found a school that was just eight blocks away—the Mann
School—that seemed bigger than the first one, Heston. It was
bigger, but it was almost half-empty. I know because I went to
observe at lunch time when the kids got out. The Bulletin
Almanac listed the enrollments of the schools; I went in and
counted the number of classrooms, then compared that with the
number of kids.

The Mann School was all-white. Eight blocks from an all-black school that was bulging at the seams.

I decided I'd try this one—I didn't mind it being all white—but they turned me down flat. They said, She's outside the boundaries. At that time we had the so-called open enrollment, but now I knew that it was only one-way. And that school was forty per cent underutilized. I talked with a secretary that day; I didn't even see the principal the first time.

I wasn't really fighting this thing yet—I was only beginning to figure it out. I would stop and say, Okay; then I'd think about it; then I'd go back and ask more questions. And finally I saw that I was really on to something. One day, the day for enrollments for kids from outside the boundary, I went up to the Mann School and got in line. There were a lot of white parents on line, and they accepted the lady in front of me—they just told her she'd have to provide her own transportation, which was expected. Then they told me I was outside the boundary, that they couldn't take my kid.

The next thing I did—I have a souvenir of this that I'll always keep—I went and got a registration form from another school, filled it out, put it in a certified envelope, and sent it in to the Mann School. It came back with a stamped form for mail that doesn't reach its destination—you know, with a finger pointing to a list of reasons? It said, "Refused." They knew my name by that time.

From that point on, I started to collect information; it was the same as going to school myself—I collected statistics and analyses. It was a period of intense concentration. I collected information all summer long and decided to make my move in September.

Now, going on in the background, completely unknown to me, was the activity involving Bill Wilcox, Jane Freedman, Bob Blackburn, and the others. The reform group had gotten the Board of Education to hold public hearings on its building program before it was adopted, and I heard about one of them. There was an article in the paper, a little box in either the *Inquirer* or the *Bulletin*—a thirty-day notice of hearings. By this time a number of things were beginning to happen simultaneously—pressure was coming from all sides—they *had* to have those hearings.

I decided to go to work on the all-white school that was half full. By then my daughter was registered at Cassidy, but it was obvious to me that we needed more classroom space in the neighborhood. I got hold of the proposed building program and saw that nothing at all was planned. So my next move was to join the local home and school association for Heston. But I was ostracized immediately because I raised questions—you weren't supposed to do that in a home and school association; they had tea parties. Otelia Robinson was another fighter, another dissident member, and her pitch was that there should be a new Heston School altogether, but she hadn't been able to get support for it. At that time you just didn't criticize the schools—the principals dominated the home and school associations, and a kid could be excluded from plays and trips if the parent caused trouble. The principals had the power.

But I decided to join Otelia and make a pitch for a new school. I decided, I'll just go down and show them that their building program was wrong. When school opened that year, my daughter went to Cassidy for about two weeks—it was a mess—really inconvenient—we had to go back and forth four times a day. We already had a new baby then, and my wife had to take the baby with her on the bus—we hadn't gotten the car yet.

You had to write in and get permission to speak at the hearings, but you had more of a chance if you were part of a group. So I decided to form a little committee. I made up a circular and distributed it in my block and the next block, inviting fifty people to an organization meeting. Five showed up—Mrs. Robinson was among them—so everybody became an officer. We called ourselves the Northwest Schools Committee.

Then I sent in my request to be heard at the hearing, and they okayed it. About a week after the request was granted, though, I got an acceptance from the Mann School—they thought they could soften what I was going to say at the hearings by giving me that. My daughter went there anyway; she was the only black kid in the school.

I used to be more patient, but not any more. Just recently my wife and I went together to make a hit, as we call it, in Wynne-

field, an integrated middle-class section in Northwest Philadelphia—the turf keeps moving northward. We went to talk to a
community meeting, and we pointed out that the home and
school associations are *still* trying to maintain white dominance.
For instance, my daughter's school won't show the black culture
TV shows prepared by the Board of Education this year, even
though it's forty per cent Negro.

Anyway, I did make the pitch at the hearing. It was a setup.
I'd gotten to know people in West Philadelphia by that time, and
two days before the hearings the West Philadelphia Schools
Committee let me present my statement to them. They played
the role of the Board of Education. One guy played General
LaBrum, the president; another guy got up and had a soft, weepy
voice like Allen Wetter, the superintendent of schools—he even
cried. They offered answers like "We have certain priorities—
the [predominantly white, semi-suburban] Northeast is a growing
area."

I didn't start as a fighter. I'd never made a public statement
before in my life, I was almost an introvert. But I'd gone to night
school for nine years. That was a grind and the engineering
course was tough—it required great concentration and effort and
discipline. I learned an approach to problem-solving at night
school—I learned that if you sit and work on one math problem
for two days, no problem is so big that you can't take it apart
and put it back together and come up with a solution.

About the rehearsal. Those people wanted me to be really
hard-hitting. They really pulled the rug out from under me. I had
to develop strategies. One was to give the statement just the way
it was written and not change a thing, then to wait for comments
and blast them. I was angry that they could discount the statement, even play-acting. I had a second statement in my head as
a counterstatement when I went to the actual meeting.

It was in October 1962, and true to form their responses were
just like the rehearsal. But I was ready—I came back and clob-
bered Wetter. All these people who had been working in the
reform movement were there, and even though I didn't know it,
this was my debut for them. I'd brought about fifteen people
down there with me from my local committee, which I kept going
afterwards. But then lots of committees wanted me to work with

them—I became a member, then co-chairman, then chairman of the West Philadelphia Schools Committee. Then, in '63, I became a member of Citizens Committee; I became vice-president in '64. And finally my involvement was city-wide. By the time of the new Board they were ready to make me a member, even though I'd attacked the nominating committee during the time of the Home Rule Commission.

The biggest thing I've ever done, in March or April 1965, was helping to stop the school at 46th and Market. For the first time in the history of the city, construction on a school was actually stopped by citizen protest. A couple of times in your life you get so committed that you say, This one I'll die for—your face gets warm and stays warm.

They had planned to build a junior high school on that site—but this goes back way before '65. It was going to be a dumping ground for black kids. "That school for the colored boys and girls," they used to call it. And the concept changed as it came under criticism. At the same time, of course, they were building new white schools for the nearby University City area. I took a stand with the West Philadelphia Schools Committee to fight for other sites that would be integrated. But there were many other things wrong with the site—it was too small, badly located, many things. They hadn't started construction, but the plans were all drawn—one of my other trophies is the blueprints; I still have them around somewhere.

I was able to mobilize this time. I'd learned to boil the issue down to go or no-go, and I boiled it down so that I had the support of forty-three organizations in the city. The school administration did everything they could to prevent a showdown, but finally they held a special hearing on the school. I made one concise statement. It was very dramatic—I went in with two hundred people and they all stood up when I spoke. I didn't even hear my voice—everything came out right. Then I said we would stop the building physically if necessary. And I walked down the aisle and out of the building and they were still applauding.

At the time my wife was pregnant with George Jr. I was working in Jersey at Campbell's, and the personnel officer told me that my job might be in jeopardy if I continued in civic work in Philadelphia. I said, You're concerned that I'm stepping on toes; well, I'll break ankles. I threatened to boycott the factory. But they'd been pretty good about giving me extra time off until then, I have to admit.

The second moment for me was November 17. I was in the building at the meeting when Rizzo and his boys beat up the kids. . . .

But the 46th and Market thing—we brought all the liberals around on that one. You have to eliminate by evidence all the smokescreen material that covers up racism. One of the most blatant examples of racism I've ever seen was when the Reverend Jesse Anderson, a very light Negro, moved into Wynnefield. He moved into a completely middle-class area, with "good" middle-class values, and the day he moved in three for-sale signs went up. His children were grown—they wouldn't be "contaminating" the schools. His wife was even a teacher.

People wanted to believe that what the officials said about the 46th and Market school was true; they'd accept *plausible* statements. The school administration would say things like "We must turn these kids out of school with salable skills"—then they'd eliminate the academic curriculum. It was completely paternalistic. But that particular one was overruled. Dr. John Marshall, a beautiful cat, a Quaker who got killed in an auto accident in Uganda, defeated that argument in two-thirds of a typewritten page. Then they said they'd make it a comprehensive school; they said they'd change the plans—but they didn't. When we checked the plans, the same workrooms were still there; they'd just changed the labels and called them classrooms. Marshall, who had been president of Citizens Committee, was at the role-playing session, incidentally. Marshall lobbied and got the public hearings going in the first place; at one time his daughter was the only white kid in an all-black school. He was a Quaker who lived it.

The truth is, I'd never been a fighter before. I was an only child, brought up in a large family by my grandparents. But I couldn't see all that without doing something.

There've been some good people working together in this town. . . .

Snapshot: *The Widening Gap*

"Letter of the day" printed on the editorial page of the Philadelphia *Inquirer*, October 17, 1968, in the midst of a city-wide controversy about forced integration through busing and racial tensions in the schools:

If the U.S.A. is still a free country, the people who hire the educators have the right to know how and what they want their children taught. The fair way would be to divide the schools into two systems and let the people decide which one they are going to send their children to.

One system would return to basic, competitive, disciplined education, with written examinations requiring passing grades before promotion in reading, writing, arithmetic, grammar, geography and history.

The other system would not have any standards. Promotion would be automatic through graduation from high school. The main emphasis would be on teaching the children to dance the Paul Jones by bus.

Ten years ago, one of the generals familiar with our ballistic missiles program said that of the twenty-five top men concerned in this vital branch of science, not more than two or three were Americans. The others had received European educations with the theoretical discipline essential to orbiting large missiles. Thirty-five years ago the Communists didn't even have the engineers necessary to operate their new factories. Today they are turning out 75,000 to 100,000 engineers and scientists every year, because they went back to basic education as taught under the Czars. At the same time we went "permissive."

Today we can only graduate 25,000 of these indispensable specialists. Do we really want to disarm ourselves?

III. *New Blood*

The Advancement School

MARK SHEDD's dark-haired, vigorous good looks made him seem even younger than his forty-one years. He wore business suits and a serious expression at public meetings, just like any other official, but occasional smiles or a straight honest glance at someone in the audience—at a leader of the black community he was trying so hard to please, for example—told them he was together. His appearance reflected his background—he had spent most of his life in the hinterlands of Maine, but during his years of graduate work at Harvard he had acquired a certain amount of big-city cool. Harvard had changed him in other ways as well; it had crystallized his philosophy of change and tuned his senses to the "action" in American education. Thirty-six-year-old Theodore Sizer, the liberal dean of Harvard's School of Education, was in the vanguard of a nationwide youth movement among educators. Richardson Dilworth talked frequently about the need for "new blood." Gradually new blood and youth became synonymous; they were one of the magic ingredients for change.

Shedd's talk about "turning kids on" was enough to make the gray hairs of the entrenched elders stand on end, but he did not hesitate to make his point explicit. In a speech to the school principals in May, 1967, Shedd asserted that the entire country needed a revolution—a revolution in values and ways of relating. He expected that the principals were weary of all the talk about change and youth and new blood, he said, but he believed that new blood could flow in old veins. Moreover, he knew that the revitalized school system would offer rejuvenation to everyone who worked within it. His relations with the principals had been rocky ever since—they *were* the old veins, and the Shedd team was a greater threat to them than to anyone else in the system. But in spite of their power, the principals could not stem the tide. Not all of them opposed the changes; more important, the youth movement was too strong for them even if they did. With nearly half the country under twenty-five, an influx of young teachers into the Philadelphia school system was inevitable, especially while the draft continued to threaten young men. Not everybody under twenty-five was a revolutionary, of course, but it was not a time for nuances.

Shedd did not create this youth movement, but he gave it momentum, mainly because he and his colleagues brought to Philadelphia a definite style associated with activist youth across the country. Anti-authoritarianism was at the heart of this style; it was resolutely democratic. It emphasized the values of community, honesty, and trust, and it was more concerned with the emotions than the intellect. The style had its jargon: "turned on," "action," "gut level," "alienation," "interpersonal," "involvement." It was the style of liberation, and borrowed from the culture of "soul" and jazz, from the psychological and sociological avant-garde. It was both a philosophy and a way of life. Paul Goodman was one of the leading spokesmen for the liberated style; Nat Hentoff, Edgar Friedenberg, John Holt, and, more recently, Jonathan Kozol and Herbert Kohl, had written about its absence —or its occasional practice—in the schools.

Whatever their motives, upwardly mobile staff members throughout the school system soon capitulated, in word if not in deed, to the new way. The middle-aged principal of a girls' high school, addressing a Board meeting, could look straight at Shedd and tell him in all sincerity, "We're going to turn the young ladies on." Shedd was so terrifying at the beginning that almost everybody agreed with him.

The reformers at the Board of Education did not depend on the regular staff to seize the banner of change, however. Long before Shedd's arrival, staff recruitment had focused specifically on finding the new blood and getting it into all levels of the system. New teachers included returning Peace Corps volunteers, Antioch students and interns from the Antioch-Putney teacher-training program, uncertified graduates of several Philadelphia colleges in a special program that enabled them to work for accreditation while they taught, and undergraduates from a consortium of Midwestern colleges involved in a work-study program. All were part of the system's efforts to tap the vitality of idealistic, committed youth.

But pressure for change had to come from every direction— from inside and outside the system, from community leaders, from teachers, visitors, nonprofessionals, and anyone else who could help. With this in mind, Shedd invited the North Carolina Advancement School, widely known as one of the most promising experimental schools in the country, to make its home in Philadelphia. The Advancement School would be a transfusion of rich new blood, for the average age of its staff was twenty-six. Bringing the school to Philadelphia was something of a coup; Shedd referred to it proudly as "my baby."

The school had originated as Terry Sanford's baby in November 1964, at a time when that liberal Democrat was well known as the "education" governor of North Carolina. An offshoot of the Learning Institute of North Carolina (LINC), which Sanford had founded as a lever for change for the state's public school system, the Advancement School was designed as a hothouse for innovation, particularly in dealing with the problems of "underachievers." Located in a former hospital in Winston-Salem, the residential school drew 150 seventh- and eighth-grade boys from all over the state for eleven-week terms of way-out experimentation and intense involvement. In addition to turning the boys on, the school aimed at developing new programs and attitudes which it would spread through the state system in the form of special curricula and teacher-training programs. The youthful staff had been getting what most people associated with the school considered excellent results; seventy-five per cent of the home-school principals reported a rise in the boys' grades, and ninety per cent saw a noticeable change in their attitudes toward school. This was all the more remarkable because the Advancement School had sought out the most difficult students —in educationese, an underachiever is one who exhibits a pattern of high ability (as measured by standardized tests), little motivation, and poor performance.

Few of North Carolina's leading educators shared the boys' enthusiasm for the Advancement School's innovations, however, and the citizenry at large was incensed that one-third of the students were black. Sanford's term ended in January 1965; his successor pledged support for the school, but it was only a matter of time before the educational and political conservatives began to move in. By the spring of 1967 the school's future looked bleak; the state Department of Education had managed to find technical grounds for taking the school over, and, knowing they would be deprived of the freedom to innovate that they had enjoyed for two and a half years, the staff began to look for new jobs.

The Advancement School had already attracted national attention. Harold Howe, LINC's first director, had moved on to head the Office of Education in Washington; the original director of the Advancement School had replaced him as head of LINC; and a young New Yorker and Harvard graduate had taken over as director. These moves produced a flurry of interest in the school's activities throughout the Northeast. The Carnegie Corporation, which had contributed $500,000 toward support of the school, issued a statement calling it "among the most far-reaching and useful educational programs in America." In addition, the school's turning-on techniques had been well publicized in several national magazines.

Two of Shedd's assistants who had strong ties to Harvard (a sort of casual incest had become quite acceptable in the most progressive educational circles that emanated from almighty Cambridge) had been following the political imbroglio in North Carolina, and finally, late in the spring of 1967, they convinced Shedd to pay the school a visit. Shedd was so impressed by the open, creative atmosphere that he quickly invited the staff to move to Philadelphia en masse. There too they would be an important agent for change; hopefully, they would have something to do with turning on the entire system. The Advancement School teachers were delighted to have this opportunity to continue their work together, and seventeen of them, natives of North Carolina as well as Harvard graduates and other Northerners, looked forward to the move.

Most of the famous innovative schools in the history of education have been the work of one man. Socrates, Dewey, Montessori, Neill—all had been the driving force behind their revolutions, the revered leaders of the schools they founded. From its inception, however, the Advancement School had deliberately avoided such leadership. In the view of the school's first director, Gordon McAndrew, teachers should have complete freedom to try new ideas and approaches. "McAndrew was a completely laissez-faire sort of director," one staff member commented in a survey of the school's activities made shortly before the move to Philadelphia. "It was very rare that he would express himself on policy; he tried to get the staff to develop a consensus." Peter Buttenwieser, who took over as director when McAndrew went on to LINC and who continued to head the school in Philadelphia, echoed his predecessor's view that the administration should not "load the deck with answers." Buttenwieser said that his main goal was to "get a reasonably creative group of people together and then let them develop the philosophy in concert." This approach frustrated some staff members, but most of them agreed that they liked it.

Describing the hiring of staff for the first year, McAndrew told an interviewer: "One of the key things that turned me off on anybody and still does is if he asked what's the structure or what is my position. . . ." According to many among the school's faculty, McAndrew espoused a "supportive," as opposed to "directive," policy. It needed no justification, of course; the word had been out for years that the failure of American education was its emphasis on structure, direction, and authority—with strong overtones of repression. The Advancement School was meant to evolve as a community effort, much like the hippie groups that were building a new life style in quiet communes throughout the nation.

Even "teaching" was looked on with a certain disdain. "Many members of the faculty reported that they made use of the freedom given them by the administration," the survey reported, "to concentrate at least as much on trying to listen to students, to observe them and react to them—and to learn from them—as they did on trying to 'teach' them in the traditional sense of the word." Few of the people interviewed in the survey seemed aware that they had unconsciously expressed a clear, even rigid, philosophy, but McAndrew suggested this at one point: "Originally we didn't espouse any predetermined philosophy about how to handle underachievers; really the philosophy was not to have one, to go into the classroom and to evolve one there in working with the kids." A "philosophy" like this could prove dangerous to its followers, but a majority of the school's staff actually ignored the "philosophy" altogether and settled for the essence of Socrates, Rousseau, Dewey, Montessori, Neill, and Goodman that formed the basis of educational progressivism. Even Goodman was "old," of course; but his ideas would have to suffice until better ones came along.

The North Carolina contingent of the staff had settled in Philadelphia by early September 1967, and Buttenwieser more than doubled their number by recruiting teachers from the Philadelphia system, Harvard, and a word-of-mouth talent pool kept alive by friends and sympathizers. At the beginning there was much talk among the staff of a clear division between the North Carolina people and the "new" people; many believed that the former had come with a solidarity that would impair the growth of community. There was indeed a certain cliqueishness in the original group—several had known each other for years and had worked together even before coming to the Advancement School—but most of the staff, old and new, were so similar in their backgrounds and ideas that there was little reason for in-groups to develop. Of the forty-five teachers, eight had some association with Harvard, for example. Altogether thirteen were graduates of prestigious Ivy League schools. Only a few were natives of Philadelphia. All but six were white.

Moreover, Buttenwieser had sought "creative" teachers, people of unusual talent and ability. Several had had careers other than teaching; some had been dancers, actors, painters, or writers. One, who spent the preceding summer as a lumberjack, had also worked as a puppeteer; another had been offered a contract by a professional football team. The teachers derived a certain pride from knowing how unlike an ordinary group of teachers they were.

But most important among the unifying factors was the element of youth; probably no other school in the country, public or private, had a teaching staff so uniformly young. Buttenwieser himself was thirty-one. A few others were in their mid-thirties, but on the surface, at least, they were in tune with the junior staff members. Later, when tensions developed, one teacher who was thirty-five began to tell his friends that he had felt distinctly uncomfortable about his age all along. On the whole the staff felt that they were responsible for creating an educational revolution, and ever since the heyday of Mario Savio older revolutionaries had not been the fashion.

Their youth notwithstanding, all but a few had teaching experience. Several were refugees from the rigidity of more traditional schools; others, feeling a commitment to urban education, came from well-known suburban systems. Ted Katz, the school's thirty-one-year-old Paul Bunyan of creativity, had taught five or six different subjects in as many schools; he had also been a dancer, actor, and painter. In North Carolina he had developed a course in communications that was being used by teachers in several schools all over the country, and after the Advancement School came to Philadelphia, he regaled a group of seven hundred teachers from the public school system with a three-hour illustrated lecture about his adventures in experimental teaching. (He left the school after its first year in Philadelphia, however, to do graduate work at Harvard.)

In addition to new staff, there were several other major differences between the Pennsylvania Advancement School and its North Carolina parent. The school would no longer be residential, of course—a vital factor. There had been learning laboratories at the North Carolina school (many of the teachers considered the "discovery" method the only reasonable means of education), but there had also been departments. Now the departments would have a purely secondary role; the basic teaching units would be four teams of eight or nine teachers, representing the various disciplines (English, math, social studies, science). Like a small school-within-a-school—or, more to the point, like a community—each team would be responsible for about thirty-five seventh- and eighth-grade boys during the term and would have carte blanche to develop its own philosophy and program. (Team teaching was scarcely an innovation; several schools in the city were already doing exactly the same thing, and the Advancement School had actually lagged in developing structural innovations.) In addition, there would still be "resource areas" (labs) for media, science, math, physical education, and other fields—typing and reading were later added.

Considering that structure was anathema to the liberated style, the building in which the school began its first session in Philadelphia was remarkably appropriate. A former factory in North Philadelphia, one of the city's poorest sections, the building had not been touched when the teachers first saw it early in September—despite promises from the Board of Education that special alterations would be made. The Board had purchased the six-story, block-long factory as a center for innovative projects and research, and eventually the Advancement School was to occupy the third and fourth floors, each covering approximately fifty thousand square feet. But the alterations would not even begin until October. For its first fourteen-week session, the school would have to manage with the unaltered second floor.

This consisted of a single room a block long, interrupted only by supporting columns at eighteen-foot intervals, and two smaller wings. Two of the teams occupied the wings; the remaining teams shared the large room with the office and administrative staff. Since good acoustics had not been important to the building's original purpose, the vast space was intermittently dominated by the muffled roar of the ventilation system, not loud enough to be deafening, but capable of drowning out a normal conversation a few feet away. Throughout the first session, but particularly at times of tension, this unlikely environment seemed to be the diabolical invention of a sadistic genius. At the beginning the staff tried to be optimistic about it. "At least," Buttenwieser said, "it doesn't look like a school."

After a brief orientation program beginning September 12, the staff divided into teams and went off to their separate areas to plan for the approaching session. A small group of administrators and counselors began to send feelers into the school system, their main objective being the selection of students, but generally the entire month before the opening of school was devoted to planning. In the months that followed, staff members often wondered what had occurred in the planning sessions. There had been, everybody agreed, a great deal of discussion, a continuing "dialogue," but actual decisions were elusive. "All we did was talk about philosophy," one teacher complained. "We never discussed *program.*"

True to the principles of democracy and community—on these there was at least superficial agreement—the teams were reluctant to elect official leaders. Even when conditions forced the designation of leaders, the idea that team members should work together as equals predominated. Although the subject was not openly discussed at the time, most of the staff seemed to have taken the democratic principle to its ultimate extreme—the very existence of a leader was seen as a harbinger of tyranny. The following discussion, dealing with activities for the first day of school, illustrates the sort of confusion and emotional deafness to which these efforts at total unanimity easily and frequently led.

Five people are seated in a circle in one of the team areas; the standard Board of Education chrome-and-vinyl club chairs encourage slouching, discomfort, and apathy, all of which are in evidence. The group consists of four young men and a girl, and their faces combine an eagerness to listen with a barely discernible tension—as Buttenwieser later observed of this group, "There's a high anxiety level here." During this discussion, several workmen are moving furniture nearby, providing an ostinato of noise and confusion.

"I don't think the first day should be a fun-and-games day from eight to three," says a long-haired young man in tortoise-shell glasses. "It's a long time to keep the kids buoyed up."

"I'd like to keep them buoyed up with anticipation for the next day," offers a pipe-smoker in a tone of slightly desperate humor.

An intense-looking fellow with dark, curly hair suddenly erupts with an idea. "I wonder if part of the first day should be an introduction along the lines that we introduced ourselves to each other last week. That way we can show them we're different from their other teachers."

The fourth young man, who has long sideburns, answers sardonically, "I'd rather let them discover the difference."

The workmen scrape desks on the floor, creating a nerve-tingling screech. "I'm going to get a great big ear horn," laughs the girl, who is wearing a bright pink-and-blue dress. "Hello, I'm *different*. Speak louder."

Underneath the pipe-smoker's smile there is great irritation. "I really find that I need silence. This building's driving me crazy."

"You're acclimated to the wrong thing," says another. "What you ought to do is set up a mixed-media environment for yourself to get used to it."

Deliberately patient, the man in tortoise-shell glasses brings them back to the original topic. "I think that not only the first day but even the first week should be oriented to turning that kid on. Then you can begin to do things; then later we begin to tighten up—we begin to get organized." He is one of the most experienced teachers on the staff, and he speaks with a note of authority suggesting reluctant semi-leadership.

"I'm just wondering now what we can do to make them come back the next *day*," the girl says.

"Let's assume," the pipe-smoker begins, "that we have a period in the morning—three or four hours . . ."

"Steve is working on an extravaganza," interrupts the intense one, then explains to the newcomers in the group: "At the end of last year we had a great big casino."

"A casino!" the girl cheers.

The pipe-smoker seems to disapprove of this irrelevance. "Could we start with the same kind of turning-on things we used last year? Mystery stories and thunder rattling in the background?"

"Even something like that," offers the semi-leader, "should be saved for after the first week. Save sensory experiences for later."

Pipe-smoker: "What would happen if we started with something like a taste test?"

Finally the discussion focuses on a game (actually, as someone points out in the technical language of the school's games expert, a "simulation") called Crisis. The kids are split up into several countries, the pipe-smoker explains. At the beginning of the game a war breaks out because of a dispute among the countries over several mines that contain a valuable mineral something like uranium. "It gets you very absorbed in the problem," he says, "and you have to react to other people in a very serious way. You find that you have to talk with people about what you want—to form a defensive alliance or something like that."

This interests the intense, curly-haired fellow, who has been relatively quiet. "Could you take that game and change it into gangs instead of countries?"

"Gangs don't form alliances," someone offers.

"Yes they do," the semi-leader answers. "Wasn't there some kind of gang plan to invade Manhattan?" He says it deadpan; there could be mischievous humor behind his slight smile.

The smoker knocks his pipe out on the edge of his chair and begins to clean it. "They might think we were trying to get them to tell us about *their* gangs."

"How long does this game take?" asks the girl.

"About an hour and a half," says the pipe-smoker, who had suggested the game in the first place and who now seems to have something of a stake in getting it accepted.

"From what you said," the girl muses, "it sounds as if it would not be a good idea to end the game on the first day. . . ."

The discussion begins to wander again. No one has offered a reason why the game shouldn't be used, but no one is particularly enthusiastic about it either.

"I'm disturbed by one thing," the girl says. "They're fighting over a mineral. Okay, say this is a simulation, a simulation of international politics. To say that this is the way things are done and to have kids learning how to carry on the sort of double-dealing that our society uses. . . . Are the kids critical of these values?"

The pipe-smoker is deterred for only an instant. "It provides kids with an opportunity to talk about whether it's good to be honest or dishonest."

The girl, more insistently: "It becomes a way of behaving."

Sideburns, somewhat exasperated: "You're playing an autotelic game; it's teleological. . . ."

"I think games are embedded right in what we believe in," the girl says with conviction. "I don't know if it's autotelic, whatever you said. I don't think we're just here to *stimulate* the kids. I have values." It is the first truly aggressive comment in the entire discussion, and for a moment there is a shocked pause.

"Aren't we losing the point?" says the pipe-smoker in a tone of weary resignation. "We were really looking for a way of turning kids on. Then we can talk with them about values."

* * * * * * * *

October 16, 1967—the first day of school. The atmosphere on the second floor is that of a famous repertory company about to go on stage for a Broadway opening without any idea of which play they are scheduled to perform. "Somehow we'll get through this" is written on the teachers' faces. "After all, *Time* raved about us."

There is plenty of evidence that the staff has worked hard for instant turn-on effects. A sign on a pillar near the entrance to the building reads: "How's your ol' self-concept, kid?" Upstairs, one of the teams has created a maze with rows of chairs. Blackboards greet the curious explorer with messages: "Nothing yet!"; "It's What you Make of It." Another area is bedecked with pop and psychedelic posters: Bob Dylan, Steve McQueen, Robert Vaughn, Marlon Brando, Moby Grape.

Kids are being bused to the school from each of the city's eight districts, and they arrive in small, bewildered-looking groups, beginning to trickle in at 10:00, the agreed-upon opening hour, allowing for the unusual transportation problems. In one of the team areas the girl who had been so definite about values is pinning name tags shaped like flowers and stars on each of the arriving students. The kids mill about awkwardly. Few of them know each other, though there are small knots of friends from the various home schools. (As in the rest of the system, about sixty per cent of the Advancement School boys are black.) The kids seek the comfort of milk and cookies as they survey the team area and talk shyly with the teachers. All they know about the school is what they've been told in preliminary interviews: that they will be able to have complete freedom to learn, that the teachers want to know what *they* want to do, that the school will be different from any other school they've ever been to. Some have seen last night's article in the *Bulletin* about the new school in a "creepy warehouse," which made it sound almost frightening.

For a large number of the more adventurous ones, however,

there is nothing frightening about these quiet, friendly, well-intentioned people who might be hippies (a few have beards), and the building itself is positively exciting. Already groups have struck out on exploring missions. They have found the secret hide-out in the cellar, the groovy sliding doors, the stairways, the private cubicles which will be their smoking dens, the roof. The sixth floor itself is a sort of paradise, for in addition to the nooks and crannies, the air-shafts and balcony, it has a pool table, a pinball machine, and a juke box with soul music. Long after the building has ceased to be interesting, the turn-on power of the pool table will endure; fights over it will lead, in fact, to the purchase of three more.

A meeting of the entire school has been called in one of the smaller rooms after the milk-and-cookies hour. It is close to 11:00, and the boys no longer have any question about the meaning of "complete freedom." None of these nice people has stopped them from doing anything. They have smoked, explored, left the building, gone across the street to buy food, smoked, and run wild until even their preadolescent energies and infinite curiosity are on the brink of exhaustion (soon they will learn to wear only old clothes to school). They are just beginning to be bored.

George Mager, head of the school's media department and chief film-maker, stands on a table at the front of the room, shouting. About half of the kids are seated in chairs set up in rows, and the rest stand along the walls. George wears a snappy-looking double-breasted blazer and a flowered tie. "Hey, I want your attention," he shouts. The mob begins to quiet down somewhat. "Do you like my tie?" he shouts. A good-humored "NO!" explodes from the crowd. "Gentlemen," he shouts above continued noise, "I'd like to take this opportunity to welcome you to the Pennsylvania Advancement School." The voice is lost in commotion. "GENTLEMEN! I want to ask you that when someone is speaking to you, please pay attention." This time they see that he means it; this sudden show of firmness commands respect. Satisfied, he goes on to explain that there are certain rules at the Advancement School: no fighting, no stealing, no smoking. But again commotion breaks out; a group of students has asked to speak, and soon ten or so are standing with him on the table. One of them shouts "Shut up!" at the audience, but the noise continues.

"Do you think we should have grades?" George calls out.

A huge chorus: "NO!"

A kid in a porkpie hat who is standing on the table manages to be heard: "I think we should have grades in some classes. . . ." But before he can go on, another kid has been pulled from the table, and a fight begins. George sends the table delegation back to their seats, but detains the speaker, who continues with his explanation. "Hey, George, we can't hear him," shouts a teacher in the back. "Here's someone," George shouts, "who says we shouldn't have grades because he doesn't *like* them." Finally, after another wave of noise, he calls on Mr. Thompson to speak.

A tall black boy, leaning casually against the back wall, smiles at an attractive young white girl: "You a teacher?"

Mr. Thompson has glasses, brown hair, and a mustache. "We've decided not to have grades," he tells the students. "One of the main reasons we're not having them is because kids don't like them. Another reason is we want school to be an interesting place to be."

"Hey, this kid's SMOKING!" shouts a boy in the back of the room.

But Mr. Mager has had enough. "Back to your team areas," he shouts. The group begins to break up. "Aw, let's keep on talking," one boy says, half to himself, in a voice that mixes guilt and anger.

As the boys move out of the room, one of the teachers greets a friend from another team. "*That* was chaos," she says with a nervous laugh.

Although the teachers are shaken, they resist the pandemonium bravely. In two of the team areas, groups of boys settle down to painting the floors and walls; they are busy, interested, highly "motivated." Others watch a movie and hear a horror story in a dark room filled with flickering lantern light and weird sound effects from a tape recorder. Others play group games. A large number of them spend the entire day on independent tours of the building, with inevitable stops at the sixth-floor recreation center. Many sit in on discussion groups and admit that they like the school much more than their home schools, even though there isn't enough discipline. Interpersonal relating has occurred. The day is not without its successes.

The staff assembles at 3:30 in the huge main room. "We've gone through a process of instant learning," Peter tells them as he opens the discussion. He seems calm and relaxed, but the day's tension is visible on many faces. "You've got to watch out not to overcriticize," he continues. "For example, I got the impression from some of the kids that good things happened. They have the sense that there are nice people here; there's a sense of humanity and exploration. We ought to remember that we did accomplish things today. The second thing is a general point: We've all talked about wanting to take on the real problems of education, specifically urban education. Today we got a chance to see if we really want to work with them." Every eye is on him; it seems that his words are filling a great void. "I know what I want, and I guess what everybody wants is instant, overwhelming success and adulation, and I guess what I'm really trying to say is that we're up against a fairly difficult time." There is a pause, then on an upbeat: "I would suggest that we talk openly and freely now and get to as many problems as we can and try to come to some kind of resolution."

The first one to speak is the girl who had defended her values at the planning session. "I find myself disturbed," she begins, "by a lack of *structure.* . . ."

For an hour the group discusses what sort of structure and rules should be adopted. Most agree that there must be rules, but the question of how to enforce them causes confusion. "I don't think you need to enforce them," offers one teacher. "It's your whole job to handle these situations sensitively." Finally one of the administrative staff suggests that the counselors and administrators should be available to handle discipline problems. The suggestion has a steadying effect on the group, but as the meeting draws to a close, the only thing that has been decided on is a basic list of rules for behavior throughout the school.

Just before the end of the meeting there is a brief flare-up. One teacher insists that the students must call him "Mister," that other teachers are not to introduce him by his first name. "I don't want to be on the kids' level," he explains.

"You're not just talking about names," observes another teacher with a shrewd smile.

"I don't think we can settle this today," someone mumbles.

But one of the clearest voices from the hour's discussion comes to the rescue: "I move that we introduce each other as 'Mister' and leave the rest up to the individual." There is an almost audible sigh of satisfaction, and soon the group disperses to the separate team areas. Planning sessions last well into the night.

As the days go by, a tidal wave of memos begins to flood the teachers' letter boxes. Marty Cohen, the assistant director, gathers them in bulging notebooks. They include memos about teaching experiments, curricula, community involvement, "learning styles"; memos reporting how various staff members have handled discipline, taught a specific subject, reached a particular student; optimistic memos from Marty that start each day with a burst of humor; finally, even a series of memos in which two teachers conduct a half-serious public feud about something one of them may or may not have said and the other thought he heard. Reams upon reams of ditto paper are consumed as the fever of communication sweeps the school. But, especially toward the conclusion of the first session, a homely brand of wisdom, of which some of the following excerpts from various teachers' notes are typical, begins to mitigate the general hysteria.

December 4, 1967

Notes on where we are going
. . . Part of our problem, too, was and still is an interpersonal one. Teams which by all account should have been terrific, were paralyzed. Decision-making became traumatic, leadership was confused, and communication got bogged down. . . .
. . . [And yet] I would definitely give the team idea at least a second go around under the circumstances produced by the changes [improvements for the next session, including the completed third and fourth floors]. Furthermore, I really don't think the staff should be asked to decide this question, although their opinions should be solicited. . . .

January 18, 1968

[One of the teachers] says he came into the school and heard about how great everyone was, saw the various slide tapes, heard the various presentations, and began to gather by innuendo that everybody was going to do all these wonderfully interdisciplinary things. Then, dismayed, said to himself, "Oh (so that's what it's all about) . . . but I'm only a . . . well, what I mean is, I'm a science teacher." Everything has to be absolutely new and different, something in the air seemed to say. He didn't say so, but I'm sure he must have shrugged his right shoulder and, throwing his open hand out and up, cast away both his confidence and his abilities. What *I* mean is, I did something like that myself. So did some others. . . .

January 25, 1968

Notes on what I've learned during the first session:
. . . Our planning often had an air of "it probably won't work anyway, so why bother with the details?" . . . I get amazingly angry when a kid defies me.

January 25, 1968

Some things I've learned or re-learned this session:
. . . Buying things—mounds and piles and heaps and great gleaming globs of *things*—seems to have been a panic reaction (even after we all agreed, quite rationally, that we needed *things* in our area). We still have those mounds and piles and heaps and great gleaming globs of things, only now they are shattered, smashed and splintered things. We need to reflect, I think, on why the things were destroyed and how this destruction relates generally to the way the kids feel about the school. We need to consider also whether it is possible to have a surfeit of things when there is no clear plan about how we will use them. . . .

January 25, 1968

What Session One has Taught Me
. . . The approach to teaching which I have reconciled myself to holding at least for a few years is basically Maslovian and Third Force. I want to begin with kids' basic needs, to try to shape a curriculum which will satisfy these needs, and to permit kids to grow into a new, more mature set of needs. I want to concentrate on the skills of problem-solving: observing, using logic, intuiting, imagining, proving. By applying such skills to the problems they confront in their lives and to the problems their macrosocieties face, kids will learn how to handle not only their own problems of personal growth but also some of the larger social problems. . .

After the initial jolt, which had the staff reeling for a couple of weeks, a *modus operandi* had been established. Although students were no longer allowed to do everything they wanted, the staff realized that they had doomed themselves to a defensive battle. There were suspensions; there were even expulsions. But the thefts, daily breaking of rules, and destruction of school property continued to the end of the term. "Why aren't these rules being *enforced?*" teachers kept asking each other. And sometimes the most honest answer was, "I'm just too tired to chase another kid."

To outsiders, the Advancement School often seemed like total anarchy. One Philadelphia principal—widely known as an innovator, in fact—decided that she would not let any more of "her" boys attend, explaining to colleagues that they had forgotten all their good habits in the wild fourteen weeks. Other visitors limited their outward reactions to tight smiles and grim affirmations that the school certainly was "different." But many were completely turned on. For, whatever its problems, the Advancement School was, as Buttenwieser had proudly declared before it opened, not much like a school. Visitors came from all over the country to view this radical experiment—the list of notables even included John Holt.

As far as the teachers were concerned, romance, after disillusioned passion, was virtually impossible. With one exception, the teams simply had not been able to work together—the exception happened to be a group that was dominated by several old friends who lived together in Philadelphia. Team structure was not inherently self-defeating, but the continuing suspicion with which staff members regarded strong leadership precluded effective teamwork. One team elected a leader, for example, only to learn on the following day that he had decided he didn't want to be a leader. In the many discussions of the subject, several teachers observed that everyone on the staff was a prima donna and that no one would follow anyone else's leadership. Others took the opposite tack, complaining that there was a pervasive reluctance among the staff to assert themselves in any way. One thing was certain: participatory democracy, one of the hallmarks of the world-wide youth movement, was having a rough time at the Advancement School. Perhaps this explained the peculiar departure of one staff member at the end of the year—there had never been any real question about the position of the Advancement School faculty on the war in Vietnam, but, to everyone's surprise, this particular young man left to enlist in the Army.

Graduation day after the first session was a time of great sadness. The four-month term had been frustrating for most of the teachers, but the kids had been turned on from the very beginning. During the fourteen weeks they had played games, cultivated and studied live animals, taken hundreds of rolls of pictures, explored the city, and done a host of things they would never have been able to do at their home schools—activities, they frequently told their teachers, that didn't really have anything to do with "learning." Moreover, once they had gotten used to what seemed at first a crazy world, they had begun to see that the teachers cared about them deeply, were going to the most incredible lengths just to do something that would "turn them on." ("Well, what do you want to do now?" the teachers were always asking them.) Many of the boys were in tears that last day of school. For them there had been no quandaries about interpersonal relationships, philosophy, or styles of learning. If they hadn't been able to find something interesting to do, which was rarely the case, they could usually get a teacher to chase them. The Advancement School was a ball.

And their mood had been essentially the same since the beginning, for while they weren't always sympathetic, they understood their teachers' problems perfectly. They were only young boys, after all, and few of them would hold a grudge against a well-meaning teacher, no matter what he did. One of them had expressed this mood eloquently in his experiments with a typewriter shortly after his group had been severely reprimanded for throwing sticks out a window during the first week:

dear mr gordon you are a very nice man i like you be cause you are a very nice man. In gods way we are the samme the reason I say this his because i got battized in jesus name and i got down to parise the lord. i like the school because it has a lot of action. i like all of the teacher. and i have a lot of fun and i like the work. and mr. gordon i really like mr gordon. and i like to discuss thing. . and it makes me think when we don,t call each other black, or., white. becayuse in gods ways we are the same. and the caflic thing that mary can save them when the world come to the end. dear mr gordon i would like you to come to my church and get battized, and receive thre gitf of thre holy ghost. i don't want to burn in for eteret i want you to read this to the class. let them now that the world hias going to in soon. . and the reason they act uop. the reason his becausre they act up like this is because they no nothing about the lord. and the bible saids if you don,t get battized in jesus name and recive the gift of the holy ghost you are lost at the end of the world you are just lost. dear mr. gordon i m i want you honest and truly read this out to the class please. take my avice! !

Sincerely your

He had not signed the letter. He was a little black boy named Bruce. Eventually he was asked to leave the Advancement School, along with a dozen others. He had been an unmanageable discipline problem.

The contrast between the Advancement School's first and second sessions was as palpable as the finished, carpeted third and fourth floors of the building to which the school moved in February 1968. The awful racket of the ventilation system had been at least partly eliminated by acoustically tiled ceilings; the rooms, with their movable furniture and walls, were as flexible as a planned learning environment could be; there was an atmosphere of openness and ease, but of order and purpose too— the whole operation had a good deal of tone, and the chaos of the first session seemed worlds away.

The first session would linger as an unpleasant memory, but it had been an invaluable learning experience for the entire staff. The ideals of youth-cult and the passion for anarchy began at last, in the new setting, to be seen in a reasonable perspective. An executive cabinet was eventually elected to handle decision-making. Highly imaginative courses of study, games, and lab techniques were taking shape. "Discipline problems" were a mere echo of what they had been before.

In short, the Advancement School was getting down to the business of being successful. The real distinction of the staff, it became clear as time went on, was its being one of the best-informed, most consciously innovative groups of teachers in the country. One could spend a day at the Advancement School and find out just about everything new that was happening in the world of education. One could have discovered all of it, in bits and pieces, elsewhere, but the Advancement School was an excellent showcase.

But innovation does not necessarily imply a revolution in

values. In the case of the Advancement School, true community had been lost, permanently it seemed, in the shuffle, and the school's emerging style was slickly professional. Turning kids on might once have meant helping them to be totally alive and aware human beings, but, on another level, the process could be merely a tinkering with intellectual and perceptual machinery. The moral fervor of the first session was gone.

There was no time for it. In the growing turmoil of urban warfare, the very survival of the Advancement School was at stake. City officials took pot shots at the school's lavish budget whenever they had a chance, and at one point the school was even closed down, on a slim pretext, by the Department of Licenses and Inspections. The Advancement School was a show-case for innovation, but it was an expensive one, and as such was more vulnerable than any other new program in the system.

Surviving meant producing, and curriculum packages were not enough. Somehow the Advancement School had to show that it was affecting the school system as a whole. With this in mind the administrative staff greatly expanded the school's teacher-training facilities, and in the fall of 1968 a whole new wing of the staff began to concentrate exclusively on "dissemination" of the school's ideas, working intensively in five junior high schools. The staff had learned, perhaps too late, that the contempt for the system so many of them openly declared was a status symbol they could ill afford.

As for the kids for whom the Advancement School was so much fun and free-wheeling excitement, the results of pre-liminary research suggested that the school actually had a nega-tive effect. According to reports prepared by the research divi-sion of the Franklin Institute—which had been commissioned by the Board of Education to evaluate several new programs in the fall of 1967—the majority of the Advancement School students returned to their home schools even more hostile to traditional teaching methods than they had been before. They had glimpsed the future; they had tasted freedom. As one of them put it, with a touch of anger, after his fourteen weeks were up: "They turned me on; then they put me back and let me get turned off again."

In the flux and turmoil of urban warfare the school's effect on the kids it served could be only one of many factors in determining its future. The report of the Franklin Institute would probably serve as ammunition someday in the hands of an enemy, but the fate of the kids had to defer, for the moment, to the needs of contending powers.

Snapshot: *The Hero*
There can be no doubt that he is the angriest of the Antioch "co-ops," a generally angry group of undergraduates from Antioch College who have come to work in the inner city for the betterment of American society. He is young and impatient, and his eyes glow like Che Guevara's, or perhaps like the eyes of Omar Sharif in his screen portrayal of Che. He has been sitting quietly, listening to Mark Shedd address the staff of the Pennsylvania Advancement School, but finally, at the end, during the question-and-answer period, he has his chance to strike a blow for honesty and the good of all mankind. "Are you tired and blasé," he asks Shedd with a sneer, "or do you just look that way?"

Radical on the Way Up

I MET HIM in the teachers' cafeteria at Gratz High School, an all-black school in North Philadelphia. I was having coffee one morning with two teachers I'd become friendly with during my numerous visits. Ken Hoerauf taught metal shop and ran the drama club. Sunny Decker, an English teacher, was a live wire. Both were friendly with a group of bright "militant" students whom the majority of the Gratz faculty viewed as dangerous revolutionaries. I was the first to notice the visitor as he approached our table, since I happened to be facing in his direction.

He seemed unusually young to be a teacher. Of medium height and build, with a shock of almost wild brown hair distinctly reminiscent of Robert Kennedy, he appeared to be at most in his early twenties. He wore a dark, conventional suit, a white shirt, and a brightly patterned tie. But the round, wire-rimmed glasses were a startlingly discordant note. Granny glasses could be a cliché, but I actually welcomed them in this alien setting.

Sitting down at our table, he introduced himself and proceeded to give us a lengthy explanation about why he had come to Gratz. Throughout the conversation he spoke in a halting manner that created an engaging impression of boyish inarticulateness, lively enthusiasm, and a respect for his listeners that verged on awe.

He managed to communicate, nevertheless, and as the four of us talked, he seemed to relax a little.

He was a junior at Yale, he told us, majoring in "culture and behavior." Earlier in the school year he had initiated a project that would serve as the thesis for one of his courses: Working closely with Yale's dean of admissions, he and a team of recruiters were combing the twenty high schools in the Philadelphia public school system in search of talented juniors who had the ability to get into Yale but who would not ordinarily apply. After selecting a group of likely candidates they would conduct a one-day "workshop" in which the juniors—probably no more than eighty of them—would visit Yale for a day and really get to know the school. Ken Hoerauf taught juniors, and the visitor wanted to know if he could recommend any of his outstanding students.

The three of us responded almost in unison. How would the candidates be selected, we wanted to know, considering that they would probably fail to meet the university's admission standards?

The main criterion, he told us, would be the students' high school records and their PSAT scores (college boards); of course he was looking for the likeliest candidates, he hastened to add. Yale could not make any significant change in its admission requirements, though the dean of admissions was on record as advocating a more "balanced" student population, not just the superscorers.

Even so, Ken pointed out, the highest scores at Gratz couldn't begin to equal the records of most suburban kids; the Gratz kids simply hadn't been raised in that sort of test-taking atmosphere.

But, our visitor insisted, they weren't looking just for high-scorers; they wanted more *city* kids to apply to Yale. He himself was from a Philadelphia suburb, but he knew of only one inner-city Philadelphian in Yale at the moment. The university had received only three applications from the entire city in the previous year. And he wasn't seeking just blacks; he wanted talented kids from the city who would not ordinarily apply to Yale.

Sensing that the three of us were more or less open to what he was doing, he went on to talk about the program with a fresh burst of enthusiasm. The purpose of the visit to Yale, he explained, was to get the kids involved in a *meaningful* way; he didn't want it to be the usual campus tour. His plan was to split up the group so that a pair of Philadelphia students would spend the entire day with one Yale student. Among other things, they would talk with a professor in a field they were interested in, but in a less formal context than a class. Then they would have dinner with a faculty member. After dinner, they would be free to explore one of the university's numerous evening activities— "like, let a kid go to WYBC if he's interested in radio." In addition to the workshop, a man from the admissions office would be visiting Philadelphia to talk with the guidance counselors in the various schools and to reinforce the idea that the students could indeed aspire to what may have seemed the loftiest heights. At one of the other high schools, he told us in a conspiratorial tone, "Two old women said, 'We don't want the kids to set their sights *too* high.'"

I think he had really won our confidence by this time. There was a feeling among us that it was good to have people about who were engaged in new, interesting projects like his, particularly young radicals from outside the school. Gratz was more open to innovators than most schools, but few visitors offered camaraderie as well. In this generally charitable frame of mind, we tended to dismiss the obvious shortcoming of the program— that it would seek only the sort of kids who excelled in test-taking—and accepted both program and salesman in a package. The incident probably meant less to Ken and Sunny than it did to me, however.

For one thing, I went to Yale. When I graduated in 1962, I was at the tail end of the so-called "quiet" generation; activism was not the style of the time, and, devoting most of my nonacademic efforts to a little theater group, I was almost completely apolitical. Here was an engaging, bright fellow, obviously a staunch member of the activist generation, who offered balm to my retrospective frustration. Here, too, was a sympathetic observer who had spent time in the high schools. I wanted to talk with him again. As I got up to leave for an appointment somewhere in the building, we agreed to meet at the end of the school day.

Throughout the afternoon I was vaguely bothered about the visitor from Yale. When I had time to think about what he'd said, when my vicarious relish for the political activism of a fellow

Yale man pitched slightly toward rationality, I began to see that, while I wanted very much to like what he was doing, wanted to relive my own Yale career as an activist, the plan he'd outlined to us was basically wrong. The inequities of our society would in no way be corrected by a few of Philadelphia's most intelligent test-takers gaining admission to that elite segment of it represented by the Yale student body. That was simply more of the same, the test-taking establishment perpetuating its own narrow vision of life. The only kids in the Philadelphia high schools who were likely to qualify for Yale would be in the city's "academic" Central High School. The search in the other schools would probably turn up no more than a handful who even had a chance.

Thus I realized that while I might mention the project somewhere in my book, it wasn't worth extensive research. Would I tell the visitor from Yale about my decision? I did not have time during the afternoon to decide, and for some reason I was avoiding the decision anyway. Considering what happened later, I can see that I must have made the decision easily, then refused to admit it to myself.

The visitor from Yale was accompanied that day by one of the team of interviewers who was assisting him in the job of lining up candidates. Most of the classrooms were locked by the time the three of us met in the main hall, and, remembering a tiny conference room adjacent to the National Teacher Corps office, I led them down the corridor. The other fellow, quiet and likeable, had an air of profound naïveté, and in the ensuing conversation he was mainly a startled listener.

The conference room was not much larger than a closet, though it was used for tutoring classes. We had settled in a small semi-circle to talk, and after telling the other visitor something about my book, I was beginning to ask a few vague questions about their research experiences, when Ned van Dyke appeared in the doorway.

Ned was twenty-six and liked to think of himself as a professional radical. After a stormy college career—a highlight of which was his expulsion from Temple University for "student politicking"—he had taught for several years in the Philadelphia system and was about to leave it out of sheer frustration when Mark Shedd assigned him to supervise the National Teacher Corps team at Gratz. The Teacher Corps was a federal program that enabled college graduates to enter teaching as uncertified interns, and it emphasized, in addition to a limited teaching load, intensive community involvement. Ned's biggest triumph as a team leader had been his founding, with two Corps members, of a storefront school in a black community about fifteen blocks from Gratz. He had dark, curly hair behind a high forehead, excited eyes that almost seemed to jump out of his head, and a voice that could well be running the one-minute mile, even with slight leaps over hurdles of thought or emotion. He usually dressed in dark suits and carried a briefcase, but his talk left no doubt of where he stood in relation to the establishment.

I introduced Ned to the visitors and explained briefly why they were in Philadelphia. He nodded his understanding during my explanation, then drew a breath. "Where are you going to find kids with high enough scores?" he asked. "The average verbal at Yale is something like 680; at Gratz it's more like 450. You'll never find the kids. Unless you go to Central." His attitude instantly gave the situation a different focus; as far as he was concerned, the merit of the program was all that counted. He had no stake in the future of radicals from Yale; there were enough radicals to go round, the important thing was to find good programs. He himself stayed up at night working on new curriculum ideas.

The visitor from Yale explained that the students would have to have high test scores—somewhere, at least, near the Yale norm.

For a moment Ned seemed to stop dead in his tracks. Then: "You're not doing anything; you're not changing a thing. You're just looking for the kind of kids who would get into Yale anyway."

The engaging smile, betraying inarticulateness, flickered on the visitor's face. "Well, most of these kids wouldn't ordinarily apply to Yale," he said. "We want to give them the chance."

For me, Ned had finally brought the whole business into focus. "That's what I was trying to tell you," I said. "Your program isn't going to work as long as you depend on those goddam scores."

The visitor seemed slightly intimidated. "How else could we do it?"

"Forget the scores!" Ned shouted.

"Right!" I said. "The scores are what's wrong with the system. It's like I.Q.'s. All they test is the ability to do well in the tests."

"What you really ought to do . . ." Ned began.

I interrupted him. "The program the way you have it set up now is half-assed," I said. "It isn't going to change anything at Yale. What you ought to do is scrap the tests, get a team of interviewers down here, and spend several weeks going around the high schools looking for talent. Go into the schools, get to know who the best teachers are, seek them out, and ask them about their *gifted* students. The ones who've done something. I know a kid right here in Gratz, he's an Ethiopian Jew, has a black belt in judo, teaches in a Hebrew school, and he's semi-literate in English. Get kids like *him* up at Yale."

"He'd have a lot of trouble once he got there," Ned offered.

"Well, they'd run a program like the SEEK program at City College to keep these so-to-speak culturally deprived kids in the university. And the university would have to adjust to them as well. *That* would loosen up some of that academic constipation. Then you'd have something *real*. The university would never be the same. And the thing is, Yale's one of the few places that can afford to try something like this."

Yale's emissary was sweating slightly; he seemed trapped.

"Now I know why you had so much trouble explaining the whole thing to us before," I told him. "You've known all along that there was something wrong with the idea. Well, now you know what it is."

"Yes," he said. "I've known about this problem. I knew it wasn't exactly right."

In a minor eruption, Ned waved his hands at the visitor. "Here's your chance. You can really shake up the system!"

"But . . . This is just for a single course in my junior year. This isn't even a senior thesis."

"The hell with that," I said. "You go tell Kingman Brewster that you want to be exempt from regular courses for the next two years, and *you* administer this program. It'll be more meaningful than all those stupid *courses* you'd be taking instead. Brewster's a liberal guy; he's open to ideas, and this is a good one." In all fairness, there are some excellent courses at Yale. But I wasn't thinking about them as I spoke.

"The faculty will hate it," Ned laughed.

"Oh boy, the faculty!" I jeered. "Lounging in their paneled offices. Writing *papers!*"

"Seriously," the visitor said, "the Corporation will have to approve something like this."

That slowed me down. I had a picture of the members of the Yale Corporation—a formal portrait in my mind's eye. In that picture, they could just as well have controlled the entire world; in fact, some of them had power over sizable chunks of it. "You might have trouble there," I admitted. "They want to keep the place safe for their sons, of course." It was a serious obstacle; one lonely radical wasn't going to shake up the entire university without help from the top. "Look!" I exclaimed. "Get Dilworth behind it. He's radical enough for something like this. He has plenty of pull at Yale."

"He's a radical all right," Ned agreed. "He's a Victorian radical."

But our assault—Ned's and mine—was losing strength. Later I could see that for Ned the whole thing had been a briefly interesting moment, no more. He'd been on his way home when he heard our voices in the conference room, and he left now in such a perfunctory way that I knew this was one revolution he was going to skip.

For a moment we were silent. "You'll never be able to carry out this idea as it should be carried out," I said somewhat patronizingly, "unless you really believe in it. Ultimately it has to come from you."

"That's right," the visitor said. His forehead was moist; I thought of how embarrassed he must be to have the basic weakness of his whole project suddenly exposed like this, but better now than later. "I'm not sure I really *want* to try this," he said.

Now I was almost sorry that we'd been so blunt with him; I wanted to help him out of the difficult spot we'd put him in. "You've either got to go all the way with it or abandon it," I said. "If you're going to be honest about it. And it's a tremendous job if you go all the way. It could fail. It means two years of hard work, and it could fail." I thought the visitor seemed grateful for my understanding.

"I'm not sure that I'd have the guts to try this myself," I went on, "but the situation at Yale is very different from when I was there. In fact, I bet you feel exactly the same way I did at the end of my senior year—I'd written plays as a special project, and I'd been introduced to an agent who was interested in selling one of them to a Broadway producer. And I thought to myself, Who's going to produce my play on Broadway? I'm only twenty-two, what do *I* know? I just couldn't think of anything like that happening to me."

"No, that's not it," he answered; suddenly the nervousness of a few minutes earlier was completely gone. "You see, the kind of thing you're talking about involves action from the bottom, shaking up the system from the bottom. I *know* I could do it if I wanted to." He paused and smiled at me—I've got your number, the smile said. "But, you see, I'm not interested in working at the bottom. I'm interested in working at the *top*."

Several weeks later I was talking with a friend who happened to be an undergraduate at Yale, and I mentioned the name of the visitor at Gratz. Did my friend know him? Had he heard of him? "Oh sure," he said. "I know him. Everybody knows him. The *Yale Daily News* has done six front-page articles about him. He's the kind of guy who's involved in everything."

A Lesson in Revolution

If children need contact with adults who will
free them to face life, adults who are concerned
with large issues, adults who are accepting,
helping, understanding, positive, open to experience, tolerant of ambiguity, personally involved, does the Antioch-Putney program prepare such human beings?

If it does (as I hope it does) is this a cruel
hoax?

What happens when a group of perceptive,
understanding, accepting, adequate, involved,
committed, and capable human beings hits a
school system that is controlling, concealing,
alienated, dominating, condemning, rejecting,
negative, closed, intolerant, and educationally
bankrupt?

—from a position paper written
by an Antioch-Putney staff
member in the summer of 1968

RICHARDSON DILWORTH had known James Dixon, the president
of Antioch College, since before the days when Dixon served as
commissioner of public health in the Dilworth administration,
and the new Board president lost no time at the beginning in
talking with potentially helpful friends. As president of the small
liberal arts college in Yellow Springs, Ohio, Dixon had inherited
a tradition of progressive activism—Antioch was ripe for projects
that would involve its students in the future of America's cities.

While not everybody connected with Antioch was necessarily
a beautiful, loving, turned-on human being, the college had a
reputation for liberalism and social consciousness that attracted

a student body with an unusually high proportion of bright radicals. Antioch's graduate school of education, founded in 1964 and linked with an already existing program in Putney, Vermont, shared these values and had already begun to search for solutions to the urban school crisis—since 1965 there had been teacher-training "centers" in Washington and Baltimore, in addition to Yellow Springs and Putney. Antioch-Putney's emphasis, like that of the college generally, was more on capable people than on certified personnel, and, in short, Antioch could provide a ready-made, self-replenishing supply of graduates and undergraduates who were generally interested in social change.

During the 1967–68 school year the program introduced nearly forty Antioch students into the system; twenty-four were undergraduates who worked in the schools as part of their cooperative work-study program (they were commonly known as "co-ops"), and fifteen were teacher-interns, students in the Antioch-Putney Graduate School of Education for whom a year of teaching was part of the requirement for a master's degree. Technically, the co-ops were separate from the interns; but they tended to band together under the same Antioch umbrella in bad weather.

The program attracted increasingly larger numbers as its reputation grew and as word got around that the Philadelphia public schools were actually welcoming change. In the winter of 1967–68 the Great Lakes Colleges Association, a confederation of twelve small liberal arts colleges in Ohio, Indiana, Michigan, and Wisconsin (Antioch was one of them), followed Antioch's lead by initiating an "Urban Semester in Philadelphia." Similar to Antioch's work-study program, the GLCA program brought a vanguard group of 6 students to Philadelphia in January 1968; during the course of the following year the number grew to as many as 70. The majority of the Antioch and GLCA students, though not all, worked in the Philadelphia public schools; those who did received salaries from the Board of Education. There were roughly 125 of them by the winter of 1969, and while they rarely made headlines, anyone who had contact with them knew that they were making waves.

The program had begun with a singular advantage: Instead of trying to overhaul the system from top to bottom, Antioch-

Putney-GLCA limited its operations almost entirely to one relatively calm section of the city—Germantown, a historic community with many qualities that sustain its original identity as an autonomous village. Gradually the Antioch-Putney-GLCA network became a minor fixture in Germantown, moving from temporary offices in a municipally owned building (after some unpleasantness, with anti-left-wing overtones, from City Hall) to its own two-story house in the heart of the Germantown business district. Organization and action within the community had been one of the main purposes of the program from the beginning, and while both Antioch-Putney and GLCA continued to develop new approaches and programs as they adjusted to the environment, even in the early stages they were getting results.

During the 1967–68 school year a group of GLCA students rented a house as a coeducational, cooperative dormitory, but the house quickly became, in addition, a recreation and tutorial center for neighborhood kids. A team of GLCA students combined with a team of Antioch interns and co-ops to nearly double the staff of the Pastorius School, whose principal was well known in the school system as a friend of change. Other teams of Antioch interns and co-ops were scattered throughout the Germantown schools and were occasionally distinguishing themselves in community or school planning, extracurricular activities, and new curriculum projects.

Of friction—or worse, "confrontation"—one heard relatively little. Part of the reason for this may have been that the leaders of the Antioch-Putney Graduate School were not completely agreed, according to Robert Piper, the director of the Philadelphia center, on whether Antioch-Putney was to be a "change agent" itself or whether it should merely produce change agents who would operate pretty much on their own. The director of the GLCA program, Robert deHaan, emphasized that "we avoid the opposition—we put our kids where they can work. We're trying to set up a new reward system by giving the kids to the people who treat them well." Antioch-Putney and GLCA were interested in constructive social change, particularly educational change, but both programs were founded on the premise that this change could occur without destroying "the system." Change would have to come peacefully—somehow, perhaps by a subtle process of osmosis, because a group of vigorous young people happened to be *part* of the system.

But the situation had not always been calm. Bright young students and recent college graduates all aglow with libertarian ideals and heady thoughts from the works of Paul Goodman were the system's natural enemies. Put them in the middle of urban war, and there was bound to be trouble. Quite inadvertently, in the fall of 1967, the program's planners had touched off an abrasive, year-long conflict of generations that turned out to be an almost profligate waste of revolutionary zeal and a threat to the future of the program besides. Thereafter, if the Antioch-Putney-GLCA planners had anything to say about it, the natural enemies would be kept as far apart as possible.

You have a huge establishment here. You have a tradition here. . . . So when you engage yourself in the school system you have to come on not like you're out to change things. Let me give you an example of what I mean. I know that Mark Shedd brought with him a lot of bright guys—you met some of them—and they're the guys that pick up the phone, and they call . . . say, Fred Cowan, a guy who's been here for years. Say, he's the one that assigns our co-ops, he's the one that initially makes contacts for our interns for future use. Now Shedd's guy can call up this guy and say, "Antioch has twenty-four interns; find a dozen schools for them." Or he can do, as I'm working with him specifically now for summer school—well, this bright, threatening guy can call the other guy and say, "Uh, Fred . . . hook up Antioch into twenty-four summer spots." He hangs up, and Fred does it.

Now I'm concerned with those twenty-four spots. I'd better get to Fred, and I'd better come on like . . . "Hi Fred, I'm from Antioch!" Then I start talking to Fred. I find out some things in common that we have. And it's just a comforting thing for him to know. . . . And then I say, "Hey, Fred, about those twenty-four spots . . ." Because without it, Fred can stick our twenty-four people anywhere and that's it. But I can say to him, "Look. You know I heard that Wagner Junior High School is a good place for them." Now how do I know this? I come with what I want. And I come on this way, and before you know it chances are I get most of these things that I wanted to do by coming on a little softer and a little easier. And even doing things like this: "Well, you know Jim . . . he doesn't know. . . ." You know, I'll even agree with Fred and nod a head—'cause I'm not concerned about the battle

between Jim and Fred and how they see each other as threats.
I'm concerned with twenty-four people, and I want to put them in
the best situation for them.

Now this was *not done* this summer. This was *not* done. All of
these assignments that our interns have were done over the phone
by one guy to another. The principals were never really brought
into it. And as a result there's been all of this . . . YECCH, tearing
away at each other. You know, I don't think that has to be.

—Antioch-Putney coordinator of interns, during a taped
discussion with a group of co-ops in December 1968

Part of the trouble was that the school where the worst problems arose—Shoemaker Junior High School—was not in Germantown. Shoemaker served some of the poorest sections of West
Philadelphia and had been consigned for more than a decade to
the inevitable fate of the ghetto school, particularly the hopelessness and the undercurrents of unfocused resentment that ensue
when the last whites have departed for the suburbs. Roosevelt
Junior High School, in Germantown, had its own share of the
usual problems, but at least there was a mood of optimism in
the community—and in Germantown the Antioch-Putney program was considerably less threatening; Germantown was where
the Antioch people belonged.

Aside from the difficulties that accompany overcrowding
(built for 1,100 students, the school had 1,800 during the 1967–
68 school year), retardation in the level of students' basic skills,
racism, and antiquated teaching methods, Shoemaker suffered
from what an Antioch staff member with many years experience
in the Philadelphia schools called an unusually "tight" atmosphere. During the change of classes, teachers and nonteaching
assistants patrolled the halls with wooden prods the size of
broom handles (generously provided by the shop teacher), but
the admonition of a smart tap on the heel or calf was commonplace in the city's junior and senior high schools—children expected such minor disciplinary measures. What distinguished
Shoemaker was an almost fanatic preoccupation with "control"
that seemed to have taken hold of the entire faculty. Control is
certainly one of the major educational concerns in urban secondary schools across the country, but even viewed in this light,
Shoemaker was tighter than most.

Benjamin Kaplan, the principal, who had been at Shoemaker for twenty years, was known to have encouraged innovation, and the school could boast a number of interesting experiments. But a desperate need for control loomed large, nevertheless. In a science class which happened to be among the kids' favorites, for example, the teacher constantly repeated the word "Quiet" as he conducted the lesson; in an English class where kids were improvising plays on tape recorders, the teacher watched over a group of boys seated near the back of the room as if they might explode at any moment. The Shoemaker faculty was more nervous than it had any need to be. But the nervousness seemed to feed the kids' excitement so that, in an endless spiral of tension, control was foremost in everybody's mind.

This high-strung environment was an apt setting for a confrontation, but, as if the situation were not tense enough, the principal had assigned the Antioch people to a pair of tradition-oriented teachers who represented the antithesis of what they were likely to find appealing among the faculty. ("They were selected," reported the Antioch coordinator, "because Kaplan's interpretation of the kind of teacher he was to select was *them*. He told *me* that Rick deLone [Shedd's twenty-eight-year-old assistant at the Board of Education] told him to select *young* teachers.") Thus, while the Antioch interns and co-ops at Shoemaker did not have a corner on humanity in the school, more often than not they were in a situation that invited grumbling and rebellion.

Wherever one looked in the urban schools of America at this time, the same general situation prevailed: Young people, whether radical or not, were continually challenged to adjust to the needs and values of "the system" or fight a dreadful battle if they resisted. The situation had a mad, but precise, logic of its own; if "educationally deprived" children were constantly squeezed in huge numbers into classrooms where they were asked to do tasks for which they had little affinity, the level of frustration and anger was bound to be high, the compulsion for order among the teachers even higher. The structure of the schools alone dictated the paramount importance of control; as long as huge classes (some at Shoemaker had as many as thirty-eight students) continued to be the basic learning unit, not to have *some* kind of order would be to invite utter chaos.

It was a familiar story; young teachers in the ghetto had been writing books about it. The odds were against the creative teacher. One goal of the Antioch-Putney program was to train creative teachers. The very nature of the Antioch-Putney program virtually guaranteed a certain amount of basic conflict, and at Shoemaker the difficulties seemed to be doubly magnified.

The entire Shoemaker experience seemed grimly fated. Perhaps most important, it had Alan Donnell, an Antioch intern who saw his role in the educational process as essentially revolutionary and who completed the polarization of values within the school so decisively that a do-or-die battle was virtually inevitable.

> If I were taking more interns, I'd insist they have more control in the first month or else. I don't think it makes a bit of difference whether they're twenty-two or *forty*-two—the important thing is that they relate. Alan Donnell is a perfect example—a born teacher who doesn't have control. Alan with six or eight kids around a table would be worth his weight in gold. . . .
> —Benjamin Kaplan, principal
> of Shoemaker

> If school is a battlefield where most students lose, achieving "normality" at the price of mental health, then anything and everything is necessary.
> —Alan Donnell, *The School Experience*,
> a master's thesis in which the author
> maintains that the normal state of the
> urban school is insanity

> I must have been advised by well-meaning children to "get mean," "get a stick," or "send so-and-so to the office" at least once a day during my year of teaching. . . .
> —*The School Experience*

Alan Donnell, a 1967 Harvard graduate who taught seventh-grade geography for a year at Shoemaker, did not look like a man who considered himself a revolutionary. Confrontation seemed as alien to Donnell's personality as authoritarianism, but even though co-ops had clashed angrily with the Shoemaker establishment on a few occasions, Donnell was, in his own quiet way, a source of much greater provocation. The main reason for this was that while the two other interns at Shoemaker had better "discipline" as the year went on, Donnell's discipline seemed to get progressively worse. It is unlikely that Donnell would have been able to crack down on his classes even if he had wanted to. He gave every indication, however, of not wanting to at all; it was as if he was so determined not to succumb to the general mania that he had gone out of his way to avoid even the possibility.

Shoemaker was undergoing renovation during the year when Alan Donnell taught there (this may have accounted for at least some of the hypertension of the place), and at one point a teacher in an adjacent room, separated from Donnell's room only by a thin temporary wall, told the principal, "Either he gets moved or I leave!" (The principal moved the complaining teacher.) Frequent protests notwithstanding, the noise level in Donnell's classroom continued high, and his students had a good deal of unaccustomed mobility. During what was, according to reports, a fairly typical lesson, Donnell presided over a seminar with a group of ten or so students in the front of the room, while various clusters of students—some boys tossing an eraser, a few girls interrogating a visitor—generally ignored their teacher's reasoned efforts at involving them in the discussion. By any standards, the situation was chaotic.

There was indeed an almost palpable crying out for the stick— so much so that one sturdy-looking boy, apparently an unchallenged student leader, patrolled the aisles in an effort to calm his classmates down, frequently stopping to hit various offenders quite hard in the chest or shoulder with a simultaneous warning to "SHET up" that carried overtones of even worse punishments to come. At one point the boy was superseded in his role of disciplinarian by a severe-looking vice-principal, who enforced a good forty-five seconds of total silence merely by stepping inside the door and glaring. (He was the same vice-principal whose office was usually packed with semi-petrified children lined quaking on a bench as they awaited sentence.)

"It would have been great," observed an Antioch-Putney staff member a few months after Donnell left Philadelphia, "if he'd had the kids all day so that they didn't have to go to other teachers." But the other teachers belittled and resented Alan Donnell. Finally they even persuaded the principal to relieve him of one of his classes—the notorious 7–8, the "worst" class in the school, which had become even wilder during the months in Donnell's room. The removal of 7–8 was a tremendous relief to the other teachers, of course—and a kind of subtle triumph as well.

But meanwhile, even in the midst of chaos, Donnell was doing some of the best work in the school. For a unit on Africa, he wrote his own textbook in the form of short stories. After the murder of Martin Luther King, he handed out ditto sheets to his students, told them to go ahead and write anything they wanted, and produced a series of class magazines. With many of his students he had relationships of profound trust and friendship. At the end of the year, students crowded around him to say goodbye, and one boy even presented him with what must have been the greatest tribute that a seventh-grader in the ghetto could offer: a live bullet.

But certainly one of Donnell's greatest successes was his rapport with Richard, the tough kid who so dutifully beat up on his classmates to keep them quiet. Donnell had "reached" his student early in the relationship—Richard's disciplinary measures were obviously meant as a gesture of support—but it was not until one evening when Richard saw his teacher play in a faculty basketball game with teachers from another junior high school that the boy was moved to write the following letter:

A MAN NAMED DONNELL

In Shoemaker Jr. high school there is an adviser in 7-7 name Mr. Donnell he is nice and likes all types people he is in the school basketball team and can play very well. he tells people he is going to send them to the office and never does, and takes a lot of stuff other teachers wouldn't. And to my mind is a perfect Americain he isn't perchedise he likes other people the same as you do no matter what color and above all he's a good teacher!

Reassured by Donnell's performance on the basketball court, Richard had seen that his hero could conform at least part of the time to the values of the system—a huge doubt had been mercifully removed.

But Donnell's troubles at Shoemaker reflected a constitutional inability to adapt. There were other libertarians who had compromised, who had struck a balance between tyranny and humanity; this could have been said of most of the Antioch interns. And to the extent that Donnell's gentle determination not to relate to students in a threatening way, to encourage only friendly intimacy, confronted the values of Shoemaker Junior High School, the clash was destructive to both. Even during his year at Shoemaker, Donnell decided that the structure of the conventional school was too antithetical to his humanitarian goals. After Antioch he decided to do graduate work in clinical psychology because, as he put it, "I want to work with people, but mainly I want to work with individuals." He had cast his lot with the Kohls, Kozols, and Herndons whom he so admired; he had even written his book.

Four of the classes I had to take over are really *rough*. That's why I have to bring my meter rule with me.
> —A young woman who has recently
> joined the Shoemaker faculty to
> cover a vacancy and who patrols
> her classes with a quick,
> efficient yardstick always at the ready.
> For a beginner she has
> reasonably good discipline.

Teacher #1: Some of the problem was that Dr. Shedd gave the impression that people could do anything they wanted. The Antioch people thought they could take over without getting to know the system.

Teacher #2: The summer was a waste of time. We offered demonstration lessons and lesson plans, but the interns refused to cooperate. They won't show us their lesson plans at all and they're supposed to. . . .

Teacher #1: They claimed that you shouldn't teach the business letter because one day tape recorders will *replace* business letters.

Teacher #2: Next year they'll have a full summer of preparation before they start to teach. . . .

Teacher #1: I took over one of the interns' classes one day when he was out, and he had pictures from *Playboy* on the walls—he wasn't teaching *English*. The kids wanted to write him a letter, but I couldn't get them to sit down. They were jumping all over the room, shouting, writing on the walls. . . .

—"Cooperating teachers" assigned to Antioch team at Shoemaker

You can't imagine—no, you *can* imagine—how threatening interns and co-ops come on to regular teachers. Now, I don't like to do things like this, but I think I may have told you . . . two of the co-ops coming in have beards. So Lorraine Sheppard [a director of Antioch co-ops in Yellow Springs] writes to me and says They have beards, they would like to keep them—what do you think? What do *I* think? Now I don't give a hoot or a hang *what* they have, but I know something—I know that with some of the principals and some of the teachers, and even some of our interns, this might be the whole ball game. So I'm not going to make that decision—I don't care if the kid comes in, you know . . . But I'm going to have to do something about it. So I sat and I talked to Kaplan. And what do you think he said? *"No beards."*

—Antioch-Putney coordinator, talking with co-ops

If one takes a human view of urban warfare, there are no villains, no clearly discernible sides on most of the big issues. Urban war is chaotic, the actual enemy being no specific bad guy, rarely even some awful conspiratorial group of power-mongers—but rather that elusive, eternal enemy, the system. In the case of Shoemaker Junior High School, the single most important factor creating dissension between the Antioch people and the regular faculty was something for which the faculty bore no responsibility; namely, that the school continued to perpetuate a learning structure—the overcrowded, uniform, teacher-centered classroom—that most educators with any vision saw as the principal barrier to more effective schooling. Until the very shape and substance of the school could be changed entirely (which would require vast sums of money and political force; the social revolution, in short, that seemed so unlikely) any efforts to change the nature of the classroom within the existing structure would be at best only piecemeal and at worst totally disruptive.

One clear indication of this was that, in contrast with the beleaguered interns, the co-ops at Shoemaker had no trouble at all with their students, whom they met in the intimate setting of semi-private tutorials. Even teachers who resented the interns' lack of discipline admitted that the co-ops had made tremendous progress in improving the attitudes and skills of their private tutorees. Sequestered in a fifth-floor hall (space was always a problem), the co-ops conducted classes with two or three students at a time, worked intensively on a one-to-one basis, played games, and generally managed to create an environment of such warmth and freedom that it could almost have been another world from the one downstairs.

But the co-ops were not universally loved, either—they were too closely associated with the interns, and they tended to seek confrontations. The school had never quite gotten over an incident in which one of the co-ops—a girl who frequently came to school on her own motorcycle—discovered one morning that the teacher with whom she planned to take a group of students on a trip would be out for the day. The co-ops had often chafed against the legal restrictions that prevented them from leaving the school with students unless they had the supervision of a licensed teacher; but on this occasion the girl stormed into the principal's office and said, "We've been planning this trip for too long to abandon it now. We're *going*." They went.

Finally, in fact, the principal relaxed the rule and actually encouraged co-ops to plan trips and neighborhood walks. To a certain extent, observes Robert Piper, the Antioch people did something to loosen up the tightness of Shoemaker. As the Antioch-Putney coordinator assigned to Shoemaker told a group of co-ops who had just completed their three-month work program: "You bring incredible richness to the program. The Philadelphia public school system is a very cold place, but you *talk* to people."

In the long run, the co-ops illustrated an important point about changing big systems. They were often the most outspoken and courageous advocates of change not only because they had been freed of dreary classroom conventions but because, having a commitment of no more than three months, they could afford to lose. They enjoyed the assurance that no matter how much they upset the system's increasingly precarious applecart, they would not have to live long with the consequences.

Their influence was severely limited, however, because, as mere tutors, they had been given a back seat from the beginning. In the fall of 1968 the few co-ops who were considering jobs in Roosevelt Junior High School decided, after consulting with friends and advisers in Yellow Springs, to volunteer instead for jobs in elementary schools, where they could be a more integral part of the faculty, or in various innovative projects, where they were not only welcomed but needed. Like so many others during Mark Shedd's fateful first year as superintendent, the Antioch people had learned that the system was bigger than the sum of its parts, that to confront it was to invite a degree of frustration no one could stand for long. Junior high schools didn't seem worth the trouble.

From the bitter experience at Shoemaker and, to a lesser extent, at Roosevelt, there had emerged something like a universal law for humanitarian change in a huge bureaucratic system. Confrontation was out; cooperation was the only way; and whenever confrontation occurred, resistance increased proportionally—on what seemed to be a sliding scale—until a state of intolerable conflict forced the new, offending element to withdraw. Basically the Antiochians and the Great Lakes students were easy-going radicals when they were radicals at all; they met the school system with a minimum of threat, and after the first year they avoided head-on clashes.

But conflict was inevitable; minor incidents could flare into ugly disputes at the drop of a word. Even with things running smoothly, with the program solidly entrenched in Germantown during the 1968–69 school year, the confrontation was only inches below the surface. In February 1969, for example, a group of black leaders accused one of the Antioch interns at Germantown High School of urging his students to blow up the school building. When reports of the accusation appeared in the local newspapers, the intern's association with SDS, emphasized in several accounts, was enough to frighten just about everybody—

SDS was, after all, the symbol of revolutionary youth throughout America. Even though the teacher later emerged as the innocent victim of black-white political maneuvering, a common prejudice had been reinforced: Bright young middle-class teachers were troublemakers.

During subsequent conferences with Mark Shedd and Bob Piper, the intern insisted that he had never exhorted his students to burn down the school. He had belonged to SDS, but mainly, according to Piper, because he believed that SDS activists from outside the high school were exploiting student discontent and he wanted to counter their influence. "He wasn't for the status quo," says Piper, "but he wasn't for burning the school down either." Finally, after the commotion of the newspaper articles and an investigation by the Police Department involving numerous telephone calls to Shedd and Piper, the young teacher returned to Yellow Springs, his contract terminated. The skirmish was over.

"People in the schools have mentioned it to me," Piper reported not long after the intern's departure. "To teachers who aren't friendly to the program it's just another one of those things the Antioch-Putney people are always doing. It hasn't helped the relationship with some of the schools, but it hasn't hurt the relationship with the Board or the people at 21st Street."

The incident had been, after the glare of publicity, just another of the constant strains on the warp and woof of urban society. For the moment—perhaps because the Antioch-Putney program continued to avoid the confrontations that had caused so much distress at the beginning—the small corner of the social fabric with which the program was concerned continued to survive intact.

The Center Will Not Hold

EVEN BEFORE the arrival of Mark Shedd, Philadelphia's new Board of Education had taken steps toward a complete shake-up of the central bureaucracy by hiring a team of younger men (average age thirty-six) from outside the system for key jobs at 21st Street. None of these men were career educators. Some, like Bob Blackburn, the new head of the Office of Integration and Intergroup Education, had helped to lead the fight against the school system in the Anderson days. Others came from prestigious jobs in city planning or private business. And so many of the new team were graduates of top Eastern colleges that they soon became known as the "Ivy Mafia."

The most immediate effect of these appointments was a shout wave of panic at 21st Street. The logical consequence, according to the rumors, would be wholesale firings and reassignments. Apparently the Board, unlike so many official organizations supposedly dedicated to social progress, wasn't just talking—Dilworth seemed to want the same kind of crusade with which he and his friends had virtually transformed the city government a decade earlier.

The Board was tampering with venerable machinery. Urban school systems have perpetuated mediocrity for generations by functioning as if there were no such thing as (to borrow one of the more popular words from the lexicon of school reform) accountability. Tenure, promotions, automatic pay raises, and strict professional requirements—features of the misnamed "merit system" originally designed to protect public school systems from meddling politicians—have guaranteed a certain objectivity, an almost antiseptic means of dealing with personnel, but they have also produced generations of neglectful and incompetent teachers and administrators. If Philadelphia's top school administration had had a professional organization, it would probably have fought the Board's recruitment of noneducators—but unionism was inappropriate to the management style. When the Board later made similarly dramatic moves toward change outside 21st Street—Shedd's proposal for a genuine merit-pay system for principals is an example—it was immediately defeated. As for the teachers themselves, their union was a formidable power, and Dilworth would go to almost any length to avoid a clash—the various intern and work-study programs were a mere beginning, in view of the changes that were so badly needed.

But change did have the upper hand at least within the central staff, and the Board was able to do what the board of any commercial corporation could have done without hesitation or opposition—give top jobs to people who, in the view of the Board members, deserved them. Whether the chain of mediocrity could be broken in this manner, whether the new dynamism could somehow spread down through the school system, were questions that only time and the new team could answer. When Shedd took charge at 21st Street and began to bring in even more young assistants, however, everything seemed possible.

Shedd's recruits, several of whom had some connection with Harvard, were generally younger than those brought in by the Board. Many administrative appointments that he approved, under a special clause in the Educational Home Rule Charter that exempted five per cent of his staff from the usual professional requirements, were recommended by other recently named deputies. For a while, at any rate, all the young tigers, a gold mine of talent by anyone's standards, rallied to Shedd's banner.

A recent Radcliffe graduate in the planning office had come from a job with the Philadelphia City Planning Commission; the community liaison worker in the Office of Innovative Programs had graduated from Sarah Lawrence in 1963 and been active in the Northern Student Movement; another community worker, a Philadelphian and Temple graduate, was among the city's leading white activists; one of Shedd's closest administrative assistants, who had an M.A.T. degree from Harvard, had been fired from the Boston school system for publishing an article criticizing that system's rigidity. None of these, the younger generation of the new team, was over thirty. Although this was not the hippie takeover that some teachers in the system occasionally muttered about, it was probably as close as an urban school system had ever come to placing such a cadre of anti-establishment intellectuals, of whatever age group, in positions of power. Certainly the most articulate of them all—and for that reason in the atmosphere of continual tension the most frightening—was the twenty-eight-year-old Harvard graduate whom Shedd once called "the architect of my administration": a native Main Line Philadelphian named Rick deLone.

Even at a time when the second floor was alive with projects to turn out turnings-on, an aura of excitement radiated from deLone's office that made most of the go-go atmosphere elsewhere seem rather pale and strained. DeLone had been hired as Shedd's administrative assistant, but he seemed to have a hand in everything. He was hated and feared not just by the old guard, but by members of the new team who suffered from the intense pressure for creativity that he seemed to revel in. There were other talented people who didn't buckle under the strain either—even some administrators who had been at 21st Street for years found the new regime more to their liking—but deLone had a clarity and intensity of vision that made him outstanding. "It's actually quite simple," commented one of his admirers. "He's *superior.*"

Rick deLone generally worked behind the scenes, but he became momentarily famous in Philadelphia for what happened to be one of his least important efforts at change—the notorious budgetary memo that attracted so much public attention in June, 1968. Sensitive to the role of newspapers and other communications media in making the public aware of the school system's problems, deLone had sent the memo, suggesting a plan for publicizing the 1968–69 operating budget, to four of Shedd's and Dilworth's advisers. The budget needed to be "sexed up," he wrote, and promoted with "Madison Avenue" techniques;

the Board should create a "climate of crisis," possibly even cut such key programs as adult education, in order to emphasize the desperate need for funds.

On the one hand, the memo was a sophisticated suggestion for drumming up support in the face of increasing opposition from the financially troubled City Council—there really *was* a budget crisis. But, on the other hand, the memo had a potentially frightening bluntness. It lacked the straight face that most executives insist on in their daily communications; it was slangy, not pompous, in style. It admitted honestly what any intelligent person knows to be an important element of twentieth-century life: Public opinion can be manipulated to almost any end. It mentioned sex—a nasty enough subject for most "school people" in any context, but in connection with money, downright scandalous. In the wrong hands the memo could be a dangerous weapon against deLone and the entire Shedd administration.

DeLone never learned how a copy of the memo reached Board member William Ross, a high-ranking labor leader who was generally regarded as Mayor Tate's "man" on the Board and whom Dilworth periodically accused of being blindly committed to the status quo. Despite the rumors, there had been no direct effort to undermine deLone's work. There had been open hostility and bad talk, but if one of deLone's enemies at 21st Street found a copy and decided to use it against him by showing it to Ross, it was the only case of concrete opposition he encountered. At any rate, Ross read the memo aloud at a Board meeting, citing it as a blatant example of the irresponsibility and cynicism of Shedd's staff, and touched off a public uproar.

DeLone had been provocative before; he had made no secret of his intense dislike for the usual routine of central staff or of his desire for fundamental change. He saw himself as an enemy of all establishments; he wanted to transform the very foundation of learning in the schools. He was close to several militant black leaders, and, taking their side, he could be highly intolerant of the whites who lacked his own understanding of urban problems. Almost as a defense against the extreme conservatism of his colleagues at 21st Street, he had let his own attitudes become polarized—and the memo carried strong overtones of his characteristic arrogance.

DeLone survived the controversy—the protests by Tate and D'Ortona, the rebuke from Dilworth—that followed Ross' coup, but it wounded him. He usually reveled in his reputation of tough radicalism; now it had backfired—somehow he had ended up looking like a monster. And the entire incident proved that if the system could not defeat him with petty rigidity, it might succeed with mere ugliness.

Contrary to what some of Rick deLone's admirers believed, he was not running the entire Philadelphia public school system. For a period of perhaps half a year, however, his office was a key focus for the proponents of change. Foundation representatives, black leaders, radicals from all over the city, many of the most innovative teachers and principals—all managed to find their way at one time or another to deLone. Officially he was not at the top of the ladder, and a hard examination of the facts would reveal that countless other administrators at 21st Street could claim responsibility for one program or another that deLone had had some connection with and seemed to be controlling. But it was as if he had struck the tuning fork that brought every "change agent" in the city suddenly into harmony. He seemed to possess a magical power to accomplish what others had been unable to do in years of dedicated reform. Ultimately this may have even been detrimental to real change—it had a quality of unabashed romanticism—but while it was at a peak, it made for a heady atmosphere. And it seemed to happen naturally.

DeLone had started life with all the advantages. His father was a prominent lawyer who had once argued against Dilworth and who was chairman of the Philadelphia Health and Welfare Commission at the time when deLone worked for the Board of Education. His mother was from the aristocratic Heckscher family. He was raised in one of the stone mansions that give Philadelpia's surburban Main Line its unique elegance. But he was not just a rich kid; he was a leader from the beginning. At Episcopal Academy, a Main Line day school for boys, he led the dramatics club, participated in the student government, and became known for his eclectic brilliance.

Harvard was part of the order to which he was born. After Harvard, he went to Berkeley and took an M.A. in English. He also taught undergraduate courses in literature and creative writing, but as he was about to begin work on a Ph.D. thesis, he finally decided that the whole graduate school treadmill, of which he had grown increasingly suspicious, was "irrelevant." In the fall of 1964 he came to Philadelphia to work for the city's top-drawer evening paper, the *Bulletin.*

Even the most obtuse members of America's upper classes have glimmerings of social conscience these days, if only because they see their power threatened and want to throw slices of it to the masses. The percentage of Ivy League graduates who don't seriously believe they want to make the country a better place to live in must be negligible. And it would have been easy, even logical, for deLone to take some vaguely hypocritical do-gooding job. He was true to his class in that he automatically gravitated toward power. But there the resemblance ended.

Basically, deLone was an intellectual, and, as with so many middle-class intellectuals who came to maturity during the "quiet" Eisenhower years, his thinking had tended toward the academic. Even as late as his mid-twenties he was a writer and an academician, not a political activist. He left Berkeley just before the tumult that launched an era of upheaval in higher education, but again, like so many middle-class intellectuals, he was becoming, to use the jargon of the New left, increasingly radicalized.

DeLone's radicalization was not so much political, however, as educational. His questioning mind had been encouraged by a few good teachers at Episcopal Academy. At Harvard he had become a close friend of Theodore H. Sizer, then head of the Master of Arts in Teaching program in the Graduate School of Education, later dean of the graduate school. Sizer was emerging as one of the unofficial heads of the youth movement in the nation's schools. DeLone talked frequently with Sizer about schools, and he had also read Jerome Bruner's *The Process of Education,* a progressive statement of learning theory that made him even more critical of existing educational institutions. The stagnant atmosphere of graduate school had finally convinced him that something was fundamentally wrong with American education, but when he began working as a reporter for the *Bulletin,* he had hardly begun to translate his criticisms into a sense of mission.

After six months of general reporting, deLone grabbed at the opportunity to take over as assistant education editor when the departure of another editor created the opening. He was just twenty-five years old, but he already had a reputation as a reporter of uncommon ability. Parts of the new job were fairly predictable—he covered Board meetings, the selection and installation of the Dilworth Board, and occasional crises—but he also had an opportunity to observe the public school system at close range. He even did some teaching himself, working as a substitute. "I kept hearing educators talk about innovations," deLone says of the experience. "Multiethnic readers, reading adjustment teachers, home and school coordinators—and I was always bored without knowing why. I kept wondering why they all made me so tired."

In the summer of 1965, deLone found relief for his impatience when he went to observe classes in an experimental, foundation-sponsored summer program run by a young English teacher named Terry Borton. On the day of deLone's visit, Borton led lively discussions about Nathanael West's *Miss Lonelyhearts*, and he struck deLone as one of the best teachers he had ever seen.

Borton, then twenty-six and at the beginning of what promised to be an impressive career in education, was going through a period of transformation himself—mainly by resisting the constraints of the conventional high school English curriculum and searching for alternatives. He remembers that deLone was "one of the few visitors who had any conception of what was happening," adding with amusement that during the visit, deLone tried "to do all the exercises in the drama class and take notes at the same time, jumping up and down with his notebook in his hand." DeLone's article about the program was highly appreciative, and, as far as he was concerned, the visit was a key moment in his decision to "go on in schools."

His next step was, typically, a move towards leadership: He became chairman of the board of the Philadelphia Cooperative Schools, a summer program which Borton had organized around his new "affective" curriculum, and which drew on students and faculty from public, private, and parochial schools throughout the city. According to Borton, deLone was in charge of the "power tactics." Principally through his connections with the public school system, deLone was able to get money from Title I; the public schools also provided the building in which the 1967 summer program took place, and, in order to qualify for federal funds, the program drew largely on public school teachers and students.

It was a high-powered board, deLone recalls—the membership included Alex MacColl, the headmaster of the Friends school where Borton had initiated his program; Graham Finney, who later became head of the school system's planning office; and Milton Goldberg, the school system's director of curriculum—but "I was a very autocratic chairman. Terry would ask for board decisions, and I'd give them to him right then over the phone." As far as deLone was concerned, there was nothing particularly wrong with this manner of decision-making. There was very little need, in fact, for the board to meet on any regular basis. More to the point, decision-making and leadership were so much a part of deLone's character that he would probably have dominated the board anyway. He was only twenty-six at the time, but he projected an almost awesome authority. DeLone stayed with the Cooperative Schools for two summers, and it was during this time that his plan for "infiltrating" the public school system began to take shape.

It was not really a plan so much as a basic commitment to humanitarian values and the liberated, anti-establishment style of the turned-on youth movement. DeLone had found a ready-made wing of the movement in the Cooperative Schools program, and he continued to rely on Borton and his colleagues for recruits when he later joined the school system. But lively comers were recognizable almost at a glance; deLone had the perceptiveness of a first-rate journalist. All he had to do, it seemed at the beginning, was find *his* people and put them to work. But first, of course, he needed power.

In a year and a half of writing about education for the *Bulletin*, deLone had come into contact with just about everyone of any importance in Philadelphia who was working for change in the schools—as well as those who opposed it—and he had always gravitated toward the leaders. He had become an ardent admirer of John Patterson, who was primarily responsible for all the system's innovative programs in the early days of the new Board, and he was friendly with Bill Wilcox and Bob Blackburn, the organizers of the city-wide movement that led to the Educational Home Rule Charter. His real hero, however, was Richardson Dilworth.

Dilworth had missed his chance in national politics—he had resigned as mayor in 1962 in order to run for governor, and lost —but in Philadelphia he was still something of a legend. Whatever Americans say about the perpetuation of democratic values, huge numbers of them are ready and eager to love an unselfish aristocrat. Among such Americans there is an almost childlike desire to be governed by those, like the Kennedys and the Rockefellers, who exemplify the success they themselves aspire to or dream about—a desire that flourishes regardless of the basic inequities of the country's political system. Dilworth was an aristocrat to the marrow of his bones. He was handsome, youthful-looking—though in his late sixties, he appeared not much older than forty-five—outspoken, and tough; he could be compassionate; he had what seemed to be inexhaustible humor and pluck.

Among the many rumors that surrounded deLone after he began working for the Board of Education was the story that his family had a summer home next door to Dilworth's in a posh town on Cape Cod. There was no truth to the rumor, but it gave expression to the common feeling that somehow there was a profound connection between the two men going back for many years. In fact, deLone met Dilworth for the first time when he went to interview him in 1966, shortly after the appointment of the new Board. Dilworth made devastating comments about the school system, many of which, he told deLone, were "not for attribution," but when deLone wrote up the interview, he included them. The next day, when the interview was printed, he was to meet Dilworth again at a press conference in the *Bulletin* offices; when he came back from lunch, just before the conference, the city editor told him, "Holy Christ! Is Dilworth mad at you!" During the conference, Dilworth ignored deLone—who went there, he recalls, trembling—but finally, at the end, he looked at the young reporter and burst out laughing. And, as deLone puts it, "I've loved him ever since."

It had become increasingly clear to deLone that he could have almost any job he wanted in the growing school reform movement. He spent hours talking with Dilworth and Patterson about the problems of the school system—"a lot of things; who was good, who was bad"—and both men had offered him the opportunity to work with them. But deLone, much too ambitious to be Dilworth's or Patterson's assistant, was waiting for the position where he could be most effective.

It was about this time that the Board decided to look for a new superintendent. Patterson had already turned the job down, and the Board was searching among the younger generation of school administrators. DeLone made two suggestions: ". . . talk with Sizer and look at a guy named Shedd. Shedd had given a rabble-rousing speech to the American Association of School Administrators. He attacked his fellow administrators for pussyfooting. He sounded good." When deLone later wrote an exciting cloak-and-dagger story describing how several Board members had slipped out of a meeting and driven up to Englewood to interview Shedd in preparation for the final decision, participatory journalism had certainly reached one of its peaks. DeLone began working as the new superintendent's assistant virtually on the day Shedd was hired.

Shedd's major achievement during the eight months in which he worked as a consultant to the Board before taking office in September 1967, was his series of visits to community organizations, a gesture that set the tone of responsiveness he wanted in his administration. But because of his excellent rapport with deLone and their general agreement on what needed to be done in the school system, the new superintendent's public speeches became the responsibility of his young assistant—deLone wrote all of the major policy statements for almost a year. Many were inspiring, eloquent, brilliantly conceived. The speech of September 11, 1967, alone, which Shedd delivered to a huge assemblage of teachers in Convention Hall, articulated a program for system-wide change that would really have revolutionized the Philadelphia public school system if it had ever been completely implemented. Ultimately it became difficult for anyone inside the administration to know which parts of the evolving program were deLone's and which were Shedd's.

The question might never have mattered if Shedd and deLone had continued to agree on every question, but under the best conditions this was unlikely. Shedd may well have been one of the best school superintendents in the country, but he lacked his young colleague's swaggering brashness. The new superintendent, having worked his way up through the ranks, was heading for the summit of a successful career—the Department of Education in Washington seemed to be the logical next step if he could do even half of what he promised in Philadelphia. DeLone, on the other hand, had no intention of staying in school administration; he could be careless, he could be daring. When the action at 21st Street got really sweaty, Shedd often failed to act upon the bold words that deLone had written for him.

The relationship of Shedd and deLone simply reflected a phenomenon that began to emerge after the honeymoon ended for the new team in the crises of late 1967. Pressures at 21st Street —for change, for adaptability, for ideas, for compromise—increased on an ever-spiraling scale. DeLone thrived on crisis, reveled in it as if it were some kind of fascinating game. For him, juggling the threats and the possibilities of disaster was fun; he could almost always come up with some kind of ingenious solution. He was creative while others were merely frightened.

But the more his natural energies prevailed, it seemed, the more he intimidated his colleagues. It bewildered him to realize, as he finally began to, late in the fall, that simply by doing what he found perfectly normal and even enjoyable, he had created severe strains among the members of the new team. But, as Shedd's key adviser, as the "devil in the building," according to one of his co-workers, "who handled things while Shedd was coming in," he had unwittingly dominated the scene.

Part of this was due to deLone's ability and drive—few people could oppose him or outsmart him. Part of it was due to his contempt for the pettiness of his fellow administrators—the more he saw of the inner workings of 21st Street, the less respect he could have for the whole operation. But, in addition, he often seemed to think of his job as a game. The name of the game, of course, was cops-and-robbers, but in this case the good guys were humanitarians and the bad guys organization men.

In the course of several months, deLone polarized just about everybody at 21st Street who came in contact with him; he began to have followers, to be the center of a cult—while, at the same time, the number of his grumbling enemies steadily grew. For his followers, deLone's office was like the headquarters of a good college or underground newspaper. Wit was one of the keys of regular admission; humor, imagination, and a commitment to radicalism helped. Even while the phone rang with news of the latest crisis, deLone had time for jokes, for buckshot blasts at the intransigency of the bureaucracy, for a nibble of hard candy from the box on his secretary's desk. Well over six feet, with dark blond hair that varied in length in direct proportion, it seemed, to his hostility toward the system (during the summer vacation in 1968 he grew a mustache), deLone was heavy-set, casually—perhaps deliberately—unkempt, and in constant motion. One of his favorite gestures of camaraderie was to tell a visitor, "Let's get the hell out of here so we can talk."

But deLone was not just playing; his power was real—he was a one-man brain trust, and he made things happen. He wrote the speeches. No matter how much other administrators at 21st Street disliked him, virtually all of the new team regularly asked him to sit in on their meetings, and, as an unofficial member of Shedd's executive cabinet, he had an important role in top-level decisions. In addition, he was primarily responsible, because of his close connection to Shedd, for speeding up the machinery at 21st Street whenever it slowed down in resistance to one new program or another. But his pet project, the one that represented more than anything else an actual program to implement his humanitarian goals, was his attempt to "infiltrate" the system with people who shared his ideas and values.

As a result of deLone's efforts, for example, two of the teachers who had worked in the Cooperative Schools program later became principals of a junior and a senior high school. He helped another teacher from the Cooperative Schools, who had assisted Marshall McLuhan at the Fordham Center for Communications, to set up a film-media center in one of the more progressive outlying districts. With deLone's help, a talented husband-wife team who worked with films and taught communications were able to run a staff development seminar, an indirect precursor of the media center, that spawned several media-oriented teams throughout the system; this same couple was responsible for *AE*, the anti-establishment "magazine of the Philadelphia public schools," for which deLone obtained foundation and Board support.

It was deLone who persuaded Shedd and the Board to hire Terry Borton, first as a full-time curriculum specialist, then as a consultant, to institutionalize the program of affective development. Borton and Norman Newberg—who had also worked in the Cooperative Schools program and who took over as head of affective development when Borton went to Harvard to work on a doctoral thesis—were responsible not only for a growing revolution in curriculum but for the group-encounter sessions that Shedd adopted as a principal means for clearing the stale air of the system and encouraging honesty and creativity on all levels. DeLone also assisted, through his connection with Borton, in the creation of the Pennsylvania Advancement School.

Another of deLone's projects was the Mantua-Powelton Minischool, the independent community school which was founded under the Board's auspices by a group of young radicals in West Philadelphia. The Parkway Program, one of the most truly innovative educational projects in the country, relied to a great extent on deLone for support, at least in the crucial early stages. He had found the money to hire a group of reformed gang leaders who had made a nationally known film about ghetto youth and who worked in several junior and senior high schools throughout the city. The infiltration process also included projects whose purpose was to bring young noneducators into the system; deLone organized a summer intern program for administrative trainees and arranged the contract for the Great Lakes Colleges Association's "Urban Semester" in Philadelphia.

The Board of Education had to approve all this infiltration, and deLone admits that in the beginning, because "I let my power go to my head," he had irrevocably alienated several Board members. Consequently he often had to resort to what he called "guerrilla politics." In one case a team of deLone's Cooperative Schools comrades had been indirectly hired by being "brought through the back door," as he put it, *via* a private, education-oriented enterprise receiving funds from the Board of Education. Using one loophole or another, he had also helped

large numbers of people get jobs who would otherwise have
been quickly eliminated by the requirements of the usual certification process. Perhaps the most spectacular example of
deLone's guerrilla politics was the Board's hiring of a group of
black militants from North Philadelphia to work in a training
program which aimed at changing teachers' attitudes toward
the community. The militants were connected with a community
organization that had long been an enemy of the Board and
whom Board members had strongly objected to on other occasions; but deLone skirted the problem by simply adding the
militants' names to a long list of prospective appointments—the
kind of list that the Board would automatically approve without
a glance.

As the network grew, supporting it became a full-time job.
Occasionally one of the network people suffered because of
deLone's mounting work load, but he and his secretary, an
attractive middle-aged woman who had quickly taken to his
irreverent style, managed to keep the lines of battlefield communication open most of the time.

After a while, however, even coups like the hiring of the
black militants began to lose their kick. There was no precise
moment when deLone began to question what he was doing—
rather, he felt a growing disenchantment. Many of his plans
went awry; the failure of new projects which had not originated
with him and were destroyed in one crisis or another added to his
discouragement. The late winter and spring of 1968 was a key
period in the struggle of the Shedd administration to make its
program work, and by the summer it seemed obvious that the outcome, of the first stage at least, was not the revolution so many
people had hoped for. The seemingly unending budget crisis and
the attendant feud between Tate and Dilworth had reached
almost ludicrous extremes (Dilworth's magic had also been somewhat tarnished by the utter banality of the exchanges), but
palpable damage had resulted from the Board's continuing uncertainty about money. The "firing" of the 381 administrators had
been a severe blow to the entire central administration, and even
the morale of Shedd's assistants never quite recovered. Perhaps
most disheartening not only to deLone but to his other colleagues

on the new team was the fact that Shedd, who had seemed so sympathetic at the beginning, became increasingly unavailable and uncommunicative. It was as if some evil giant, some overwhelming historical inevitability, had taken a huge hammer and smashed the whole glittering apparatus for change into paltry fragments.

It is easy, of course, to blame "history" for the failure of an urban administration of any kind in mid-century America, but the Shedd team would have had serious problems even if it had not been encumbered by crises and self-contradictions. One of the worst of these—the tendency to see the central staff in terms of good guys and bad guys, extremes of partisanship—probably had its greatest encouragement from deLone himself. Inevitably, what might have been considered a reactionary force among the "new" people, a group that wanted to reconcile the good guys and the bad guys, added to the chaos at 21st Street, and the process of partisan disintegration was virtually complete. It was the American crisis in microcosm: No one was to blame, but everyone was responsible.

Finally, the situation reached a level of almost self-destructive bitterness. A relatively unimportant, but graphic, example of this occurred when Shedd told a group of recent Harvard graduates, deLone among them, to handle preparations for the 1968 alumni conference of the Graduate School of Education, for which Philadelphia was host. The previous conference, reflecting Sizer's growing interest in urban schools, had taken place at New York's famed IS 201, and the choice of Philadelphia, aside from the many close personal ties involved, was meant to provide a glimpse of the school system's numerous innovative programs. With strict instructions to "avoid confrontations," Shedd had assigned the topic of "The Teacher and the Urban Schools." A week or so later, however, flyers went out announcing that the conference would deal with "The Radicalization of the American Teacher"—despite the obvious fact that, as one of the conference planners put it, "Mark will be furious."

By this time, some of the younger members of the new team had taken to joking about how the slightest inconvenience might serve as a pretext for quitting their jobs. It was desperate joking, but in the opinion of one of the more analytical observers at 21st Street, it reflected "suicidal impulses." The dismal atmosphere seemed to infect everyone on Shedd's staff; it was as if the younger members of the team were so bitterly disappointed that they wanted to blow up the entire school system before they left it. They resisted the impulse, but nevertheless they began to leave.

Rick deLone's departure was quiet and gradual. In October 1968, he agreed to join Graham Finney, the head of the planning office, as a staff member of the decentralization commission that the Board had formed in order to come up with a comprehensive plan for the entire system. Finney had become so exasperated by the constraints of his job, that he had told Shedd he would continue to work for the Board only in this semi-independent capacity and only outside of 21st Street. Another of Finney's requirements for even this provisional continuation of his service was that deLone be one of his assistants. Thus, in less than a month, two key positions had become battle victims. For a while, deLone continued to nurse a few of his pet projects from his new office, but he had clearly chosen a graceful means of withdrawing from what had become, in his view, an intolerable situation. DeLone and Shedd parted on friendly terms, but as far as any of deLone's followers were concerned, his move, with Finney, to a separate office a few blocks from 21st Street marked the end of an era.

In a moment of extreme humility, deLone once remarked that the job he was doing "won't change the system, but maybe it will get us over the hump." Few of his friends, however, were so clear-sighted. About a month before the departure that everyone who knew him realized was imminent, one of his followers said: "I have to remember when I pick up the phone that I can't call him. I have to find someone else." For many of them, he had been the center of the world, the single concrete hope. It was a tiny world at best—deLone's efforts had never affected more than a small minority of the teachers in the Philadelphia school system. But it was a world where, in the midst of the urban war that plagued America, there existed a modicum of humor and imagination. DeLone had been a strong leader at a time when leadership seemed an old-fashioned idea; for a while he was a source of magic. No one who had seen him working to keep his network together could doubt that eventually he would be back where the action was.

Snapshot: *Swingy Chick*

It's late in the afternoon. I've been at 21st Street, talking with several different people, for most of the day. Usually I schedule brief visits, salt them with glimpses of the real world—the New Jersey Turnpike, Center City (Philadelphia), even a school. I am heading down the marble hall toward the elevator.

A good-looking dark-haired chick in a miniskirt appears from a room nearby. She seems lively, bright, awake. We are walking together. I notice that she carries a copy of *Death at an Early Age,* Jonathan Kozol's book about the failures of ghetto schools in Boston. "What's going on there?" I ask about the room she just came from and from which a small crowd of people now emerges. "We just took the local exam for English teachers," she says with a friendly smile. "You a teacher?" I ask. "Yes, I teach at Roosevelt." "English." "Yeah." We take the stairs.

"I've heard about Roosevelt," I say. "There are some good things going on there."

"What have you heard?" she says, as if she can hardly believe that I could be so misinformed.

"Don't they have some good people there? And they've been trying some new teaching approaches?"

"Oh *that,*" she says. "Well, they've been *trying* some new things."

"Isn't the faculty pretty much . . . young?"

She considers this. "It's a fairly young faculty. There *are* some people I like."

We are standing now in the first-floor marble hall, near the door to the board room. People rush by, leaving the building, their working day over. "What don't you like about it, then?" I say. This is not the first time that I've heard something favorable about an innovation from a reliable source, only to have it roundly contradicted by what I assume to be another reliable source.

"It's the kids," she says. "They're *horrible!* You can't do anything with them."

"Oh," I say.

She has been getting her bearings. "What do *you* do?" she asks.

"I'm interested in innovative programs," I answer. "I'm a writer." She smiles; she is quite pretty and sure of herself.

"Have you read *this?*" she says, indicating the Kozol book.

"Yeah. . . ."

"Boy, would I like to have a word or two with *him!*" I can see her telling off Jonathan Kozol, in endless detail. We smile goodbye.

IV. *Community*

All Together for Gratz

AT ONE TIME, Simon Gratz High School was the epitome of inner-city education in Philadelphia—a model of everything that should not be. It was the kind of school that most people who had never been there were afraid even to visit. The very name could evoke images of dark halls teeming with knife-wielding gangs. Gratz was a dumping ground, and students who had a choice did their best to go somewhere else. More important than any of the specific faults—the antiquated, inadequate facilities; the high ratio of permanent substitutes; the low morale of the faculty; the students' sub-normal reading levels—was the fact that Gratz was a poor black school, the ultimate symbol of failure. People in low places as well as in high ones simply tried to pretend that Gratz didn't exist; it was easier to ignore the utterly hopeless.

But like the city itself, which was close to ruin by the late 1940's, Gratz would not have been such a perfect target for reformers if it had not suffered from such general deprivation. Moreover, Gratz was a disgrace to the black community in particular; no black man in the city could really hold up his head as long as the school continued as it was. And through a series of extraordinary events that spanned several years of continuous struggle, Gratz came to represent the essence of the black power movement in Philadelphia's educational system. At the height of the struggle, every important black leader in the city rallied to the cause. No Ford Foundation had backed the movement for community involvement, as in New York; no white administrator had sparked the grass-roots interest. Rather, Gratz became the center of a spontaneous uprising; the community, in effect, seized control.

"It's a lousy, corrupt, no-good system," says Mary James, for several years president of the Gratz Home and School Association, "and it needs to be rebuilt. We're trying to help them." Mrs. James is typical of an informal sorority that has emerged throughout the city of Philadelphia and other cities as well. These are the strong-willed, outspoken black women, usually the mothers of several children, who have chosen education as their main sphere of interest and their own neighborhood schools as their principal target. Most of them have risen from poor backgrounds; while many have husbands, they are unquestionably the dominant figures in their families.

Mary James was born in a nearby New Jersey town, but she received most of her schooling in Philadelphia. She was one of the lucky ones who made it through the system's little traps into the prestigious, closed-enrollment Girls' High School, one of the city's two "quality" high schools (the other one, Central, is for boys). From there she went on to business college, then finally to the Bible College of Philadelphia, where she studied religious education. At the time of her association with Gratz, Mrs. James ran a preschool in a North Philadelphia church and served as director of Christian Education for the Lutheran Church of America. Mary James had made it; she had not only survived the system, she had prevailed.

Like Annette Temin, who hammered away at the Anderson administration for so many years, Mrs. James had made her pursuit of a broad spectrum of change in the Philadelphia public schools virtually a full-time avocation. For many years her principal lever for change consisted in "busting" various home and school associations. Each school had one, and traditionally these groups of mothers from the neighborhood were dominated by the principal—they were the administration's way of giving parents an occasional glimpse of what was happening to their children in school. But the individual home and school associations were effectively dominated, in turn, by the city-wide Home and School Council, composed of powerful recruits from local groups, and virtually an offshoot of the Anderson administration.

The entire home-and-school apparatus, in short, had been a subtle but effective instrument for relegating parent involvement to the harmless level of occasional afternoon teas.

The apparatus had been under attack since it was invented. Anyone who cared to think about it could see that in its own innocent way it was part of the massive structure that kept real education from happening. Though no longer paid by the Board, the Home and School Council continued to be among the most predictable defenders of the status quo even after the Anderson days, and the fight against it continued as well. But most reformers despaired of changing this particular aspect of the system and found other ways to affect the educational process in their neighborhood schools; this was true of Mrs. Temin, who eventually turned her energies to forming a completely independent citizens' coalition.

Mary James had decided that she could work within the system. There was no written law saying that home and school associations were supposed to do nothing but serve tea and cookies every few weeks. Home and school associations could be "organized." Mary James became an organizer.

She began in the late 1940's in her neighborhood elementary school in North Philadelphia; but the system's policy of open enrollment—in theory, any student could voluntarily transfer to a school outside his immediate neighborhood—allowed her considerable flexibility. Moreover, she had four children of various ages passing through the school system over a period of almost two decades. After several years she and her children moved on from the North Philadelphia school to a junior high school in one of the city's better-integrated sections. There she became the first black parent on the home and school association's executive board. "I went there," she explains, "to integrate it." And then, in 1962, just as she was beginning to run out of school-age children, she answered the call for increased membership in the home and school association of Gratz.

"They used to say Gratz was the worst school in the city," Mrs. James recalls. "And they said the kids were bad. The school was going downhill rapidly. There were very few children going on to college, and those that did go weren't prepared. The principal wasn't able to conduct the school as he should have, but he was near to retirement." In addition, by this time Gratz was ninety-five per cent black. Technically, the school was not in the inner city, for it was located at the northern-most part of the district from which Gratz students were supposed to come. Even though the huge semi-Gothic building was set amid several blocks of middle-class homes, however, the poor neighborhoods to the south could easily be classified as ghettoes. Gratz was indeed a ghetto school.

Ghetto school, inner-city school, slum school, culturally deprived—they are all educators' jargon for the same idea: poor, usually black. Nor were the problems at Gratz unique. In Philadelphia, as in so many other American cities, there is an almost predictable similarity among such schools. Since gangs are an important factor in the kids' socialization, for example (Philadelphia still has one of the most active gang networks of any of the nation's large cities), gang tensions naturally "spill over," as the administrators like to say, into the schools. Ghetto family life spills over, too. Within five minutes at Gratz one day in the winter of 1967, a young teacher was approached first by a student who despaired so much of school and family life that he was enlisting in the Army, then by another who had gotten into several fights while defending his just-pregnant girl friend against the taunts of her classmates. One learns to accept such things in poor schools; after a while, they are as routine as pink slips, hall passes, or the late bell. As for the kids' actual readiness for traditional schooling, this is a subject so thoroughly researched, so widely discussed, that it needs no elaboration. Large numbers of the usual graduating class at Gratz, during the period of extreme neglect that preceded Mary James' struggle for change, left the school as functional illiterates.

But Mrs. James knew better than to attack the general failures of ghetto life; there were enough specific problems at Gratz to fuel a campaign that might last for years. One of these was the building—although identical to two other (integrated, largely white) high schools in other parts of the city, the forty-year-old monolith was seriously overcrowded. By 1968 the school, which had been built for 2,000 students, had to go on separate morning and afternoon shifts in order to accommodate 4,300. And while Gratz remained untouched, with its dreary classrooms, its undersized gymnasium with flaking walls, and its primitive lunchroom, the other two schools were being refurbished and expanded. Mary James started right away to work on an expansion for Gratz.

Armed with specific requests for a new gymnasium, more classrooms, and a playing field, she soon joined the growing crowd of parents who made regular appearances at 21st Street to fight for their territory. "I got a committee of women to go to Add Anderson six or seven years ago, before I came to Gratz," she says, "to get a new elementary school in the neighborhood. He said he'd review the situation with us. But he was *lying*. He never reviewed the situation, and he never listened." Anderson was just as unresponsive when Mrs. James went to him as a member of the Gratz Home and School Association, which had drawn up a detailed plan for the expansion. Once she even resorted to taking the president of the school's Student Association along with her. "You don't listen to these *young* people enough," she told Anderson. "You're in a different generation."

But the central administration did nothing. The school's white principal, Mrs. James points out, didn't exactly sabotage the move. "'If you can get it going,'" he would say, "'that's fine.'" And for several years, despite the efforts of Mary James and her co-organizers from the community, Gratz stayed at the bottom of the totem pole.

"The black community" is a virtually meaningless cliché from America's almanac of race and poverty—there is no community, in the true sense of the word, among any city's blacks, just as there is no real community among its whites. Nevertheless, the Philadelphia *Tribune*, founded in 1884 and now published twice weekly, could well be considered the strongest public voice of the city's black people, however diverse their views. Like New York's *Amsterdam News* and Chicago's *Daily Defender*, the Philadelphia *Tribune* had played several different journalistic roles during its long history. On the other hand, it had been a powerful instrument for perpetuating a black establishment— its society pages identified a black elite, just as the society pages of the Philadelphia *Bulletin* identified a white one.

There was never anything particularly radical, however, about "black power," a phrase that terrified many whites when Stokely Carmichael first used it, and the *Tribune* had been a natural defender of the movement through its detailed reporting of the achievements of black business, political, and educational leaders. The paper had also played an educational role, as in the case of a lengthy series on consumer fraud. But one of the *Tribune*'s greatest coups, in exercising responsible black leadership, was the hard-line muckraking that occupied its front pages for several weeks in the winter of 1966, when it publicized conditions at Gratz High School.

J. Brantley Wilder, who joined the *Tribune*'s staff in 1963 after several years as a regular and substitute teacher of English in the public schools, was the paper's chief education reporter at the time. For several weeks in 1957 he had subbed at Gratz. Neither then nor in his subsequent wanderings through the public school system had he found anything particularly conspicuous about the school. One day early in 1966, however, he had a talk with a Gratz student who complained that school had become such a terrifying place that she was afraid to go there. The reason, she said, was the rampant gang terrorism—one result of a tremendous increase in the city's gang warfare, which reached a peak in the bloodbath of 1965, when some weeks saw a murder a night.

Wilder went to Gratz to check the report and stayed there, posing as a teacher, for six weeks. He had friends on the faculty, he was already known there as a substitute, and when he walked in to the teachers' lounge for a chat, no one ever questioned his reasons for being there.

"PARENTS CLAIM GANGS RULE GRATZ HIGH SCHOOL," shouted the front-page banner headline of the *Tribune*'s March 8 edition. "Principal Denies Reign of Terror Exists There," proclaimed a subhead. But the editors' note introducing the main article was itself sufficient to rouse the community: "Beatings, gang rule and surrender by teachers," it said, "—these are but a few of the grim facts of life at Gratz Senior High School. To get the full story behind GANG TAKE-OVER, reporter J. Brantley Wilder, at the risk of his own personal safety, spent six weeks in closed-door sessions with parents, teachers, and students. Here is his eye-opening report."

Wilder's main point was that the school's gang activity was "so bad that students cannot walk down the halls without fearing for their safety" and that teachers had given up trying to keep order. But he also cited other, more familiar, causes for the low morale: a purported third-grade average reading level, the unsanitary conditions of the lunchroom, the poor quality of the teaching, and even the waste of time on "highly advertised modern programs." The Gratz Home and School Association, whose executive board Wilder had interviewed at Mrs. James's home, was named as a principal source of information. The group's officers later denied that they had tipped Wilder off to the story, but they could only rejoice at the bad publicity and the pressure for change it was bound to build.

Immediately after the first article appeared, the *Tribune* was bombarded by angry letters, but few of them actually denied Wilder's claims. The predominant reaction from the students, for example, was outraged pride. More than a hundred students signed a protest letter demanding a public apology. The students of Gratz, wrote one girl in another letter, "are some of the most wonderful people in the world. We love Gratz High and will do everything in our power to see that Gratz is talked about only when you can be proud of what you say." Students even threatened a march to the *Tribune*'s offices.

Many of the school's senior faculty members insist that whatever the problems were, Gratz was never the terrifying hellhole Wilder described. One department head joined the faculty with great trepidation and reluctance, after years at an all-white high school in Northeast Philadelphia, only to discover that the school was a "calm, friendly place with very tight discipline." Discipline, says a teacher, was "tighter than it is now. The school was actually *dull*. Nothing happened. You could go into the classrooms, and the kids were just sitting there in silence." Tight discipline did not preclude an occasional eruption, of course—a discreet stabbing on a stairway during the change of classes or a beating in an out-of-the-way, fifth-floor hall.

But Wilder's claims had sparked an uproar that no simple expedient could quell. Replacing the plastic forks in the lunchrooms with silver ones (this was done shortly after the first article) would not make Gratz the kind of school the community wanted. Half-measures would no longer satisfy; there would have to be important, highly noticeable changes—basic changes. It was only 1966, and the top administration at 21st Street wasn't yet familiar with the sensation of being backed up against a wall every day by angry community representatives; but the first ghetto riots had already happened—the image of a lid blowing from a cauldron had a corner in the imagination of every public official who read the papers. The Gratz situation demanded immediate action from the top.

Despite the high noise level generated by the issue of community control of public schools and the fact of racism in America, black teachers and administrators have made real progress in many urban school systems—particularly Philadelphia's—within the last decade. Whether this progress has been fast enough or sufficient to the proportion of black children in the schools is another question, but in Philadelphia in 1968, five of the twenty-two high school principals were black. Public school systems have been a means of social advancement for other underprivileged minorities in the past, of course—the Jews in New York, the Irish in Boston. Blacks, from one point of view, were merely late in getting their share.

The qualitative differences were tremendous, however. Schools have traditionally been an almost mechanically safe means of climbing the social ladder, and for the white minorities the next rung has always been fairly easy to reach. The first middle-class generation spawns a new generation, more sophisticated, "cultured," and "educated": the principal's son, the lawyer. For whites there have always been leaders; there have always been the prominent WASP's at the top, providing the universally accepted image of propriety, respectability, virtue, and reward. Whatever success meant in America, it was definitely white.

A black principal was the logical answer to the furor produced by the *Tribune*'s Gratz stories, and it is likely that any man with dark skin would have satisfied the community's demand for justice. But there was no necessary connection between a principal's skin color and his sympathy or understanding. The cry for black leadership in the schools generally ignored the almost inevitable identity crisis that black school administrators in the 1960's were heir to. One of the most respected senior high school principals in the city (according to student militants) was Walter Scott of all-black West Philadelphia High School—a white man. Several black principals, on the other hand, were known to be such infallible machine-cogs that they were actually retarding the progress of their schools. What Gratz needed more than a man with black skin was a strong leader who had the community's welfare at heart.

At forty-three, Marcus A. Foster had already distinguished himself as a highly promising career educator. Born in South Philadelphia, he was graduated from South Philadelphia High School in 1941 and attended Cheyney State Teachers College in nearby Chester. He also had a degree in education from the University of Pennsylvania. After nine years of teaching in elementary schools, he had gone on to be principal first of an elementary school in one of the poorest sections of North Philadelphia and later of a disciplinary school. In March 1966, he had made another move up the system's ladder when he was hired to be one of the idea-men in the Shedd administration's Planning Office. This promotion was clearly an acknowledgment of what most people who knew the public school system had recognized for years: Marcus Foster was not just a strong black leader; he was one of the brightest and most imaginative men around.

His innovativeness was almost legendary, in fact. He had taken over the principalship of Catto Disciplinary School at a time when disciplinary schools were virtual prisons for the disrupters and rejects who couldn't fit into the already prisonlike regular schools, and he had raised attendance levels higher than they had ever been. For years the policy at Catto was to ignore truants and be grateful that they stayed away, but within the first year of Foster's administration he had created programs for parent involvement (before, most parents were reluctant to admit that their children attended Catto), new curricula, and such offbeat attractions as a fashion show for the boys and their families. Some observers claimed that in three years as principal of Dunbar Elementary School, he had transformed it into an institution that could rival any school on the Main Line. Foster was so highly regarded in the black community that Mary James had already, a year earlier, asked officials at 21st Street to make him the new principal of Gratz.

The Gratz faculty was not quite so eager to welcome Foster, however, when they learned, thirteen days after the first *Tribune* article, that he would take over as head of the school. It was not that the former principal had elicited great feelings of loyalty or that anyone believed he was the best man for the job. Rather, many faculty members objected to the precipitous nature of such an important change—"Just overnight," complained some as much as two years later, "the old principal was gone, without a word of warning." There were racial overtones as well; many on the Gratz faculty protested the appointment of a new principal, as one teacher put it, "just because he's colored." And Marcus Foster had not reached his position through the usual bureaucratic channels; he was appointed under the Board's rule that exempted five per cent of the superintendent's administrative staff from the usual qualifications.

Thus, on the afternoon of his first meeting with the Gratz faculty, Foster did not exactly enter a climate of friendliness and eager anticipation. Protests against his appointment were still strong. Several deputy superintendents had been sent from 21st Street to smooth Foster's way (among the official excuses for the change was the former principal's alleged poor health), but, listening to the elaborate officialese while he fidgeted in his seat, Foster became just as impatient with it as the audience. "Of course," he recalled in an interview in *AE*—the magazine published by Philadelphia teachers, which did a cover story on him in December 1968—"the people weren't buying it."

Finally it was Foster's turn. "It seems to me," he began, "that if one's friend is moved out rather unceremoniously, one must be upset. Or else I question his loyalty. So you have loyalty to your former principal. You should have. And now there is the possibility that your loyalty can be transferred. So make no apologies for feeling kindly toward your friend." Marcus Foster had a way with an audience; it was almost impossible not to like him.

As he remembers it, one teacher finally said, "'Well, Marcus, you're up there, and every new principal is due for at least a year's honeymoon.'" Foster replied, "Well, the thing about a honeymoon is that it's a time when you can fall in love. So I'll take the honeymoon. We'll see what we can do with it."

What Foster wanted to do most, what he had always been best at doing, was to bring the entire community "together."

"Stay together" was Marcus Foster's answer to almost any adversity, and with few exceptions, he made the answer work. Though there was never any official directive establishing Gratz as a demonstration school in community involvement and though the changes that occurred during Foster's administration were almost entirely the results of his unique leadership, Gratz became one of the best examples of the black community keeping itself together to be found anywhere in Philadelphia. Foster was more than a principal; he was one of the most highly regarded black leaders in the city. Noting that "no field in Philadelphia has been more responsive to talent in the last few years than public education," an article in the liberal *Philadelphia* Magazine entitled "The Black Tigers" cited Foster as the most impressive figure of all. "He has an incredible future," says one of his super-loyal faculty. "He can go anywhere—politics, anything." And, savoring the extreme irony, another comments, "Marcus Foster is *really* The Man."

Foster could address a large audience and give the impression that he was talking to every member of it individually. For him, a walk through the halls of his school was an uninterrupted series of greetings, warm smiles, handshakes, and words of praise—signs that he knew exactly who each one of the students was and cared about them all. He had perfected the feat of talking to people in his office and at the same time—the door was always open in welcome—carrying on a nonverbal conversation with people he could see outside. "Come on in," he would say if visitors hesitated on the threshold. "You just have to barge right in and start talking; that's the only way you can get to me." Or into the telephone: "Hello old buddy, how're you doing?"—the "old buddy" his own special, magic touch.

But Marcus Foster was no teddy bear. He was an imposing man—six-foot-five, on the portly side—and, in his usual business suits (or even his blazer with "Gratz" embroidered on the breast pocket) and thick round glasses, he projected firm authority. He could have been the head of a corporation—most likely a conglomerate. His message—"I'm a black leader; my time has come"—was unmistakable to any observer who saw him in action.

Foster's first move as principal was hardly in the style of the corporation executive he often resembled, however: Visiting one home after another, he scoured the Gratz district, trying to recruit more students. The higher achievers had at least a limited choice of schools, and, until Foster's regime, any student who had managed to demonstrate a certain measure of scholastic ability also managed to avoid Gratz. In his effort to bring these better students back, Foster promised special "academic" courses, extra help in college admissions, and a thorough revision of the curriculum. He brought several hundred new students to Gratz in his first year. Ironically, overcrowding, one of the greatest problems, became even worse than it would have been ordinarily—for in addition to bringing better students back to the school, Foster cut the dropout rate in half.

Nonetheless, Foster did so much to improve Gratz that the overcrowding could hardly be seen as an error. By the end of one year there were few aspects of school life that he hadn't changed in some way. Like the massive rehabilitation program that the new Board of Education was trying to effect throughout the school system, the changes that occurred within Foster's early administration may not have been entirely revolutionary, but they were impressive.

In curriculum:

—The vocational education staff rose from eight to twenty-three, with a corresponding rise in the number and diversity of vocational classrooms.

—A humanities program was developed for approximately forty academic students; a combination of English and social studies, this was similar to many "core" programs in suburban high schools.

—An authority on African culture was hired part-time to introduce African themes whenever possible into the ordinary course work. He was responsible for such novelties as dashikis in the tailoring shop and African sculpture in art classes.

—Gratz became the first school in Philadelphia to offer Afro-American history (though only as an after-school elective).

—The school established a highly advanced biology program (Biological Sciences Curriculum Study) that offered special two-hour labs and a much greater opportunity to do actual experiments than did the conventional science course.

—Perhaps most important, seventy-five teachers, students, and community representatives were paid to conduct a ten-week study of curriculum changes. Funded by a federal grant of $30,000, the curriculum workshop became a laboratory for curriculum change throughout the city's high schools, focusing on the role of Afro-American culture, the problems of the inner city, and the restructuring of course material according to a more logical basic plan than before.

In nonacademic school activities:

—The Honor Society was reinstated, and accepted sixty members in the 1967–68 school year.

—A band, a drama club, and a class prom were organized; there had been none before.

—The athletic teams were provided with new uniforms (they had previously worn castoffs from other schools or none at all). Gratz teams began to win. A former Harlem Globetrotter joined the physical education staff.

In college preparation:

—A small group of students participated in Saturday morning study programs at Haverford College.

—Usually through Foster's personal efforts, Gratz seniors began to receive offers of scholarships from colleges throughout the country.

—In the spring of 1968, one hundred seniors were planning to go on to college. This contrasted with eighteen seniors two years before, and while the figure fell far short of the national average of fifty-one per cent, it amounted to a five hundred per cent rise for Gratz.

Ties with the business and professional community:

—Two hundred seniors in the 1968 graduating class had lined up jobs, one result of Foster's campaign to involve the city's business community in the life of the school.

—Foster arranged for entire grades to visit a variety of businesses and factories.

—Business and professional leaders made a grant of $21,000

to Gratz for establishing a vocational guidance center and a summer training program.

Morale:

—Because of Foster's interest in innovation and his encouragement of new ideas ("I was going to leave just before he came," said one teacher, "but now he's letting me do anything I want"), Gratz received the largest number of grants from the Shedd administration's teacher grant program.

—The local soul station, WHAT, awarded Gratz first place in its 1968 School Spirit Contest.

While there was rarely any concerted opposition to Foster's efforts within the school, he was able to overcome such opposition as there was with good will. "He's like a man walking a tightrope," a Gratz teacher once observed. "He has to be everything to everybody—white to the whites, black to the blacks, everything." Foster was not above firm measures, in fact, when this delicate balance was at stake. On several occasions he had to deal strongly with critical student militants, many of whom participated in the November 17 demonstration. A select group comprised of some of the most articulate and outspoken students was shuffled into what amounted to a genteel club for the alienated. And several left-oriented community leaders failed in their attempt to stage a minor coup at a time when Foster was seriously ill only because he made an almost miraculous eleventh-hour appearance after rising from his sickbed to stop them.

While most people believed that Marcus Foster could do no wrong, his very insistence on togetherness tended to impose an artificial homogeneity on the Gratz community. He could always justify this approach by citing the array of benefits that the community had gained from working together; but this was galling to the dissenters. Some—the older teachers usually—were interested in keeping things just as they had always been, though they were reluctant to admit this publicly. Others—the militant students, many of the teachers—had little faith in Foster's goals, which seemed to be to make Gratz exactly what people said he had made Dunbar Elementary School: just as good as any school on the Main Line. Foster and his family were among the very few black residents of an elegant Philadelphia suburb, in fact. Entirely a product of the system, even an embodiment of the good old-fashioned American Dream, Foster rarely seemed to doubt that a high school on the Main Line was as good as a high school could be.

Nevertheless, there had been noticeable, concrete, and unquestionably positive changes at Gratz. Within his first two years, Foster had raised huge amounts of money in addition to the school's regular budget to bring these changes about. Nor was he completely satisfied with the record. He was often the first to admit that there were still serious problems—though the particular problems he had in mind concerned the failure of his program to be even better than it was, not the value of the program itself.

Although he and his staff had helped three hundred graduating seniors find either colleges or jobs in 1968, this left six hundred who still had no idea of what they would do after school. There were still classes with as many as forty students. The basketball team still played league games in a gym that was undersized even when it was built. And after two years of change, finally it became clear once again that something had to be done about the building before Gratz could be the kind of school that Foster and a majority of the community wanted. It was the old question of the expansion that Mary James had raised years earlier, but now there was a difference; now the Gratz community was ready—they were together.

The school system was somewhat more together as well. The new planning office at 21st Street had already been working for almost a year on a proposal for the expansion and had finally come up with a solution that would, through a series of progressive steps, virtually double the size of the school and give it the extracurricular and athletic facilities it needed. One step of the plan involved a smaller building, a junior high school adjacent to Gratz which was due to be replaced by a proposed middle school. When this building eventually became available, it would increase the space at Gratz by almost two-thirds. Another step involved the purchase of large tracts of property close to the school which would be used for playing fields, tennis courts, and general recreation. But the most immediate relief was to come in the form of a small addition (sixteen classrooms and a gymnasium) that would occupy a triangular block on the

north side of the main building. This part of the expansion was
already under consideration by the Board of Education.

In order to execute this first stage of the Gratz expansion, the
Board had to take fourteen homes which faced Hunting Park
Avenue, the northern side of the triangular block. These homes
were owned almost entirely by Polish families who had lived in
the neighborhood for as long as fifty years and had attended
services for every holy day of those many decades at the Roman
Catholic church on the adjacent corner. Expansion of public
facilities was a growing source of controversy in Philadelphia—
residents of South Philadelphia were battling a proposed ex-
pressway, and homeowners throughout the city were opposing
suggested school sites—but this time the story had a new twist:
Usually the victims of these moves by public institutions were
black; now they were white. And finally, Mayor Tate—who had
watched the multimillion-dollar University City Science Center
destroy a huge chunk of the West Philadelphia black ghetto
without batting an eye—decided to take a stand.

The Gratz expansion could conceivably have been carried out
without the cooperation of the city government, but it would
have been almost insurmountably difficult. For one thing, the
City Planning Commission, over which Tate had indirect control,
could have blocked the move by refusing to allow the necessary
closing of a street that ran between the triangular block and the
school. More important, Tate's vendetta against the Board of
Education could have serious consequences for the budget of the
entire school system; Dilworth wanted Tate's cooperation in the
Gratz expansion, if possible.

Soon after his re-election as mayor, however, Tate and his
sometime right-hand man, City Council President Paul D'Ortona,
came out against the proposal. D'Ortona's argument was that the
expansion was an invasion of the rights of homeowners. "Pretty
soon," he said at one point in the dispute, "between the schools
and redevelopment we'll be chasing everybody out of their
homes." In an almost saintly effort at diplomacy, Dilworth
agreed to a joint study by the Board's planning office and the
City Planning Commission of possible alternatives to the expansion—though he commented publicly that he doubted any
alternatives could be found. But by this time, almost two years

to the day after Marcus Foster had taken over as principal of Gratz, the pressure from the black community had become virtually irresistible.

Beginning early in 1968, a network of community leaders throughout the city, most of them black, had begun to make plans for a confrontation with the Board, and the result was a feat of organization that could have made a confirmed revolutionary envious. Foster himself was one of the outstanding leaders—the school was so together on the issue that the entire faculty petitioned the Board for the expansion and the entire student body agreed to refrain from participating in the demonstration, lest they trigger any repetition of the November 17 disaster. The members of the Gratz team of the National Teacher Corps promised to ask their headquarters in Washington to withhold all help from Philadelphia in the future if the Board did not meet the community's demands. And the home and school association, still under the leadership of Mary James, raised enough money to hire ten buses to take people to the Board meeting scheduled for Monday afternoon, February 26. Even some of the militant leaders who had said they would have nothing whatever to do with the system made an exeception this time for Gratz.

The question of the Gratz expansion did not come up until late in the meeting. The Board's usual business preceded it, and, ironically, so did protests from a group of about fifty white parents who had descended on the Board to complain about racial tensions at Germantown High School. At any other time a group of fifty parents en masse would have seemed a formidable power bloc in the large, elegant board room at 21st Street, which could hold approximately a hundred people comfortably. But the meeting of February 26 was unusual; as many as six hundred people had come to confront the Board on the Gratz issue. The crowd had overflowed into the second-floor auditorium, where the meeting could be seen on closed-circuit television.

In the briefing session held earlier in the day, Dilworth had convinced his colleagues, despite protests from the two black members of the Board and others, to stand by the agreement with Tate until the next Board meeting, which would be on March 11. As Dilworth later explained, during the public meeting, to a gathering of vehement speakers who had hours of reasons why the expansion must be approved immediately, Tate had the power to endanger everything that the Board was working for. But the speakers, and finally the dissenting Board members, would not wait.

One community leader elicited laughter and applause when she told the Board that she was still trying to relocate black families who had been forced to move within the last year as a result of school expansions. "The fourteen families at Gratz don't have any problem," she said. "Just take them out to the suburbs." Another threatened to "mobilize North Philadelphia" if the Board didn't move ahead with the expansion. And, one by one, Philadelphia's black leaders virtually overwhelmed the increasingly astonished Board members with their eloquence and anger. "In view of the patience, forbearance, and long suffering of the Gratz community," concluded Board member George Hutt, "we cannot pass the buck any longer." That afternoon, in the board room of the Philadelphia Board of Public Education, hundreds of years of injustice had come to a dramatic climax. It was the kind of decisive moment in which the wrong move could have touched off civil disorders throughout the city.

Finally Dilworth called for a vote on a resolution that the Board move to take the fourteen homes immediately. He and William Ross, the only Board member who seemed to represent Mayor Tate's views to the letter, voted against it. Hutt and Reverend Henry Nichols, the vice-president of the Board, who was also black, voted yes. One new member abstained, and the two others who were present at the meeting, though they had voted against the resolution earlier in the day, finally decided to listen to the community. The resolution passed by two votes, and the audience got to its feet and yelled.

For weeks after the meeting, black leaders throughout the city were claiming that the Gratz triumph was the beginning of a new stage of the movement. Riots were out of style, they said; working through the democratic process was the only answer. The following summer in Philadelphia would be cool (the city had suffered only one major disorder, in the summer of 1964). The time had come for blacks to build a political coalition, a sort of black ADA. West Philadelphia's Novella Williams was hard at work, organizing voter registration in preparation for it. Briefly, the bitter social climate of urban America was warmed by a spirit of optimism. In retrospect, and in the light of later events—the dreary routine of civil strife and racism; the presidential conventions, the elections; the continuing inequality and injustice; the severe cuts in federal aid to the schools; Mayor Tate's unflagging inability to respond to the needs of the poor—this moment of joy seems roughly equivalent to a champagne supper on the eve of an execution. But the champagne bubbles stayed alive for a little over a month—at least until the execution of April 4—the murder of Martin Luther King.

Snapshot: *Protection*

He is a huge, beautiful black cat, and as he strides through the halls of Germantown High School, he could be a visiting prince. He wears an elegant dashiki and fila, and he mingles with the crowds of students during the change of classes amid an uninterrupted flow of smiles and greetings. His voice is low and rich, confident, strong. "Hey, we gonna see you down at the center?" he asks one of the boys. "Yeah, man, I'll be there," comes the answer. "How's that little thing comin'," he shouts to another. "Oh, we're workin' on it."

He has been pointed out to me as one of the most militant of the militants, and as we talk, I discover that he is not a student at Germantown at all, that he graduated from the school several years ago. Nonplused, I asked him what he is doing here. He glances at me as if the answer ought to be obvious. "I'm just lookin' after my brothers and sisters."

Two Con Artists
Call It a Day

SHE WILL PROBABLY TRY to sue me no matter what I write. I'd
like to identify her and describe her work in detail, but I'll have
to call her Ethel Dobbins—it seems an apt *nom de guerre*—and,
unfortunately, I can't say much about the numerous ways in
which she struggled for a better future for black people in Philadelphia. She was one of the full-time fighters—those usually
hefty black women, varying in overweight from plump to gross,
with shy children and quiet husbands ("She's probably off somewhere *do*ing something," her husband once told me on the phone.
"I don't know where she goes.")—who have devoted their lives
to social activism. There were at least a dozen in various parts of
Philadelphia just like her. Everybody knew them. They were the
leaders, the ones who always turned up at public meetings armed
with rounds of invective and denunciation; "this sick society,"
"this racist school system," "this sick . . . ," "that racist. . . ."
It was part of their whole familiar routine.

The routine also included periodic assaults on City Hall ("You
pick up this garbage," I once heard Ethel shouting into her office
phone, "or I'm closing the streets at four-thirty this afternoon"),
the state Department of Welfare, Police Commissioner Rizzo,
and, when they had time for it, big business and the Vietnam
War. But they were revolutionaries in only a limited sense;
haranguing the "colonialist" forces that continued to keep them

down, threatening and demonstrating, sitting-in and leaking scary plots to "the media"—these were merely the tools of their trade. The more they denounced the society, the clearer it was that they wanted in. They were the contemporary believers in the American Dream—tragic evidence of the lies that have governed the country since its inception.

Ethel Dobbins could never have seen the tragic element in her crusade; she was much too single-minded to bother with that kind of subtlety. I don't mean to belittle her intelligence—her thinking was as hard and clear as diamonds; she was so shrewd she could probably have defeated the NLF if she'd put her mind to it. Unfortunately, in my view of it, she had no time for contemplation; forty years of struggle had hardened her outlook into an almost grim absolutism. She might become a heroine of sorts, but she had to forfeit such lesser virtues as trust. I am not sure that she would have reacted much differently to the events I am about to describe even if I had been black.

Like so many of her comrades in the black liberation movement, Ethel Dobbins was always getting her name in the papers, and it didn't take me long to find out that part of her crusade involved the school system. The community organization with which she worked had put so much pressure on the Board of Education that the group was actually beginning to play an important role in key policy decisions involving various neighborhood schools. Mark Shedd had granted them the usual advisory board, which later became synonymous with token "community control," but they had turned the gesture into an important move toward power simply by pushing so hard in the right places that they finally got whatever they asked for. It was tremendously effective de facto community control—an example of involvement comparable to the community school districts that New York had made official through the agonies of legal battles and strikes—but it had grown spontaneously with the rise to power of the Women for the Embetterment of Black Society (or WEBS, as I'll call Ethel's group), one of the most dynamic citizens' organizations in Philadelphia.

The success of the community-directed program, which affected every facet of school life and included the hiring of new

administrators and the development of curriculum, simply proved
what in theory should have been obvious: No matter what the
"law" said, power belonged to those who worked at it. Ethel
Dobbins and her friends, like good Americans of frontier days,
had taken the law into their own hands. Community school districts, with legally established advisory boards, are probably
inevitable in most large American cities. It is more than likely,
however, that at some point, community control—a term whose
meaning varies with almost every speaker who uses it—will
cease to be the magic answer to America's social problems and
will go out of fashion, leaving in its wake a great many community advisory boards with varying degrees of legally established power that will have proved themselves no more effective
than the original centralized boards whose deficiencies provoked
the movement in the first place.

For in Philadelphia, as in other cities, real community involvement—when it occurred—was the result of extensive, dedicated
organization. In the fall of 1967, Novella Williams's citizens'
group in West Philadelphia, with the authority of years of
activism behind it, refused to allow the school board to put Sayre
Junior High School on double sessions. The Board capitulated
and even heeded their demands for increased facilities by renting
unused buildings in the neighborhood to relieve the school's overcrowding. When a group of citizens in Germantown demanded
the ouster of the principal of an elementary school, the Board
agreed; but few communities in the city could match Germantown's network of hard-driving civic organizations. Where there
was genuine power, in short, the Board had no choice but to
respond.

My first contact with Ethel Dobbins came in December 1967,
after the principal at one of the schools whose business she
minded so well told me, with a mixture of resentment and boast-
ing (no principal in his right mind will miss the opportunity to
proclaim strong community interest, whether he likes it or not),
that Mrs. Dobbins and her group had an important role in running the school. I had visited the school mainly to observe a
friend's English classes. The talk with the principal was prompted
by idle curiosity, but the obvious fear in his voice when he told
me about the community group (they later persuaded him to

find another job) aroused my interest. I'd heard about Mrs. Dobbins's various demonstrations of militancy, and, not without a certain amount of trepidation myself, I decided that I'd try to talk with her.

On at least one occasion a well-known Philadelphia militant had refused to see me altogether. The more Ethel Dobbins growled at me over the phone, when I finally reached her at home one day, the more intense were my pleas for at least a brief audience ("I'm writing this book completely on my own," I told her. "And I've heard so much about your work. . . ."). Finally she agreed to talk with me—I managed to convince her that I was clean enough at least to continue pleading my case in person—and we agreed to meet one afternoon a few days later. She hadn't committed herself to anything yet; the purpose of the talk would be for me to expound at length my theories on education and my experiences in the school system—and, of course, for her to get a chance to size me up.

I took great care to be there exactly at the appointed hour, for I sensed that here, at least, I was the underdog. I'd been anticipating the interview with such anxiety that by the time it arrived, I think I must have convinced myself that I alone was responsible for three hundred years of racist oppression. Ever since our conversation on the phone I had been haunted by the thought that the future of black and white together hung on our ability to make contact and establish a reasonable give-and-take. But, aside from this exaggerated humility, I fully expected an atmosphere of complete honesty to prevail. She, of course, had nothing to hide and it never occurred to me to do anything but tell her the truth about myself. I was on her side, and I wanted her cooperation in writing about her work. There was no other way to approach the situation. She would have to judge for herself whether I was honest or not.

But she was not at home. A squinty, frightened old woman answered the door and told me that she had no idea where Mrs. Dobbins was, nor had she been told anything about my appointment. She thought that Mrs. Dobbins would be back later in the afternoon, but she wasn't sure. The old woman guarded the doorway carefully and slipped back inside as soon as she could.

When I reached Mrs. Dobbins by phone later that afternoon,

she told me that she'd been tied up with appointments all day and had no way of getting in touch with me. I soon learned that since I lived in New York and more or less commuted to Philadelphia, it would be necessary to double-check all appointments; this was the first time an appointment hadn't worked out because of my not having a local phone. Annoyed, but still humble, I made another appointment to meet her at the WEBS office during the following week.

It amuses me to think that Ethel Dobbins took pleasure in standing me up that afternoon, that while she really was busy, she couldn't have cared less. But she *said* she was sorry about the mistake. She said she was sorry each time it happened afterwards —and it happened at least half a dozen times during the following year. After a while I was certain that I detected a note of insincerity in her voice.

The WEBS office had a rather makeshift air, but it remained essentially the same during the year of my visits. Overlooking one of the main streets of "the ghetto," it was a small, cramped room that contained a desk with a phone, a folding table and chairs, and numerous posters on the walls, one of which was a sort of hot-line list that included the phone numbers of the Fire Department, the Police Department, the Board of Education, the Department of Welfare, and several congressmen and city councilmen. Some community organizers adopt poverty as a pose in order to gain sympathy from the people with whom they work, but WEBS, unlike so many antipoverty groups, was really poor. "We don't take any money from anybody," Mrs. Dobbins informed me at one point in our conversation. "We're completely independent."

She was on the phone when I entered the office, and she beckoned me to a chair next to her desk so that we could have a good look at each other while she finished her conversation. There were only two important things about Ethel Dobbin's appearance aside from her dark skin. One was her eyes—they were unusually large and so clear that they seemed capable of extraordinary feats of perception. It would be difficult to imagine those eyes tired, runny, glazed, or in any other condition but absolutely wide open and alert—she probably slept with them open. The other was her decidedly martial bearing, a composite of many things—her incontestable bosom, the clothes she wore (I remember the semi-Nehru hats; she could have been a soldier), the carriage of her shoulders, even the booming nasal voice, which she was so accustomed to projecting at crowds.

It didn't take me long to give her what had become an almost routine narration of how I'd started to work on a book about change in the Philadelphia school system. I'd been a teacher myself, I said; I'd left teaching to write; I'd decided to write whenever I could about education, particularly experimental education, though I did occasional articles and book reviews (the most recent, I said proudly, was a rave for LeRoi Jones's *Tales*); I'd come to Philadelphia to do research for an article on the Advancement School (yes, she knew about the school, she nodded solemnly); I'd heard about all the other things that were happening in the city; and I was interested in her particular role in the school system because it seemed to me that even the sincerest reform movement within the central administration couldn't get very far without pressure for change from the community. ("Yes *indeed*," she said in the voice of a revivalist, "yes indeed.")

Then we talked briefly about WEBS. The group was primarily involved in community improvement, she told me. One of the principal goals was reforming the school system; they'd worked with the neighborhood schools, of course, and they'd been involved in the controversial sensitivity-training retreats. "We are totally black," she said. She spoke with great deliberateness; key words were like small blasts from a cannon. "That's one thing we take PRIDE in being." On the whole, she seemed favorably impressed with me. No questions, no challenges. She'd even overlooked what I recognized, to my annoyance, as an element of dishonesty: I had deliberately flattered her by embellishing my usual routine with the comment about pressure from the community—I wasn't sure it was true, but I'd said it anyway.

And finally she got to the point. "I have a story here," she quietly boomed, "and I knOWWWW it." The cannonball-words come hurtling across the table, reaching peak force at the point of impact. "This is a story of national importance! Everyone should know what we've been doing here in Philadelphia. The future of black people in this racist society is at STAKE!"

It was the first hint I'd had that, as far as she was concerned, if her story could only be published in the right place by the right person, the mere fact of its publication would almost automatically revolutionize American society. We never agreed on this point, but it didn't matter, since I wanted to publish the story anyway. But I was relieved; apparently I'd passed the test. "I think it's very important for your story to be part of my book," I said, not knowing quite how to respond.

"You BET it is!" she said. "People MUST know about this." Then, with a look of slight disgust that seemed to be intended for whatever imaginary conspirators had been keeping the story secret (her coverage in the local papers was almost as good as the mayor's), she shifted emotional gears. Her voice took on a conspiratorial tone. "But I am not GIVing this story away," she went on. "It's too important just to give away. I've got something valuable here that people are going to WANT to know about." She tapped the top of her desk, as if the whole story were written there in invisible ink. Then she looked up at me with eyes that communicated so effectively that she could easily have dispensed with words altogether. "Do I make myself clear?"

"Hmmm," I said. "Aahhh . . ."

"YES," she continued, pushing her advantage. "This is too important to give away."

Finally I got myself together. "I never pay for information," I said. "I scarcely have enough money to live on as it is. I am *not* working for a wealthy corporation."

"Well, I am NOT giving this story away," she said. "It's too important."

We stared at each other for about a minute. I have rather large eyes myself. "How much do you want?" I said.

Here she faltered. "I'm not setting any price on it. I'm just saying that I won't give it away. There are plenty of other people who could publish it. . . ."

"Since I don't have any money to pay you now," I said, "I can't even begin to know what I could offer. What would you consider appropriate?"

Her eyes told me that I was trying to pull a fast one. "That's for YOU to decide," she said. "Then, once we've worked this out,

I'll give you interviews, I'll make a tape recording, I'll tell you the whole story from the beginning. . . ."

A tape recording? Who had said anything about that? The idea suddenly appealed to me; in the past, if a subject agreed to my using a tape recorder, it was only with great reluctance. "Well, I'll have to think about this," I sighed. "We shouldn't try to reach a final decision now."

"You THINK about it," she said with a smile—not so much triumphant as encouraging.

As I prepared to leave, we told each other again how important her work was, how bad the schools were, how much remained to be done. She seemed to be making up for the harmful effects of the assault. At one point we asked each other which leaders might help the country get back on its feet. Maybe Stokely, she suggested, but definitely not King; not Bobby either, he couldn't be trusted. In our militancy and uncompromising demands, at any rate, we were on the same side. There seemed to be no doubt in her mind, in fact, that we were actually good friends—except for that one little question which, her manner conveyed, she was sure we could work out.

Since the next step in the negotiations was obviously up to me, and since my decision was probably not the best one, or even particularly sensible, the double perspective I now have of the incident—what I know to be true about it now and what I thought motivated me then—is at least illuminating.

What I see now: Ethel expected me to come out swinging, and, much to her surprise, I was merely grateful that she would talk to me. She talked to white people all the time—shouted at them, browbeat them. Not talk to me, indeed! Talking to white people was her *job*; and her responsibility was to take advantage of them if she could.

What I saw then: Most of my exposure to the "black community" up to that time consisted of what I'd read. It seemed to me that white people really had no right to go snooping around black people's affairs while the latter were trying to get themselves together, and I considered myself lucky to gain tolerance from a militant, to say nothing of actual acceptance. I expected that if I made a false move, I would not only be thrown out of the black community forever (and somehow barred by an imaginary network of black leaders), but I would have struck a damaging blow to human relations. Disgusted by the effects of white racist power on the black community, I went to Ethel Dobbins on the assumption that I, at least, had no power at all.

Conclusion: Like so many whites who, out of conscience and compassion, have dedicated at least part of their lives to the struggle for a just society, I allowed my outrage at the society's injustices to become the burden of personal guilt.

Now: I was furious with Ethel Dobbins for demanding payment in exchange for information. The last time a would-be subject had asked for money ("What's in it for me?" had been the snide opener to the interview), I'd stormed off without the interview—but not before I'd told the would-be interviewee that people like him were the main thing wrong with America.

Then: Swallowing my anger (not completely however; I stayed slightly angry with Ethel for most of a year), I decided that because Ethel Dobbins was black and because it was the responsibility of whites in America to do everything they could to counter the effects of racism, I *ought* to pay her for the interview. I should be happy to pay her; I should have thought of it myself.

Conclusion: I leaned over backwards in thinking up an expensive scheme that would reward her more than she either deserved or expected. She was obviously so delighted at the thought of being the focus of a chapter of my book that she probably would have done it for nothing.

My plan was to offer her a share of the book by donating a certain amount of the profits to a sort of black community chest. It would be, in fact, the most honest way of approaching the black community, for it would assure the black people with whom I had contact that I was not out to exploit them, that I was writing the book for them as well as for myself. In exchange, I would do a taped interview which, transcribed, would enable Ethel to tell her story in her own words. (Although I still believe that my plan would have been a more honest approach to black-white relations, it was simply a clever way of rationalizing a position that I had let her force me into.)

The bizarre history of my association with Ethel Dobbins, beginning with our first confrontation in her office, follows directly from the analysis I've outlined above. Without this perspective on my decision about how to handle the situation, what happened later makes almost no sense. But it took me several days to work out my thoughts on the subject; once committed to the plan, I began to believe in it.

I never bothered to tell anyone all the reasons for my working agreement with Ethel Dobbins, but I did mention it to a few white community workers I knew, partly because I felt like broadcasting what I thought to be a kind of victory—after all, I had managed to elicit the complete confidence of one of the most outspoken black militants in the city. To me, Ethel Dobbins would tell *all*. One friend who had years of social activism behind him said, in what I was sure was an admiring voice, that the plan was "radically different." Actually, in my ignorance, I was proud of my ingenuity; it seemed to me at the time that I'd turned an almost certain defeat into an advantage.

My agent, who was also Eldridge Cleaver's agent, laughed when I told her what had happened. A letter of agreement, she said, would be sufficient to make the plan legal.

But before Ethel and I could get to work, there would have to be a long delay. The immediate cause was my being perpetually on the brink of running out of money. No matter what we finally agreed on as a fitting sum for an initial payment, I could not afford to pay it when I scarcely had enough money to live on. Ethel grunted assent to the plan, when I phoned to tell her about my decision (it never occurred to me she might be overjoyed). She was willing to wait until I could afford to pay.

First we waited for an advance from my publisher. But before I (we) could get that, we (I) had to finish several introductory chapters in order to secure a contract—even though the publisher had been verbally committed to the book since December 1967. The world of book publishing moves at a leisurely pace; lunches last for hours, vacations for months. The contract was finally signed in June, and I used most of the advance to cover debts. I told Ethel, who by this time had become something like, though not very much like, an old friend, that we would have to continue waiting—this time for a foundation grant. Shopping for a nice, responsive foundation is a huge job that involves letters, phone calls, interviews, and waiting every day for the mail. My efforts finally paid off in the fall of 1968, about ten months after my first conversation with Ethel Dobbins.

For most of a year I had been confronting the exhilarating prospect of going broke any week or so. I had managed to survive, however, by living on my steadily depleted savings until they were almost gone. The federal government had returned some extra tax money that would otherwise have been used for bombs and napalm. I had sold a few articles and book reviews. And, finally, Ethel Dobbins and I were ready to get down to business.

In retrospect I can see that the amount of money I would have had to give her was not so large that I couldn't have scraped it up somehow. I was just angry enough with her, however, to wait until I could make the initial payment without any trouble to myself whatever. I certainly wasn't going to make any sacrifices to a deal that I had been blackmailed into.

Even though my business with Ethel was deferred for ten months, we continued to meet and talk quite regularly during that time. We always said hello at meetings of the Board of Education. Twice I wrote brief letters informing her that I was still plugging away at getting us money for our book and congratulating her about her latest threat or demonstration. And occasionally I saw her when I visited schools in the neighborhood where WEBS was active. While I knew relatively little about what had been going on at these schools before my arrival in Philadelphia, I had been watching them carefully since my conversation with the frightened principal.

Even if Ethel didn't revolutionize the schools in which she worked, she had initiated several potentially beneficial programs. One of these involved a relief to overcrowding. Another was the introduction of the courses in black culture and history that were becoming a symbol of community involvement. Perhaps more important, she had contributed to a growing fashion throughout Philadelphia and in other cities as well: extensive programs for changing teachers' attitudes toward their students and the black communities from which they came.

The theory behind these programs (according to many studies—most notably, *Pygmalion in the Classroom*, a scientific investigation of the subject that created something of a stir in

the fall of 1968) was that teachers' attitudes had a strong effect
on students' learning, and that since getting rid of thousands of
teachers with bad attitudes was virtually impossible, intensive
exposure to ghetto life would at least establish in these teachers
a modicum of contact and sympathy. In Philadelphia, the programs ranged from inviting black leaders, many of whom were
school dropouts, to visit the schools to tell-it-like-it-was (this
almost always meant giving whitey hell) to the somewhat
gentler and more effective neighborhood walks, which included
visits to such strategic spots as bars, roach-infested movie
theaters, and the jails where so many of their students spent so
much of their time. "If you're not sensitive and you feel we can't
sensitize you," Ethel bellowed at an audience of hostile teachers
during a "staff development" session which I attended, "I feel
SORRY for you. Unless you shape up and do what you're paid to
do and TEACH, you're going to be OUT." Ethel told me, during
one of our usual meetings, that a group of teachers had attacked
her for using "street talk." Her answer: "Street talk is the thING
now. Mr. Webster just might have to change his DICtionary."

But she knew better than anyone else that her cannon-blasts
were merely part of a routine, that she would be among the last
ones to actually carry out her threats. Why bother, when she
could get what she wanted by threats alone? In fact, she had
been receiving an unusually privileged education during her
brief career in community-school involvement; partly through
her own observations, partly through talks with genuinely radical
teachers, she'd come to realize that demanding an equal share
in the system that was failing all students, white and black,
wouldn't be enough any more. Even during the year in which I
knew her, her absolutism shifted from its original black power
axis to a significantly deeper commitment to real educational
change.

The majority of black parents who visited the schools seemed
to think that more discipline and thorough drilling in basic
skills would solve all the social problems of America—a black
businessman who addressed a group of mostly white teachers
at one of the staff development programs expressed this attitude
perfectly when he said, "I'm interested in the black community
being a viable community. What I want to see is a lot of success-

ful black people making *money*." But by the fall of 1968, Ethel was telling groups of parents, "We have to get away from this DISCIPLINE hangup." She had, in fact, become radicalized; there was nothing really radical about black power, she had learned, and now, with her new ideas, she was beginning to be a part of a division in American society that went far deeper than race.

Ironically, Ethel was being "radicalized" by being "co-opted." It was true that WEBS took no money from the establishment, but she could hardly be regarded any more as totally independent. She was beginning to receive a fairly steady income as a consultant to the Board of Education. ("Ethel told us that the Board had always given her a consulting fee of $150," one of Shedd's assistants laughingly informed me once, "so that's what we gave her. Later we found out that she never used to be paid at all.") The school system, so much more open than most, had virtually made her militant-in-residence. She must have invited this—it involved a good deal of power, in addition to the money —but it took some of the dignity from her campaign.

By this time it had become clear to me that my original fears about being somehow ejected from the black community and never allowed to return were largely the result of knowing about it only through the papers and the super-amplified threats that grew from its horrible despair. Ethel and I sincerely respected each other's work, and more than ever before, we were on the same side in the steadily increasing polarization of society. Moreover, we both knew that the polarization, despite the ranting and lying of "the media," actually had very little to do with race. Race conflict had been America's dirty little trick, a cover-up for a real questioning of the country's political and economic structure. I had always known that something was fundamentally wrong with the way the majority of Americans lived, but my childhood and young adulthood had been as whitely supreme as anybody's. Only by fighting my way past the stereotypes and fears that I unwittingly carried underneath my surface of liberalism did I come to this conviction. Ethel Dobbins was part of my education. So were the kids at the charity camp where I worked in the summer of 1961, and where, perhaps unnaturally late for a self-styled liberal, I made my first moves out of the white cocoon. And so were all the black people, ranging from those who accepted me openly to those who refused to speak to me at all, with whom I came in contact during my investigation of the urban war in Philadelphia.

In short, during those ten months of getting to know the people of Philadelphia's inner city, I had begun to eliminate in myself the racism into which I had been born. To those who are determined to remain racists, this confession can only seem a smug rebuke; to those who consider themselves full-scale radicals or, better yet, "revolutionaries," and who, for all I know, were never racists at all, it must seem a dubious claim to virtue, at best. Racist feelings were one of the last barriers, however, to my joining Ethel Dobbins in a relationship of genuine honesty.

During the waiting period, Ethel Dobbins and I had come as close as we ever came to being real friends, but the waiting period was now over. I had the money, and we were ready to do business. We were ready, that is, to do battle; with some minor differences, the stereotypes still prevailed in spite of everything both of us had learned.

Before writing the letter of agreement, I phoned Ethel to tell her that at last we were ready to go. She accepted the news with stolid approval. There would be an initial payment, I said, and then, something in the manner of my own royalties, there would be additional payments each time a certain number of copies were sold. And I needed to know to whom she wanted me to make out the checks—did she want the money to go just to WEBS, or did she want to include other groups as well? "You can make out the checks directly to ME," she said. "This is my own THING." I tried to laugh away my outrage by telling her that she'd certainly worked for it.

My agent considered the terms of the agreement "generous." She checked over it with her lawyer; my rights were protected. Two weeks after sending it, however, I had still received no answer. I had assumed that it would take Ethel at least a few days to consult her own lawyer about the letter, but finally I phoned her. She just hadn't had time to do anything about it, she told me, but she would let me know in a few days. We made an appointment to meet for lunch; she would have her final word, and we could begin preliminary talks about the actual interview. We'd already discussed this; since I still knew virtually nothing about her background, I wanted to find out all these precious facts she'd been withholding from me before planning the final interview. My idea was that since I would be paying her handsomely for her work, for once I would make an interview as exhaustive as I wanted and not worry about taking advantage of my subject's kindness.

She did not appear for the appointment. We were supposed to meet after one of her social-action seminars, but I searched for her and learned that she had not been to the seminar either. When I reached her the following day at her office, she said that she had indeed been there and looked for me in the lobby for twenty minutes. It was a lie; I had examined every corner of the lobby for half an hour. But I think she actually believed she was telling the truth. We made another appointment.

This time I called about fifteen minutes before the appointment to make sure she would be there. She was there all right, but, she said, she was so busy with so many things—couldn't I come tomorrow? She really *wanted* to talk, she said, because there were several things about my letter she needed to discuss—she'd consulted with her advisers.

We met in the morning. I waited for several minutes at the door, though I could hear her on the phone inside. Finally she let me in and went back to resume shouting. The office was somewhat less elegant than usual, having been only slightly damaged by a recent bomb attack, which, Ethel assured me, was a result of a battle she'd been having with the Mafia. Finally she was through terrifying whatever public official she had on the phone at the time, and, having beckoned me to the chair next to her desk, she fastened her great eyes on mine in what was clearly an unbroken crescendo of righteous indignation. "They're all ROTTEN," she told me. "They tell you yes, but all the time they're busy taking care of WHITE folks. And they keep saying yes yes yes, we'll get to you. Well, they're gonna get to me NOW."

I could only agree that she sure had given it to 'em.

She went on to list a few more injustices she had suffered at the hands of "this racist system," then titillated my curiosity with some inside gossip about the role of the Mafia in the recent presidential elections. It occurred to me that she was holding out the promise of more inside gossip to come—displaying the merchandise, as it were. This seemed to lead logically to my reason for being there: What about the agreement? I asked.

"Well, I've been consulting with my advisers and my board," she began. We both knew that there were no advisers; there was indeed a WEBS board of directors, but we also knew that she wasn't letting them in on this particular deal. "And we don't find the agreement satisfactory at all."

"What isn't satisfactory about it?" I asked, more surprised than I had expected to be, considering that I had outlined the agreement in full detail over the phone before writing it up.

"I don't know WHAT I did with my copy," she said, hardly pretending to look for it. "I guess my advisers have it." This meant, of course, that she had lost it somewhere, probably thrown it out by accident. We both knew that was what it meant; she lied easily, and always with the complete transparency of a guilty child. "But I don't need it anyway, because after talking it over with my advisers, we've decided that we want a perCENTage."

"What per cent do you want?" I asked.

I watched her eyes shift around while she thought this over. If she had given the matter any thought at all prior to my arrival (she probably had), it was obvious that the notion of asking for a percentage had only just begun to crystallize in her mind. She and her advisers, therefore, needed a minute to figure out how much they would ask for, and since none of them had any idea what a percentage of a book's profits could mean in terms of actual money, they were on somewhat shaky ground. Finally, their conference was over.

"We want SIX PER CENT," she said.

"Six per cent?" I muttered.

"SIX PER CENT!" This time she was certain. My astonishment obviously convinced her that she had asked for a great deal of money, a fact which she half-suspected anyway.

"Well . . ." I said. "I don't know exactly how much that would amount to, but if the book's sales are low, it might even be less than what I've offered."

She smiled confidently. "I'm willing to take the CHANCE. I've always been a gambler."

"Well, I can't answer you now," I finally concluded. "I want to consult with *my* advisers."

"You DO that," she said. "And I hope we can work this out soon and get finished with it. We've been waiting a long time to settle this. Just as soon as we've worked it out, I'll sit down and tell you EVERYTHING."

"I'm not at all sure this is going to work," I said, beginning to savor the feeling of not caring, for the moment, what happened. "I made a generous offer, and you agreed to it a long time ago. I've been planning my book with this in mind. I thought we were ready to go ahead on this, and now you tell me you want an entirely different agreement. I'm not sure we can work it out."

Following me to the door, she seemed anxious. I realized as I stood there that if I'd acted decisively in the first place, this whole charade would never have happened at all. But it was too late. When Ethel Dobbins committed herself to a position, she didn't back off easily. "This is going to be a VITALLY important chapter in your book," she called after me.

"That's what I was hoping," I answered.

For several days I refused to think about the problem at all. With plenty of work to do (I was well into the actual writing of the book), I had no trouble avoiding it. Finally I called my agent. Her advice—she'd been a tough haggler for years—was "Offer her $25 more."

But I continued to delay my decision. More than a week had passed since my talk with Ethel, and I still hadn't bothered to figure out what six per cent of even the lowest profits might amount to. I'd been surprised when she suggested it, but for all I knew, it wasn't half as much as what I'd already promised. On the other hand, as I finally began to come to grips with the situation, I realized that if the book were to make a great deal of money—if it became a best seller in hardcover and paperback; if it were made into a play, a movie, and a musical; if it led to a sweatshirt fad and a new kind of hamburger—Ethel's six per cent might really amount to something. I actually sat down one morning—I'd decided that I wouldn't let the decision linger for another day—and, straining my mathematical resources, figured out the several possibilities, ranging from not selling out the first meager edition to vast riches. And it was then that I realized that while vast riches seemed a most unlikely consequence of a book about a school system, however entertainingly written, I'd been determined from the beginning not to share them with Ethel Dobbins.

It was a shattering realization; for as I sat there at my desk in front of my frenzied jottings, I knew for the first time that ever since the beginning of my involvement with Ethel Dobbins I had fully intended to withhold from her as much money as I could. I, who fancied myself such a friend of the blacks, such a pillar of social justice, would be *damned* if I'd give her six per cent of the profits. I was worried, of course, that if I didn't at least meet her halfway, she would have to live up to her convictions and refuse to do business—even though by then I knew that she wanted the fame she was sure I would bring her more than she wanted any amount of money. But percentages were out; percentages were too much; percentages left me no pride. It had come to that.

I revised the original agreement so that it was several cuts more generous and mailed her a copy that morning, including a letter of explanation that ended with the following paragraph:

> I want to do a chapter about your work in the Philadelphia school system, in the manner outlined in the agreement, but aside from the extra time I will need for research, I could easily do it in some other way without your help. If the terms of this revised agreement—which I have prepared against the protest of my professional advisers—are not to your liking, I will have no choice but to abandon the effort to work with you.

My agent hadn't exactly protested, but it wasn't a complete lie—she had grunted. As for the revised agreement, the best I can say about it is that it was the least dishonest compromise I was willing to offer.

I was no longer intimidated by Ethel Dobbins' pose; when she growled into the phone several days after I'd mailed the letter that she certainly HAD received it, I could hear the theatricality in her voice. She had consulted with her "board" again, she said, and they were adamant: six per cent or nothing.

Again, I was astonished. I fully expected that we might not be able to work out an agreement, having backed ourselves into such intransigent positions, but I thought that Ethel cared so much about the chapter, this great national tribute to her work, that she would at least try. "I've always worked this way," she said, "and I don't want to do it ANY other way."

"Have you ever done this kind of thing before?" I asked.

Even over the phone, she lied like a child. "Yes," she said, after a moment's pause, "but it was a magazine article."

I could hear her listening to my mind clicking.

"It was a LONG time ago, but I got a percentage."

"Tell me, Mrs. Dobbins," I said. "Have you given any thought to how much you could make from this? I mean, have you really investigated the trade book market?" I realized in an instant that if I had not been so intent on giving her as little as possible from the beginning, I would have explained the book market to her in detail, including the market for best sellers, foreign rights, TV, magazine, and movie rights. But I didn't wait for whatever feeble answer she might think of. "The first printing of this book will probably not be any more than 7,500 copies," I said. "And, unless the book's sales are really unusual, there won't be a second printing."

"Oh?" she said. She was beautiful.

"There is a *chance*," I went on, "that the book will sell large quantities of the paperback, but . . ."

"Well, we're counting on the paperback." She said it as if anyone in his right mind knew that you couldn't count on the hardcover edition, that the paperbacks were the real money-makers. What she never realized for an instant, though she may have had some vague suspicions, was that my specific approach to cheating her was to deprive her of all the *other* rights; the original agreement, especially, had focused on the hardcover and paperback editions.

"I want you to know," I said, "that I can do this chapter completely without your help, if necessary. . . ."

"I have an agreement," she interrupted, "with the Board, with the schools. . . ." I forget who else she said she had an agreement with, but it was preposterous. "Nobody is ALLOWED to write about my work in the school system without my permission."

And here, much to my delight, the blood started to rush and the words started to come without the slightest inhibition of reason or wisdom. "You can SUE ME!" I shouted. "You can drag me to court, but you won't have a leg to stand on! Anything that you've done is a matter of PUBLIC INFORMATION!!"

"That isn't SO," she shouted back. "I have agreements with everyone in THIS CITY."

But then, suddenly, it was all over. "Look, Mrs. Dobbins," I said. "I don't think we're going to be able to work this out. But I'll let you know one way or the other."

"You DO that," she said, and I could hear her smiling. "I certainly don't want to end something badly with people I LIKE."

"Well," I said bitterly, half to myself, "we all have to do our thing."

Her voice was, it seemed, deliberately hearty. I don't know what to make of her last words. But what she said was: "You're GREAT."

Snapshot: *An Honorable Contract*
Pledge sponsored by the Philadelphia Police Athletic League and distributed to all junior and senior high school students in the public school system in March 1967:

To the Honorable Lyndon B. Johnson
President of the United States of America
White House, Washington, D.C.

We, the undersigned, do hereby affirm our dedication to respect for law and authority, and promise to follow the precepts set forth in the Police Athletic League pledge which reads:

"I pledge to learn and practice the rules of fair play, to respect the rights of others, to obey the laws of our city, state and country, to be a credit to my family, friends, and myself, to be a leader for the good things of life and thereby prepare myself for the task of adulthood."

Students are not required to sign.

"The Education of Our Children Is Through Power"

THE MANTUA-POWELTON MINISCHOOL was conceived as a truly "human" institution that would be both an integral part of the community from which it grew and a genuine community itself —all part of a continuum of honesty and trust. One of the incidents that marked the school's early months, however, was the divorce of a couple who happened to be among the founding staff members. As the school struggled for its life throughout the winter of 1968–69, the gap between theory and practice seemed only to widen.

The Minischool was not exactly doomed as it moved toward its second year of operation; but it had gone through a series of strains that reflected a quintessential alienation. The Rockefeller Foundation, following its policy of increased involvement in grassroots poverty programs, had upped its initial grant of $100,000 by half to keep the Minischool alive, the Board was contributing more money as well, and it would be wrong to say that this bold experiment in community education was a failure. Who could *ever* say that it was a failure, after all? The opinions about evaluation ranged all the way from the basic-skills theory (if the standardized tests indicated a rise in the students' basic skills, the school was successful) to the principal's own belief that as long as students wanted to come to school, the experiment was worth continuing (the rate of attrition became a cause for alarm a few months after he had voiced this opinion) to the vague notion that as long as anybody in "the community" wanted to keep the school going, it ought to be done. But ultimately the question of whether the Minischool would survive or not was a political one, and in the vagaries and maneuverings of politics, perhaps more than in any other aspect of the school's operation, the role of the community—or whatever any substantial group of people could decide on as being the community—was vital.

"Community" is a word-in-the-news that in recent years has gone beyond the usual level of cliché to a point of hideous travesty. Partly because of all the *talk* about community in Mantua-Powelton, there were probably few better illustrations in America of how little real community there can be in a city at war than in the so-called community that the Mantua-Powelton Minischool was supposed to serve. "The Mantua-Powelton community" was actually two separate communities, each quite distinct, in a number of readily obvious ways, from the other.

The general area of Mantua-Powelton was located close by the Penn Central's 30th Street station, west of the Schuylkill River and north of Market Street, in a triangle-shaped space roughly twelve blocks at the base and ten blocks high, the hypotenuse being the railroad tracks along the river. Powelton— or Powelton Village, as it was commonly called—had once been a semi-downtown residential neighborhood of considerable substance. In the 1960's, with seven thousand residents, Powelton was still middle-class (and approximately half black), though most of its Victorian town houses had been divided into apartments.

Powelton was Philadelphia's closest equivalent to New York's Greenwich Village. The converted houses were generally occupied by students who attended the University of Pennsylvania or Drexel Institute of Technology, both nearby to the south of Market Street, or by young married professional couples; there was also, throughout the mid-sixties, a scattered, but sizable, group of poets, artists, and writers. Yet Powelton remained a place of tree-lined streets, wide porches, and distinctive, often quaint, architecture, all mingling to create an air of frayed grandeur.

Mantuans and Poweltonians were not entirely agreed on the boundary between the two "communities"—some said Spring Garden Street, some said Hamilton Street (the Hamilton interpretation allowed for a block of more substantial houses in Mantua)—but the division was visible to the most casual stroller. Mantua, with an almost entirely black population of 22,000, was terribly poor and had been built primarily, in the late nineteenth century, as the "service" community for Powelton, housing domestics and other people useful to the comfortable class to the immediate south of it.

In the 1960's few blocks of Mantua were free of shell houses. Rats and roaches infested the place. Broken windows, uncollected garbage, streets filled with refugees from the squalid rows of brick and frame dwellings—this was the city-scape of Mantua, the usual setting of poverty and despair that one could find, with only minor variations in style, in almost any city of America. But Mantua was unlike other poverty areas in one important respect: In the early 1960's several community leaders had taken steps to overcome the apathy and hopelessness that poverty breeds by getting themselves "together."

Whatever real togetherness there was in Mantua was due in large part to the efforts of a young former gang leader named Herman Wrice. A tall, gentle-looking black man, Wrice transformed his gang into a community redevelopment group in 1965 (as in the city's poor neighborhoods generally, gang conflict was rampant in Mantua) and called it the Young Great Society. Under Wrice's direction the group turned its energies to such tasks as rebuilding some of Mantua's ruined houses, running recreation programs for neighborhood children, and generally avoiding the usual course of incessant warfare that formed the main activity of most gangs in the city. In the summer of 1967 the "Young Greats" were hired by the Board of Education to participate in a neighborhood-oriented training program for new teachers in the school system. And within two years of its entry into the field of urban redevelopment, YGS had branched out to include several neighborhoods in other parts of Philadelphia as well. YGS still had a long way to go in transforming Mantua, but Wrice had built a broad power base with amazing speed.

In rising so far so fast, however, Wrice had left a large crowd of people behind. He became the object of petty and not-so-petty jealousies; some Mantuans thought he was too much of a big shot and cared too much for himself, not enough for them. But the "black community" could ill afford a public feud; quietly, with a minimum of fuss, a few of Wrice's colleagues broke away from YGS and, in January 1967, formed their own neighborhood renewal group to serve Mantua exclusively. Led by thirty-year-old Andy Jenkins, a black man who had been a close friend of Wrice's for years, and directed by a board representing a number of smaller community groups, the new group called itself the Mantua Community Planners. Within half a year or so, MCP was solidly established as the "umbrella group" that would unify all the neighborhood organizations—including YGS, various church groups, and the local branch of the federal antipoverty program. MCP's motto was "Plan, or be planned for!"

Despite the occasional rivalry between Jenkins and Wrice, Mantua was well on its way by this time to a degree of relative unity. Other communities in other parts of the city were well organized, but in terms of immediate survival, Mantua was more threatened than most. The University City Science Center, a brainstorm of white supremacist urban renewal, was encroaching on Mantua directly to the south and dumping untold millions into the pockets of establishment business leaders. And as the year of the American Bicentennial drew nearer and Philadelphia began to vie for the prize of being exposition headquarters, the planners "downtown" who had the city's future so much at heart began to talk avidly of a huge exposition area just north of 30th Street Station. The bicentennial space would occupy the air rights above the Penn Central tracks, but no one in Mantua could have been surprised to learn that the city was buying up vacant houses in their community at the alarming rate of a hundred or so every month even in 1968.

The day had long since passed, however, when white business leaders could casually wipe out poor black communities without a fight. In the case of Mantua and the neighborhoods of West Philadelphia affected by plans of the University of Pennsylvania, the Drexel Institute of Technology, and the Science Center, the leaders would have to contend with the—by then—usual angry minority of middle-class whites. (Penn had even made the liberal concession of lending its support to MCP.) They would also have to realize that enough Mantuans were concerned with not being planned for to cause a good deal of trouble. And considering the general chemistry of the situation, it was probably inevitable that leaders of Mantua and radical whites in Powelton would get together at some point. Thus was the Minischool born.

A good deal of the initial thrust for the Minischool came from a small group of friends in Powelton, both black and white, most of whom were involved in an influential organization called the Powelton Neighbors. In its own quiet, middle-class-liberal way, Powelton was fairly together too. For several years, Powelton parents had been running a cooperative nursery, and the Powelton Neighbors were active in political battles in which they frequently took on big business, city, or university interests. During the noisy fall of 1967, however, with all its talk of revolution and Mark Shedd, a small group of Powelton activists began to turn their attention to the school system.

The climate was right, they agreed, for a community school, like the cooperative nursery, that would help to bridge Mantua and Powelton. Too many of the Powelton parents were moving their children to private schools in the later grades; the upper grades in the local elementary schools were eighty per cent black. Something had to be done.

A few of the Minischool founders also cite as an influence a brief article by Paul Goodman that appeared in the *New York Review of Books* in December 1967, in which Goodman proposed tiny schools staffed by community residents, and so closely tied to the community's culture and language that the problems of the typical system-dominated urban school would almost miraculously vanish. With so much healthy, ruddy-cheeked middle-class radicalism behind it, the Minischool would always have an unmistakably white tinge, and later this became a problem. As the various struggles for power throughout the Mantua-Powelton community grew more vicious, one often heard complaints that the Minischool was dominated by "those Powelton people."

There were already several strategic bridges between Powelton and Mantua, even before the Minischool opened, and these promised at the beginning to establish the necessary links for further cooperation. Most important was the Mantua Workshop, an offshoot of the Mantua Community Planners devoted exclusively to the physical rehabilitation of the community and headed by a young white dropout from the Penn School of Architecture named John Ciccone. Ciccone actually lived in Mantua, but he was more a temporary guest than an integral part of the community. In the best manner of modern community organizers, he had offered himself to Mantua as a constantly available resource with which the community could do pretty much whatever it liked. Among other services, he directed a staff that planned renovations of buildings, helped contract (almost always to community people) the work for getting these jobs done, and trained black architects and planners who would eventually relieve him of his job. Ciccone had a perfect combination of humility and personal dynamism; he could make it clear at a community meeting that he knew more than most people about the work he was doing, but at the same time, like a young Saul Alinsky, he projected complete unselfishness in doing it.

The Workshop was, in short, a hip haven for radical activists and radical intellectuals, and it was to the Workshop that the Powelton activists turned with their idea for a Minischool. Finally, in March 1967, the newly formed bridge group was ready with a proposal to submit to the Board of Education. Paul Goodman's article may have sparked the group's thinking at the beginning, but the concept had become something much grander by the time it reached 21st Street. It had also become one of the pet projects of Rick deLone, whose network of power plays within the Shedd administration resembled, by this time, an underground three-ring circus.

The initial proposal was for two minischools, each serving seventy-five children, which would be located in two converted houses on what one of the Workshop staff called the "spine" of Mantua-Powelton, the block between Spring Garden and Hamilton Streets. Each minischool would have eight permanent staff members and several volunteers from the community. The curriculum would center on the urban affairs and communications courses that had been developed during the three summers of the Philadelphia Cooperative Schools program—generally oriented to the philosophy and practice of humanism, the founding group was eager to get away from the "traditional" curriculum. And, to cap off the utopian dream, the minischools would serve as a model for a new middle school (grades five through eight) that the Board of Education's demographic studies had slated for the area sometime around 1970.

This part of the proposal was the most radical innovation. Instead of building the typical educational institution, with its warren of classrooms, endless halls, and cold uniformity, the Board's planning office, under the enlightened leadership of former city planner Graham Finney, was actually willing to use the minischools as a model for a "scattered site" middle school. According to the plan, there would be several minischools dotted throughout the community, causing an absolute minimum of disruption (many would be located in already existing buildings), and one central building for various recreational and cultural services that would function as a community center as well. In one page of proposal-ese, the whole suffocating structure of the typical American school was being erased. The new middle school would truly be a part of the community, not just something that The System imposed on it from outside.

Not long after deLone had shuttled the proposal through the Board's planning office (it was not officially approved until late in September, however) the Rockefeller Foundation came through with a grant of $100,000. The Board agreed to provide an additional $27,000, and the Minischool was on its way. Scheduled to open the school on September 6, the staff and community would have the entire summer to prepare the buildings and develop an innovative, "human" curriculum.

The fall and winter of 1968–69 featured a series of minor explosions, and even a few major ones; but no matter who happened to be the *cause célèbre* of the moment, there was a hard core of staff people who could well be considered the foundation of whatever community the Minischool actually attained during its first year. For a long time the acknowledged leader was the Minischool's principal, a young black man named Forrest Adams.

Twenty-seven years old when he took over as head of the Minischool in June 1968, Adams had had a busy and eclectic career. He had gone to public school in Philadelphia, graduated, joined the Air Force, and attended several colleges for varying periods of time, including a stint at Trenton State Teachers College while he was in the service. As part of his Air Force training he had spent several years in England, studying civil engineering at the University of Reading. Back in America, he had worked for General Electric for a while ("I was starving to death," he explains), taught himself draftsmanship, worked for an architectural firm as an architect and planner, and finally, in December 1966, joined the Mantua Workshop. During this time he had also done a good deal of teaching—mainly of electronics —and worked on developing such new curriculum ideas as a "ghetto game," which he tested in public schools and which featured such relevancies as a player's getting picked up on the street by the police and having to raise his own bail bond.

Adams had the volubility and outward self-assurance of a man who has learned to make his way in the world. He made friends quickly and managed to convey warmth and openness with what sometimes seemed an uninterruptible patter of dry, sophisticated humor. In the dark days of the winter and spring, when Adams's activities as principal came under attack, his defenders insisted that he had exceptional charisma, that he was "great with groups," and that the "community" respected him. Indeed, even when the school seemed to be hopelessly bogged down in problems of communication, both internal and external, Adams managed to preserve a certain cool that could be dazzling when one considered the difficulties he faced.

Whatever the school's problems, Adams remained a vital link between Mantua and Powelton. He lived in Powelton; he was closely identified with the Workshop; and he provided the strong black male "image" that the school's founders considered at least as important in a principal as actual experience, though he had plenty of that as well.

Conveying images—of himself, of the school—was, in fact, Adams's chief forte. His mind was as eclectic as his resumé, forever jumping about from one idea to another, consistently inventive and witty. Usually outfitted in round, rimless glasses, jeans or slacks, and a dashiki, he had the look of a young black militant intellectual, yet he was outwardly friendly and tolerant. He had managed to get him*self* together, it seemed—to come to terms with being black in mid-century America. He did not need to hate whites, and even a brief conversation led one to believe that he was thoroughly tuned in to the most up-to-date educational and social theories, covering the whole spectrum from McLuhan to Goodman to Malcolm X to Cleaver. It seemed at the beginning that he would provide not only the major intellectual and emotional thrust for the entire school but the school's essential identity. Strong, black, intellectual, committed, integrated with white society, profoundly humanitarian, freedom-loving, together—this was Forrest Adams's image, and the founders of the Minischool hoped that it would be the school's image as well. Or rather, they hoped that this was what the school would actually be—none of them could be charged with the slightest trace of conscious deceit in the Madison Avenue sense of image-making, though their images often had a slickly professional tone.

Two others on the Minischool staff were also officials of the Mantua Community Planners, and, together with Adams, they provided ample evidence that at least a few genuine leaders of the community were solidly behind the school. Doris Hamilton, whom one admirer had once called "the mother of almost everybody in Mantua," was a round black woman who seemed to possess as much understanding, depth, and compassion as several ordinary people. For years she had been a part-time volunteer one-woman trouble-shooter and psychiatrist for hundreds of Mantua families, and she was also treasurer of MCP. Cassie Stuart had taught for eleven years, nine of them in an elementary school in North Philadelphia, and was the most experienced teacher on the Minischool staff; she lived in Mantua, she was corresponding secretary of MCP, and she had decided to give up a comfortable job to work for the Minischool, because, she explained, she believed in doing things for the community.

David Fleischaker, twenty-six years old when the Minischool opened, was a graduate of Swarthmore, a resident of Powelton, a close friend of Forrest Adams, and another of the Minischool's leading founders. Throughout the tempestuous first year, Fleischaker remained Adams's loyal assistant, though his official position went through several changes. Soft-spoken, modest, dark-haired, and white, Fleischaker shared with Doris Hamilton

the job of "community liaison." Frank Lamont, the other principal founder, had taught for two years in the city's Catholic
school system. A burly, moon-faced twenty-six-year-old who
smiled a great deal and talked and sang in a rich bass voice,
Lamont had an air of guilelessness belied by the fact that he had
helped to organize a strike against the city's Catholic school
system.

There were a great many others who came and went. Among
the permanent staff there were one occasional leader of SDS, a
recent graduate from Penn who taught urban affairs; a young
white woman who taught communications and who was active
with her husband in community affairs and New Left politics; a
painter who ran the art program; an actress who offered classes
in creative dramatics; two young black men who had grown up
together in Philadelphia and served together in the Army; a
dozen or so students from Penn and Drexel who visited the
school to do part-time tutoring; and two mothers from Mantua,
in addition to Doris Hamilton, who had children in the school.

The ratio of black to white varied considerably, increasing in
blackness as the size of the staff grew—by the spring of 1969,
out of twenty staff members, fourteen were black. This was
important, the entire staff agreed, in establishing a sense of
identity among the almost entirely black student body of fifth-,
sixth-, and seventh-graders. But while the need for a sense of
black identity was vitally important, the Minischool was never
separatist. The white staff considered themselves emphatically
on the radical side, and generally they adopted a realistic, re-
spectful attitude of wanting to serve the future of blacks in the
most unpatronizing, yet unobsequious, way possible.

On the surface it seemed that if a genuine community school
of any considerable size—that is, larger than a mere neighborhood club or church group in which an integral community was
ready-made—could sustain itself at all in Philadelphia, the
Mantua-Powelton Minischool offered a promising test case. The
implications for the future of the public school system were vast:
Here was a grass-roots organization that wanted to run its own
schools. Here was participatory democracy, social equality,
brotherhood, and the revitalization of the American Dream.
Long after it became widely known that the Minischool was

having problems, visitors and observers continued to talk about it as one of the most "exciting" educational experiments in the nation.

Even at the worst times there were enough good things happening in the Minischool to make it several cuts better and more humane than the typical urban middle or junior high school. The tone was distinctly innovative; teachers had unusual autonomy. The school's administrators were always ready to trot out statistics proving how large a proportion of the staff came from the immediate community. And a majority of the children, eighty per cent of whom came from Mantua, were certainly better off in the Minischool than they would have been in the regular schools—in which many of them had experienced a subtle rejection because of their inability to conform or their deficiency in basic skills.

Whether the Minischool was a "community" school and whether it was a good school even if it wasn't a community school, however, could not be shown with statistics. But, fortunately for those who had a stake in the school's future, the question of power eventually overshadowed that of quality and program. Power was something that a community getting itself together could understand and deal with much more easily than the complexities of educational theory and practice. This did not become clear, however, for several months.

July:

The sites of the two minischools have been chosen, and the Workshop is making moves to buy and renovate them. They consist of a double house on Hamilton Street back to back with a single house on Spring Garden. Already a team of young architects is at work drawing up plans that will enable the converted buildings to conform to the laws of the city's Department of Licenses and Inspections. John Ciccone is directing the entire project.

The other components of the summer are extensive training sessions for the staff and a recruiting program run by Doris Hamilton and Dave Fleischaker. By the middle of July, forty or so kids are committed to entering the school in September.

Recruiting has been difficult. Working from lists of students in the four elementary schools that ordinarily serve Mantua-Powelton children through the sixth grade, the community liaison people have been selling the minischools to parents from door to door—Doris in Mantua, Dave in Powelton. But selling the minischool is difficult, Dave reports, because there isn't much to show at this point. The proposal stipulates that the schools must serve 150 children, at any rate, also that a curriculum outline for the first three months must be submitted to the Board of Education. Several of the minischool's founders have been in touch with various staff members of the experimental Cooperative Schools Program, the freedom-oriented, student-centered curriculum project to which the liberal-radical wing of the minischool faculty is unanimously committed.

In staff development sessions, however, there is already some disagreement about what will be taught in the school and what style of teaching will prevail. While most of the teachers are interested in the Cooperative Schools approach, a rift has developed over the question of reading. Some staff members want to set up a reading clinic, strongly teacher-directed, strict, and product-oriented. Others favor a much looser and creative method in which the students' interest in reading should be cultivated and the teacher's main job would be to provide motivation; technical skills would be de-emphasized, the theory being that emphasis on skills in reading and writing to the exclusion of motivation through meaningful content is what kills students' interest in the first place. Reading is the single biggest "community" concern, and it is one of the biggest concerns within the school as well. The question of philosophy and technique is never resolved, however, and the dialogue of July foreshadows the strife of November.

The Minischool's founders have not been able to recruit a genuine community of teachers, and already Adams's antipathy to structure has produced discord. Adams, Fleischaker, Lamont, and the others might have found nine people who shared this educational philosophy if they had had time to look for them, but the likelihood of finding such a group within the borders of Mantua-Powelton was far too dim to make the effort worthwhile.

At times there has been a last-minute quality to the hiring of staff; priorities remain flexible. Two of the original nine teachers live in other parts of the city.

August:

The basic faculty of nine has been meeting during the last one and a half months at least four times a week, and there has even been a four-day sensitivity-training retreat. So far the mini-schools have initiated two meetings with adults in the community; twenty-five people were invited to each of the meetings, and in each case, eight showed up. One night the poor attendance was due to a gang war that made walking about the streets of Mantua-Powelton too risky for most parents. At a staff session, Doris Hamilton observes that one of the teachers tended to dominate the second community meeting and that the parents were intimidated by him and other outspoken representatives of the Minischool.

The staff session has begun late, with several stragglers still arriving. Adams follows Mrs. Hamilton's remarks with a pep talk in which he explains that the lack of structure in the school is deliberate and that they will be running a pretty loose ship—specifically, referring to an employment contract that each teacher is expected to sign—as regards the length of the school day. There will be no overtime pay for teachers, but staff will be expected to remain after school for planning sessions, Adams says. Adams's manner suggests that the contract is a mere formality, that of course the staff is much more dedicated than the usual staff of the usual school, that people should be happy to stay until five o'clock for planning sessions when true community is involved. Defiantly cocky, Adams tells the group with a laugh that he has been talking with people who lay odds of ten to four *against* the school's succeeding.

There are some bad vibrations in the room, however. One young man challenges the daily schedule, threatening to refer his case to the teacher's union. All the other teachers leave school at three o'clock, he says—why shouldn't he? (A perennial disrupter, the young man is dismissed a few days later.)

When the discussion moves on to other business, the room is filled with heat and boredom. Several people whisper; one teacher falls asleep and begins to snore. The talk is all of community and mutual sharing, and the intent of everyone in the room, except the disrupter, seems to be one of honest commitment. But the group is quite visibly not together.

Even though administrative officials have already received a check from a local foundation to pay the expenses of the summer training program the money has been held up at the Board of Education. Meanwhile, Rick deLone has managed to borrow money from emergency funds in order to pay the staff. With time so short, the Workshop has virtually had to give up the idea of converting the buildings, and there is talk of opening the minischools in an unused factory owned by the Philadelphia Redevelopment Authority. (At this point the concept of a single minischool for 150 students begins to supplant the original idea of two minischools, each for 75). The unused factory is located at 33rd and Arch Streets, just a few blocks from Drexel and the 30th Street Station. It is much more a part of Powelton than of Mantua, but the group will be lucky if they can get it at all; the Redevelopment Authority is not wholly in favor of the idea.

There are plans for a community board consisting of three people from the faculty, three from the community, and Adams, that will evaluate the minischool every twelve weeks, but so far no definite action has been taken, aside from the tentative meetings with parents. It is too early for a board; the minischool staff is already learning from the controversy in New York that community boards and their responsibilities are no casual matter.

The debate about curriculum more or less resolves itself toward the end of the month, striking a balance, according to Adams, between "pure emotionalism and pure academia"—the basic curriculum will consist of courses in communications-reading, math-science, urban affairs, and gym. Also available will be courses in art and drama.

September:
First Week:

The Redevelopment Authority has agreed to rent its building at 33rd and Arch Streets to the Mantua-Powelton Minischool for a dollar a year. With the opening of school only a few days away, there is an air of rather strained excitement in the offices of the Mantua Workshop, which are located in an old rowhouse on a bedraggled street in the heart of Mantua.

A second-floor room of the rickety building has been set aside as Forrest Adams's office, and it is filled with a constantly circulating stream of people checking on last-minute details and decisions. For the first two weeks of school, the faculty has been divided into two teams; each teacher will have 18 kids (157 have been recruited so far) and will conduct a community orientation session. Part of the tension and excitement arises from the fact that over the weekend the slides and materials prepared for the first days of the orientation session were stolen from the Workshop building. Several of the Workshop staff suspect sabotage, though others say no, robberies are common in the neighborhood.

On the wall of Adams's office there is a huge sign with a list in Magic Marker headed "Things to Do." The list features follow-up procedures on "recruits"—letters to the district superintendent, the Board of Education, and the principals—and questions about lunch—who will prepare it? who will pay? The list indicates that the bus route, at least, has been settled: Stops will be made in each of the nine gang turfs, thus avoiding conflicts that would arise if some of the gang members attending the school had to walk on other gangs' turfs.

Rushing off to an appointment and looking every inch a harried, but brilliant, executive, Adams asks one of the Workshop staff if he has purchased the bus yet. The young man answers that he hasn't. "When you get the three thousand tomorrow," Adams says, "buy the bus."

"We spent that *last week*!" answers the young man in a voice that could almost be a muffled scream.

"Buy the bus!" Adams says in a voice that defies contradiction. The young man is speechless as Adams sweeps down the narrow stairs.

At times, Adams conveys the impression that he can accomplish just about anything on bravado alone. It is still uncertain whether the Department of Licenses and Inspection has actually cleared the building for use; but the Minischool opens—with full bus service—on September 6.

Second Week:

Like the Pennsylvania Advancement School when it opened in an unconverted factory, the Minischool doesn't look much like a school. The first floor of the building is almost entirely open, with only blackboards and an occasional bookshelf, in addition to huge pillars at twenty-foot intervals, dividing the various classroom areas. At the end of the room is a wall of frosted windows, beyond which can be seen the shadows of ivy growing on the walls outside. The floor is gray-painted brick, the noise level seems calibrated to make thought impossible, and usually there are a dozen or more children either in transit from one place to another, or merely lolling on the outskirts of a classroom area. The over-all effect is near-chaos.

The second floor of the building will not be usable for several weeks, but "community" people, many of them wearing YGS identification tags or sweatshirts, are already at work on the renovation. Most of the teachers agree that very little can be accomplished while the student body is gathered in its entirety on the first floor. Fortunately, during the second period of the day, about half the students—there are eight sections, each with roughly eighteen kids—go off for physical education or other activities, and the noise level drops enough to make the place seem at least sane. The periods are one hour and fifteen minutes long, however—double the normal length—and the horrendous first period of the day can be devastating.

Some of the better features of the program are evident even in the midst of the noise and confusion. In the urban affairs class, those students who can hear the teacher—usually the ones within earshot of his hoarse shouting—readily volunteer answers to questions about their neighborhood and its community organizations. Students who have earned recognition for good deeds are rewarded with dashikis, and clearly the kids covet these status symbols. There is relevance; there is identity.

Also, there is a positive emphasis on individual creativity in the afternoon period called "contract time," one of the Minischool's most constructive innovations to date. During the allotted hour, each student is free to engage in a project of his own choosing. After he decides what he wants to get involved in, he actually signs, with his teacher and his parent, a printed contract which becomes a statement of honorable intention to finish what he has begun within an appointed time.

Doris Hamilton, always wary of easy talk, observes the tremendous difficulty of building a sense of true community among Mantua's blacks. Recently, she says, she referred to one of the students as a "black kid." The boy became angry and repeated what she had said to his mother, who threatened to remove him from the school. "I went to talk with his mother," Mrs. Hamilton says, "and I said, 'What color is your boy?' His mother said, 'He's colored.' Then I said, 'What color are you?' and again the mother said, 'Colored'" As far as she herself is concerned, Mrs. Hamilton continues after a rueful sigh, it doesn't matter what labels they use—"I just want people to *live*, and to have a sense of dignity."

Fourth Week:

Forrest Adams has come up with a brainstorm for soliciting community support which would probably delight Marshall McLuhan. The device is a recorded bulletin that one can receive simply by dialing a Workshop telephone number. Adams's voice answers, rich with charismatic urgency, and says:

> While the Board of Education has been dealing with the madness of racists in order to decide whether or not black children should get a good education [this is the week of the huge anti-busing demonstration staged by parents from predominantly white Northeast Philadelphia] we of the Mantua-Powelton area have built a school for 137 children from fifth to seventh grade. In this insane world of racist power we have decided that the education of our children is through power. However, if this school is to be a success, we need the support of all the people in the Mantua-Powelton community. Come out to our meeting Thursday, September 26, at 8 P.M., at 3304 Arch Street and learn what a community school can truly do when it's run by the community. Dial in next week for a new message about our community. This message has been sponsored by Mantua Community Planners.

September 30:

Although about fifty people showed up at the meeting last Thursday, Forrest Adams observes, "People don't like to talk at big meetings." There is still no real sense of who the community is or how it can be involved in running the school. "You could get a group of people and ask them what color that wall is," Adams says, pointing to the other side of the first floor area, "and you'd get seven or eight different answers. Maybe at best you'd get some kind of consensus." Part of his job, and that of the two community liaison staff members, he continues, is to go out into the community and "find out what the community *is.*"

Nevertheless, the Minischool continues on its usual daredevil course in an attempt to build an effective school for the community, whatever that may be, to support. Today, Monday, is the day of the Board meeting at which the final Minischool resolution is due to be passed, and Adams is all prepared—slide-tape, public relations spiel—to convince the Board that it is worth doing. Rick deLone arrives from 21st Street for a last-minute conspiratorial visit. He assures Adams that everything is O.K., that in the usual premeeting briefing session this morning the Board agreed to approve the resolution. "We told them you had five certified teachers," deLone tells Adams. "You'd better produce them quick." Four of the permanent faculty meet most of the requirements for certification to teach in Pennsylvania, Adams tells him. "At the briefing session," deLone continues, "one of the Board members said 'But we don't even *know* Forrest Adams,' and Graham Finney said, 'Damn it, I know him!'" Finally, at any rate, Dilworth had prevailed on his colleagues and a compromise was reached: The resolution would pass, and several Board members, trusting Finney and his staff, would visit the school during the week.

After deLone has departed for 21st Street, Adams urges Fleischaker and Lamont to push for another T-group retreat the following weekend, not so much in order to plan curriculum, but to get the group together. "When [one of the female teachers] cried the last time," Adams tells the others, "that really did a lot for her." Lamont becomes annoyed when Adams accuses him of preferring to remain home with his pregnant wife, rather than go to the retreat. "I can see you getting red," Adams says with a laugh. "You're going to explode. Go ahead. Go ahead!"

The tension passes after a while, and the three founders of the Minischool agree that a retreat is necessary fairly soon, if not the

following weekend—that several teachers are beginning to use
the "black-white" thing as a defense, that they are withdrawing
from the rest of the faculty. "That's why we need this weekend,"
Adams says. "To break down the black-white thing."

October:

The kids at the Minischool have so much more freedom in this
unusual environment than in their regular schools that they seem
much happier. There is another side to the coin, of course—
several kids complain to visitors that the school is "too noisy."
Construction on the second floor continues; crews of "community" workers are constantly going in and out of the main
room. Whatever the students' reactions to all this confusion in
general, one boy has been moved to write a poem, which is
prominently displayed on the bulletin board near the main office.

MINI SCHOOL

Mini School is a boss boss school
Mini School doesn't carry fools
It gets cooler and cooler every day
And if you would like
With all your mite
To help the Mini School
Just come rite in and *Volunteer*
To ask other people to please come here
With pleasure to help our children learn
And hope they have a better life earned

No one has attempted to survey the attitudes of the Minischool
students scientifically, but despite the chaos of the place there is
a discernible mood of trust and optimism. The students' behavior
suggests that they know how much the teachers want this effort
to succeed and that for the moment they will do anything they
can to help.

Even so, discipline is already beginning to be a serious problem, and some teachers are so frustrated by the noise and confusion that they incessantly shout to be heard and frequently collapse into petty anger. It is very difficult to love a child when
twenty others are destroying the room. The administrative staff
has set up a Minischool court, an attempt to instil self-government
and discipline within the community, but the court has done vir-

tually nothing to keep order, in spite of a few scorching public humiliations that some students have received at the hands of others.

In mid-October, several of the black men on the staff initiate an organizational shake-up in which, rather subtly prying loose some of the power from Adams, they take over a good deal of the discipline. Tyrone Shields, a six-foot-five former basketball player, gives up teaching to become head of discipline for the school and begins patrolling the main area with a stick. In the confusion of the last several months some coalitions have begun to form, and action to be taken. John Fennell, Shields's boyhood and Army friend, who teaches math and who told Shields about the job in the first place, has the quietest, most orderly class in the school. While other classes, clearly visible from Fennell's semi-enclosed teaching area, are milling about in confusion, Fennell's class is lined up in rows, just as in any other junior high school in the city, and his students are more or less occupied in completing a written math exercise. Complimented on their department, Fennell waves a yardstick and says, "Yes, this is how I get it."

The libertarian educational wing would say that he is a monster, that he is conducting a reign of terror in the classroom. Later, however, when he becomes a center of controversy, large numbers of students take his side. And the tacit agreement that this is the way school should be, that all the noise outside is sacrilege, hangs over Fennell's students like a soothing mist.

The black men on the staff are beginning to assert their identity, at any rate, after the initial confusion and the hippie-intellectual whiteness of the early days. Doris Hamilton reveals to observers, who can only admire her inventiveness, that for some visits in Mantua she wears a straightened black wig, for others her own real bush.

The newest addition to the permanent staff is a young white man named Eric Olson, a skinny, wispy-bearded Oberlin graduate who has come to teach in urban schools after two years of community work in India. Supposedly working in partnership with Fennell, Olson has been given a few weeks in which to build a discovery-oriented math lab. He is using the only large enclosed space on the first floor, and he has already attracted a

substantial following of kids who like to hang around his room
and share the casual, relaxed atmosphere. One of them has even
contributed a mural, in the style of Jackson Pollock, to the decor.
He would like to reproduce it in his room at home, he tells
Olson, but he has to share the room with a brother who won't
let him do any painting. Olson explains that Adams and
Fleischaker hired him only with the greatest reluctance; they
needed a math teacher, but they would have preferred a black
man.

November:

At a faculty meeting held in the newly created math lab,
which often doubles as a teachers' lounge, several teachers make
rather pointed exits long before the business of the afternoon
has been finished. There is a great deal of tension and anxiety.

In spite of this, the staff spends most of the meeting considering the Minischool's proposed report card, which will not be a
report card at all, but a written summation of what each student
has been doing in his classes. Each homeroom teacher eventually
does one for his students, consulting with each student's other
teachers before writing the final report. True to the beliefs of
the original founders, the Minischool has kept grades and testing
to an absolute minimum. This attempt to support humanistic
values notwithstanding, most staff members agree in private
talks, though trying to put a good face on it, that morale is at
an all-time low.

November 29:

It is the Friday of the Thanksgiving weekend, and the Minischool faculty has organized a huge "community" party at the
Green Trees, a homely and prosaic restaurant next door to the
school's Arch Street building. Some estimates place the attendance at over 100, out of about 150 people from all facets of the
Mantua-Powelton community who have been invited. The guests
begin to gather at about 7:15 and continue arriving for the next
forty-five minutes. Most of them are black and all have done
something outstanding in "the community," but it is clearly not
a group that is used to being together. A few small cliques
stand out in the crowd.

There are officials from the various home and school associations of the neighborhood schools. There are prominent businessmen. A few of the "young professionals" from Powelton are here. The guests wear name tags, and the room is filled with aggressive conversation. A black undertaker from Mantua confides to a white Poweltonian that he seriously questions whether "these people can really make this thing work," implying that people in Mantua have never been able to make *anything* work. Yet the guests, in their hearty efforts at meeting other people, seem tremendously eager to make a success of the evening, despite the air they have of not knowing exactly what it is supposed to accomplish. Many of the black people present are just beginning to reap some justice from American society through employment in community-action programs. The majority of the guests, when asked, admit that they have never been inside the Minischool and know very little about it.

After a dinner of turkey, fixin's, and ice cream and cake, eaten at tables that seem to be composed half of cliques, half of strangers, Forrest Adams, Andy Jenkins, John Ciccone, and even Herman Wrice greet the gathering in turn and say a few words. Jenkins and Wrice affirm their friendship and remind the guests that they started out together. A film with a rock 'n' roll score is shown; narrated by Jenkins, it depicts the severely depressed conditions of Mantua, the community's efforts to do away with gang conflict, and, finally, the specific achievements of MCP and the Workshop. The film features a few off-color comments from various community people that cause a minor stir in the audience, many of whom seem straighter than John Fennell's yardstick. And finally, after the film, Forrest Adams, at the top of his charmingly cerebral form, introduces an all-black rock 'n' roll band with the explanation that it is "somewhere in the vicinity of an octet."

The dancing begins, and black is really beautiful in the Green Trees Restaurant this strange, crowded night. At 10:30, after an appropriate climax in the music, several volunteers conduct readings of black poetry while the subtle music of the band slides along to their rhythms. Some of the poetry is very cool, very black, very angry; some of it is even anti-white. "Black meat is TOUGH!" shouts a young girl in an Afro, concluding a poem

—and the audience cheers. It is the first real suggestion of to-getherness in the entire evening.

December:

Doris Hamilton sees the school as being very successful in a number of ways, especially with some of the most difficult kids. "Everybody can clearly see change in the attitudes of the kids," she explains. "We have one girl who used to be a very *bad* kid and she's gone completely straight, helping around as an assistant to the secretary. Her attitude has even changed at home. And there's Bill, a big shy boy who's never done *anything* before—he could have been a mute for all we knew. One day he cut a class and fooled around with some of the other boys, and his mother was glad that he even got in *trouble*—at least he was involved!"

But the politics of Mantua-Powelton are not the only factor in the school's uncertain future, Mrs. Hamilton continues. For one thing, the school system has not exactly been helping the project along. She has encountered resistance on several occasions from the district office, particularly in regard to meetings with parents. And it was at the promptings of school officials, she suspects, that several parents have withdrawn their children from the Minischool—there are now 132 students. Nor has the situation been helped by the school system's school-community coor-dinator program. True, each of the coordinators is a resident of the community, and Mrs. Hamilton is quick to acknowledge that they do excellent jobs (so good in fact, that the program is cited as one of the most successful Title I projects in a national survey early in 1969). But, however effective they may be, the school-community coordinators necessarily compete with their counter-parts in the Minischool.

There is still no semblance of a unified program. The too-long classes have been shortened, contract time has been made con-siderably more flexible, and the second floor is in almost full use —but the grumbling over coffee in the Green Trees continues unabated. "I don't think they have any money left," smirks a teacher in the Green Trees one afternoon. "And I just can't stand that chaos."

"You can't take a bunch of amateurs," observes another, "and put them in a factory and expect to have a school. So many of these people are supposed to be from the community, but that's a myth. This whole place is riddled with myths. Forrest Adams may be a bright, sensitive guy, but that doesn't make a school successful."

January:

During the first week of the new year, John Fennell, the strict math teacher who has never agreed with the free-thinking philosophy of so many of the Minischool staff, receives notice of dismissal from Forrest Adams. The main reason Adams gives for firing him is that he did not fit in with the group and did not do his job. Some staff members add that Fennell behaved "childishly" at the weekend sensitivity-training retreat held during the Christmas vacation, that clearly he could no longer be tolerated. Others say that however uncooperative Fennell may have been, Adams's sudden dismissal without notice was hardly fair, either. And Fennell, seizing on the question of due process that the lack of notice has raised, decides to seek more powerful support than he can derive from those few staff members who openly take his side. The logical power to appeal to, of course, is that mysterious entity commonly known as "the community."

Fennell goes to Andy Jenkins of MCP, and once again the question is raised of who exactly "the community" is and to what extent it is in charge of the Minischool. According to Jenkins, MCP is the "overseer" of the Minischool and will call a meeting of its own board to decide on Fennell's status. All of this is duly reported in a lengthy article in the *Evening Bulletin* emphatically partial to Fennell and written by the paper's education reporter—who has admitted privately on at least one occasion that he is opposed to the kind of freedom the Minischool offers its students. The article stresses the fact that Fennell was the only teacher at the school who "gave tests and grades, as well as nightly homework." It also quotes several parents who support Fennell and disapprove of the school's lack of discipline. "'We all got the feeling that it would be good for our children when we heard about it last summer,'" one mother is quoted as saying. "'Now my child comes home and says the students don't have to go to class if they don't want to. There is no discipline.'"

But there is no community board, either. Through the exertion of pressure from the MCP board, Jenkins prevails on Adams to take Fennell back on a thirty-day probationary basis. If Adams had refused, according to most of the Minischool's friends, Fennell could easily have wrecked the school with the publicity alone.

"If it's not community-controlled," Jenkins observes a week after the conclusion of this incident, "we might as well forget about decentralization in the future." At the moment he plans to bring up the question of a board of directors for the Minischool at a community-wide meeting that will be held on the 28th of the month; probably, he observes, the board of directors will be chosen at that time. There has been difficulty in forming a board up to this point, Jenkins admits, mainly because "the community" had been active in so much planning for the school's basic operation that there was no time to set up a board; but "now we're settling down." And, Jenkins says, the people who worked on the Minischool at the beginning, the original founders—Adams, Fleischaker, Lamont, and Mrs. Hamilton—will have to understand that, once formed, the new board of directors will take precedence.

Jenkins talks with the self-assurance of a man who knows it's in the bag. He observes that Forrest Adams has been doing an "excellent job," and one can almost hear the sound of heads rolling.

But Jenkins's community board never materializes. The Minischool's founders are able to rescue themselves through legal safeguards; long before the planned confrontation they manage to pacify Jenkins by pointing out that the Minischool's charter as a nonprofit corporation lists *them* as the governing board, and that there is no formal connection between either the Minischool and MCP or the Minischool and the Workshop. In short, the school's association with these groups has been useful merely as a toehold on power. Now that the factions are exposed, Adams and the others immediately proceed to set up *their* community board. The threat of disaster has been skirted.

By the time of the planned confrontation on January 28, Adams and Jenkins are friends again; the meeting that evening becomes a strong, apparently unified plea on the part of most of the community groups in Mantua-Powelton to get themselves together. Adams's contribution is a show of highly impressionistic slides which are supposed to represent what the Minischool is all about. The only jarring note of the evening comes from a mother who complains to anyone who will listen that her son's official transcript was not returned to his original school when he transferred out of the Minischool. By the end of January the constantly fluctuating enrollment is down to roughly 110.

But the end of January is a crucial time for the Minischool for other, quite different reasons than the fact that a struggle for power has been more or less resolved. On the final weekend of the month, Eric Olson, despairing of any possibility of real community within the school, has gone out and, with his own money, purchased enough plywood to erect walls separating all the classrooms.

On Monday morning January 27 the teachers arrive to discover that the open first-floor area and most of the second floor as well have been completely transformed. Where once there was a huge open space downstairs, there is now what seems to be an enormous hallway, with walls on both sides. The second floor, with a much larger open space outside the classrooms, is similar. Each staff member will now have the privacy and quiet that the chaos of the last few months has precluded, but, in addition, the walls have made alienation a visible reality. And throughout the day, as puzzled students wander about in a state of almost complete disorientation, Olson and a crew of volunteers from a Quaker weekend work camp continue to hammer and saw with a frenzy.

Olson stops his work—he has been going all weekend long—to offer a brief explanation of what he has been doing. "People had asked me before if they could have walls like the ones in the math lab," he says. "So I didn't just dream this up myself. I know that people *wanted* it. It was a very hard decision to make, but I just felt that these people had to have some *support.*"

Later, downstairs, Fleischaker smiles enigmatically when asked how much money has been spent on this admittedly temporary building to date (in March the lease is renewed until June 1970). "I know exactly," he answers. "Forty-six thousand two hundred dollars." It is still a month or so before the Minischool will run out of money completely and turn to the Rockefeller Foundation for an unanticipated second grant.

Things did not get much better at the Minischool during the spring, especially with money so scarce. There was an ugly incident in which one of the teachers chased a student out of the building one day and beat him up. There were more confrontations, with threats of gang vengeance, at meetings of the newly formed fifteen-member board of directors. But by the spring of 1969 the Mantua-Powelton Minischool had become so much a part of the local urban battlefield that it seemed likely to remain so at least for another year, possibly even longer. The Minischool might be a failure as a model for true community, but this clearly had very little to do with its political future—it would survive. The real questions were: Who would run it, how would it obtain money, and what would be its relation to the Board of Education?

As far as officials at the Board were concerned, there was no definite answer. In March the Board's planning office—no longer under the direction of Graham Finney, who had taken his leave several months earlier—commissioned a "study" of the feasibility of a scattered-site school for Mantua-Powelton. Although the planning office was still interested in the idea, there were, as one planner observed at the time, "serious 'buts.'" More important than the commitment to the scattered-site middle school, perhaps, was the administration's view, according to this planner, that MCP and YGS ("Herman and Andy") would have to be involved in whatever the school district was going to do for the area. The "community" was too powerful by this time to ignore.

Forrest Adams had plans of his own, however—even though, in accordance with the new regime of unity in Mantua-Powelton, he was a member of the group evaluating the prospects for a scattered-site school. "Community control usually means community terrorizing these days, but we're talking about real involvement and participation," Adams said in the spring of 1969, as he and his staff moved into a new stage of the ongoing battle. "We have to *make* something, not control it. We're creating a homework center—eight people have volunteered their homes for tutorials, meetings, and slide shows. There are a few parents who really feel the kind of excitement the school generates. 'Black is beautiful,' but not when you get down to the specifics—mass meetings are only for fighting a war, not giving useful information.

"We think the only way to do this thing is just to go and do it. When you get up to a speed of a hundred miles per hour with three thousand people, nobody can stop you."

Snapshot: *Philanthropy*

In the spring of 1969 the Black Panther Party opened an office in North Philadelphia. One of the party's first moves was to institute a program providing free meals for neighborhood children. Every day about fifty kids shared eggs, sausages, grits, bread, juice, and milk—most of it contributed by local merchants—in a room decorated with posters of revolutionary heroes and, according to an article in the *Evening Bulletin,* occasionally filled with the sound of records "espousing party doctrine."

When the *Bulletin*'s reporter asked a spokesman for the milk industry to comment on the fact that the Panthers were handing out lists naming the companies that refused to contribute, the man observed that "state law forbids the distribution of free milk to any but recognized legitimate charitable institutions."

"We do not intimidate," asserted a spokesman for the Panthers. "We ask people to contribute, but the decision is theirs alone."

V. In the Classroom

The Learning Centers

This is the point: we lack convincing alternatives, actual classrooms that people could go and see, that teachers could work in, functioning schools that would demonstrate to the public and to educators the kind of learning I've described in this series. They must be institutions that can develop and grow over time, not just demonstration classes. A tiny number of infant schools pioneered the changes in the British schools, and it is probable that careful work on a small scale is the way to start a reform worth having, whatever our grandiose educational reformers might say. In the end, you always return to a teacher in a classroom full of children. That is the proper locus of a revolution in the primary schools.

—Joseph Featherstone, conclusion of
a series of articles on the British
infant schools published in *The New Republic*
in the fall of 1967

THE TEACHERS in the Learning Centers Project rarely thought of themselves as revolutionaries, but their combined efforts could almost have been a military assault on the structure and purpose of the conventional classroom. The project offered a program for change that was beginning to transform several schools throughout the city, and project director Lore Rasmussen, who tended to think of her colleagues in the same way that Rick deLone thought of *his* colleagues, as a network, guided the operation with the aplomb of a logistics expert. Even in the midst of urban warfare, however, the staff of the learning centers tended to avoid the more overt forms of battle.

Essentially the learning centers were elementary-school classrooms filled with interesting equipment and staffed by teachers whose aim was to encourage children to learn and think on their own, rather than be directed in every move they made by an all-knowing authority. Though almost entirely free of dogma, the approach followed by the learning centers seemed to be a composite of the educational theories of Montessori, Dewey, Piaget, Bruner, Holt, and other "progressives." Similar in many ways to the extensively adopted—and officially approved—infant schools in England, word of which was circulating with increasing speed among the growing number of discontented in the classrooms of America (the Featherstone articles, like books by Goodman and Holt, were a necessary component of a liberal teacher's bookshelf), the structure and methodology of the learning centers were almost diametrically opposed to those prevailing in the normal elementary school.

Where the conventional classroom stressed order, the learning centers emphasized freedom; whereas conformity was the rule in most schools, the learning centers encouraged the growth of the individual child; perhaps most important, the learning centers avoided the tyranny of paper-and-pencil rote learning. Children were encouraged to write down their thoughts only after they had had concrete experiences—with mathematical games, for example, or with a personal discovery—as a basis for something to say. Children (and teachers) in the learning centers usually enjoyed themselves, but not simply because they had free time to fool around; the strong element of play in the activity of the centers was more an ingredient of active learning, as opposed to the passive kind one usually sees in schools.

By the 1968–69 school year, the Learning Centers Project consisted of nine learning center classrooms in as many schools; a separate laboratory school with six teachers; roughly a score of classrooms partially converted to the learning centers approach and in regular contact with designated staff; the Philadelphia Teacher Center, a sort of grown-up learning center where visitors could explore at first hand the various elements of the program; and a consulting role that ranged from administrators in charge of curriculum at 21st Street to architects involved in the design of new buildings to district superintendents. The "network" had grown, in short, to affect a large but indeterminate number of teachers—perhaps as many as a hundred—and several thousand students. It was only a tiny part of the Philadelphia public school system—but, as Featherstone had observed, a similarly tiny minority had brought about major changes in the schools of England.

Unlike the Pennsylvania Advancement School—which observers generally considered the system's most promising laboratory for educational innovation—and a host of other projects not nearly as successful, the Learning Centers Project was almost completely independent of Mark Shedd and the movement for school reform that began officially with the installation of the new Board in 1965. "Learning centers" was a recent label, but the phenomenon it described had been steadily growing for a decade. The difference was that, while before only a few officials of the public school system had supported Mrs. Rasmusson's work, now the Learning Centers were among the system's most widely hailed innovations.

The real beginning of the learning centers movement can be traced to Donald and Lore Rasmussen's arrival in Philadelphia in the fall of 1955. After thirteen years of teaching at all-black Talladega College in Alabama, Don Rasmussen had been invited to take over as headmaster of Philadelphia's ultra-progressive Miquon School, a small independent day school located in a forested valley lying between Northwest Philadelphia and the suburbs. Miquon was founded in the early 1930's by a group of parents who were tuned in to the theories of progressivism then in vogue, but, like so many such schools, it had fallen on hard times after the vogue declined, and the travails of the war years superseded everything. The Rasmussens had also been directors of a cooperative summer camp in Michigan for many years. Miquon had been run as a parent-teacher cooperative even before their arrival, and it was at Miquon that Lore Rasmussen began developing new approaches to the teaching of mathematics—a field whose formal rigidity had made it the bane of the average school child, and one in which some of the most interesting work in curriculum development was then being done.

In experimenting with the learning laboratory approach, Lore Rasmussen joined a burgeoning movement. The studies of Piaget and Bruner, which outlined levels of thought development, provided a strong theoretical focus for this movement. Curriculum laboratories, such as England's Nuffield Foundation and the Elementary Science Study (ESS), in Cambridge, Massachusetts —which later became the Educational Development Corporation (EDC)—were turning out new materials and courses of study. By the late 1950's, Lore Rasmussen had become so thoroughly involved in curriculum change that she was corresponding with the leaders of the field across the nation—Holt and Bruner, among others, were close friends, and both she and her husband were consultants to ESS.

Mrs. Rasmussen also began at this time to run workshops in the techniques of the learning laboratory for enthusiasts from local universities, private schools, and the Board of Education. Board member Elizabeth Greenfield attended one of these workshops with the school system's director of curriculum, and it was a short step from this introduction to a year-long in-service course for teachers from the school system, supported by a grant from a local foundation. This led in turn to an arithmetic guide for the primary grades written by some of Lore Rasmussen's students and put out by the Board's curriculum office, and then to an even larger workshop program, sponsored by yet another foundation.

Finally, in the spring of 1963, a group of school officials, after years of unofficial involvement with Miquon, invited Lore Rasmussen to continue her experiments within the public school system. Milton Goldberg, then principal of the T. M. Peirce School, which was to house the first learning centers, recalls that Mrs. Rasmussen was not at first convinced that the Board really meant to go ahead with the project. Nor was Goldberg, for that matter, convinced that he wanted the learning centers in his school. Thus, for several months, Goldberg and Mrs. Rasmussen visited each other's schools and homes, got to know each other, and all the time talked in terms of—as Goldberg puts it, "If we did have a program, what would it be like?"

By June, they had a program: "At the end of June we went to Creative Playthings, in Princeton, and bought the first batch of stuff. The proposal we developed called for four learning centers, including a math lab and a children's playroom. We completely transformed the dark old cellar of the building—the playroom had a piano, record players, and a wall-length easel. We wanted it to be used by any kids in the school who wanted to go there; we hoped to free up things that were happening in the classroom." And at the beginning, whatever extra equipment the learning centers were able to obtain was squeezed out of the regular school budget.

The year at the Peirce School was a period of generation and growth. Teachers from Peirce and other schools visited the labs, and interns from Temple University's graduate education program served as apprentices—and in 1965 the program expanded into two more schools. By the time of the first applications for grants under Title I of the federal government's Elementary and Secondary Education Act (ESEA), in the summer of 1966, the project was ready to move out into the school system at large. Title I was designed specifically to implement programs for raising the quality of teaching and achievement in poverty-area schools, and while many critics of the ESEA insisted (and still insist) that it was just another band-aid, Title I programs were beginning to be a tremendously enriching factor in the growth of many urban school systems. The result was, in part, that a large number of Philadelphia's poorest schools had become hotbeds of innovation, while many of the schools in the wealthier parts of the city were hopelessly conventional and almost entirely without resources for change. The learning centers would continue to be an "inner-city" phenomenon, at any rate, for some time. Under the first Title I grant, the project encompassed nine learning centers, a headquarters office, and extensive staff development programs. The movement was shifting into high gear.

One of Lore Rasmussen's objectives from the beginning had been the development of a basic learning center model that could be reproduced fairly easily in any classroom in the city, and by the time of Title I she had made considerable progress toward this goal. The immediate impression of a typical learning center was of a miniature amusement park so full of stimulating things to do that even blasé adults would find it difficult not to be enthusiastic. Though some classrooms were better equipped than others, on the whole, all of them were literally crammed with things. There was usually an abundance of mathematical equipment: several different scales for weighing; various tabulating machines; sets of varied tiles for geometric games; puzzles; Cuisenaire rods (one of the most popular mathematical innovations, these are sets of varicolored wooden rods that illustrate basic mathematical principles and also set theory, the foundation of the "new math"); all sorts of measuring instruments, including clocks and timers, rulers, and thermometers. But the focus was not exclusively mathematical: The equipment also included sandboxes, live animals, plants, drawing and painting materials, libraries, building blocks, playhouses, tiny projectors for film loops, tape recorders, cameras, puppets, and typewriters.

Often there was an air of pioneer making-do in the inventive use of raw materials, the outgrowth of a series of workshops conducted by Don Rasmussen in relation to curriculum materials under development at EDC. A sturdy cardboard called "tri-wall," for example, could be used for sandboxes, tables, playhouses, and other products ordinarily requiring expensive, impractical plywood or metal. Some learning centers had homemade musical instruments, such as banjos made out of plastic Ajax cans. Perhaps the most interesting articles of equipment in the centers, mainly because they sustained the first outburst of curiosity long enough to create an actual learning experience, were the various forms of "shoe-box labs." These were actual shoeboxes containing the materials for a brief experiment and enough provocative questions, though no answers, to challenge the user to work the experiment out, thus making the learning experience a stimulating and enjoyable game.

The other main component of the learning centers was, of course, a strong emphasis on the individual initiative and freedom of each child. This required much more imagination, hard work, and genuine concern for kids on the part of the teacher than the conventional classroom. It was easy for teachers to espouse "freedom" in the abstract, but genuine freedom, as distinct from mindless anarchy, did not happen automatically, even (or especially) in the learning centers. During the 1967–68 school year, for example, in an experimental class at the F. C. Douglass

School—the network's headquarters—two young teachers, John Harkins and George Eves, spent the entire year patiently striving for the proper balance between freedom and order. And during the year, Harkins kept a written record of their work together that, taken as a whole, could almost be the diary of Sisyphus. Here is one excerpt, written at the end of June:

GROUP TIME AND THE PLATE SPINNER

During the first week of school we started something that came to be known as "free time." Our objectives were the same as our procedure and that's why it didn't work. It was naive. It was as if a poor man who wanted to be rich opened up his wallet with the expectation of finding millions.

I had been reading Featherstone's articles in the *New Republic* and attending Lore's summer workshop where playful curious spirits were encouraged to follow their inclinations with a smorgasbord of provocative materials. I had also just suffered through a boring regimented sit-and-listen orientation for new teachers. I was ready for freedom and individuality and some academic cutting loose. George knew better but he didn't say so. Perhaps he was being polite to me; perhaps he was thinking that this was the kind of thing we were supposed to be doing; perhaps he wasn't convinced that his experience offered better alternatives. He went along with it. Together we were inundated with supplies. We had 25 sacks of Cuisenaire rods, 3 tins of tinkertoys, a cylinder of D-sticks, five calculators, two tape recorders, four microscopes, 3 boxes of beads, some games and the usual collection of classroom supplies. The kids were eager to get at all that stuff and we were eager to let them.

The result was a mess. We didn't know how to go about it. I'm convinced that something very close to our free time can work but I don't yet know how to let it. We have created a second cousin that works very well but it involves much less freedom. Someday we'll get back to "free time" and have it work.

Meanwhile it is useful to record the progress of both free time and group time so that the best parts of each can be preserved.

Free time had a supermarket atmosphere to it. The focus was on the various materials available rather than on the use of the material. We would usually begin by putting a list on the board. On an early day the list might have read:

> D-sticks
> Microscopes
> Compasses
> Tinkertoys
> Calculators

Tape recorders
Typewriters

We gave each item a place in the room. We sometimes talked about what might be done. We sometimes put limits on how many people could use different materials at the same time. In general, we just turned them loose. The kids reacted in a way that had been predicted. They sampled one thing. Then they ran and sampled another. Then they just ran. It had been predicted, but it was still hard to put up with. Materials were being broken. Clean-up was an ordeal. No one was staying with one thing long enough to accomplish anything. Fights were developing over who was going to get to use the choicest goodies. Worst of all, the situation showed no sign of improving. I had thought that the whirlwind sampling would settle down into relatively calm exploration of the materials. George said that the kids were probably thinking something like: "All that stuff and it's here now and I better get it while I can 'cause it's not going to be here long." That prediction turned out to be the case. The tape recorders were broken, two calculators were broken, my own compass was put away to prevent its being broken. Something had to be done.

We all wrote on the topic "IS FREE TIME BETTER WHEN YOU STAY WITH ONE THING." The kids produced a lot of empty pieties for us but there was no change in free time behavior. For several days we tried to get every student's name on the board next to one of the available materials. The first day we did this was very painful. There was no fair way of deciding which of six students would be allowed to fill the last coveted place in the tape recording corner. Several students wanted to do nothing if they couldn't have their choice. It took us a very boring, selfish, squabbling hour to get the list completed. When it was all done, the teachers were forced into the role of policing the assignments. Inevitably the boy who had been denied the use of the typewriter would sneak or bully his way into the typing chair and start a fight if he was asked to leave it. The liveliest corners of the room would attract other kids. If the tinkertoys seemed boring that day, they would be left scattered over several desks while the kids crept into other areas. Should the teachers have forced them back into the corner to tinker with tinkertoys? Would that have been FREE time? Would it have been a good situation under any name?

The real problem with our free time was that there was nothing to do except fiddle around. There was no reason for sustained effort. There was no promise that it would accomplish anything. There was no experience of direction to support such effort. We must have been assuming that a child would latch onto a microscope and become transformed into Antony van Leeuwenhoek inventing bacteriology. They came as close as could be expected. About half the class learned how to use the microscope. The more interested ones ran through a miscellany of things to look at: floor dirt, blood, hair, soil, leaves. But even these kids were coming around with "What do I do now?" or drifting off into other activities. In order for them to stay with it, the teachers had to be available to invent the next steps. This was not producing the independence that we wanted.

I think I know what is needed but we never got around to supplying it for the kids of 317. The British call them assignment cards. To produce them for the materials we were working with would take a lot of time, energy, imagination and experience. A child working with a compass needs some direction other than the needle. We were just turning him loose with the hope that he would find his own. The alternative we were running away from would have placed him constantly at the feet of a teacher for directions or inspirations. The better solution is a series of cards with problems and questions and perhaps a little bit of information, all set up in a way that lets the child work through the cards independently and open-endedly. There's a crucial shift in emphasis. The focus would not just be a gadget, nor would it be a teacher-centered school with a gadget as a prop. The focus would be on the things one can learn and do with the aid of a compass. The teacher would be there not as a policeman ("Go fiddle with that damn compass") and not as a fount of knowledge but as an unobtrusive but available guide.

We didn't get the cards made. We did fall into a workable pattern that lasted for most of the school year. We changed the name from "free time" to "group time." We insisted that the members of a group work together or, at least, next to each other, and that they stay in their own group. It was possible to change groups but we let it be known that we didn't expect it to happen very often. During the week before Christmas when teachers all over the school were bemoaning the difficulties of teaching in the excited pre-vacation atmosphere, we realized that our class was going better than it had ever been.

One day I realized that I wasn't needed in the workroom [a separate room where the main activity was reading and writing] so I walked over toward the classroom. I met George in the hall. Since he was coming to the workroom for the same reason, we figured we had arrived. The rest of the week was just as good.

After Christmas vacation we hoped to take up where we had left off. The general pattern was continued for months but little changes began to take place. Our "group time" was absorbing some of the characteristics of the earlier "free time" without losing the basic framework of the groups. Howard had typed enough in his reading group and didn't need to be in the competition for typewriters any more. He went to see what Martin was shouting about over his microscope, got drawn in and established a kind of squatter's rights membership in the pond water group. Shirl slipped off into the girls' half of the movie group, as did Charlene. Elaine took up the typewriter deserted by Charlene. James and David finished their movie and found different partners for their next film. There was an element of sneakiness about most of the changes. The kids had the feeling, probably valid, that the best way to get in or out of the pond water group was to ask no questions and make no announcements. They just went and avoided being quizzed and lectured. The teachers caught on to what was happening about two weeks after the kids. We did not object nor did we approve publicly. The sneakiness was serving as a useful control and seemed to prevent promiscuous sampling and roaming. There was intergroup mobility without the earlier disorders of free time.

Later in the year that pattern of group time began to deteriorate. The glamor of the gadgetry had worn off. The typewriters, for instance, were no longer coveted. Most of the ponds were "dead." New groups had developed to replace some of the older ones. Some groups would last a day. Some lasted for months. Assignment cards would have helped but we still didn't have them. There became an increasing number of students who were not loyal members of any group. For these, group time was approaching the darkest days of free time. I'm sorry to say that in this respect the year fizzled out on a lower note than we had attained in January.

Conclusions? Well, first of all, group time or free time demands an enormous amount of work. There were two of us in the classroom and we still failed to generate enough educational materials to get the most out of the physical goods. Instead of the usual lesson-plan type of preparation, it takes a catalog of simultaneous options. That's work.

It seems very appropriate to use the natural motivation that some tools and materials inspire in kids. The trick is to permit that motivation to lead into learning before the glamor is gone. Too often, in the past year, we allowed unguided, curious, playful exploration to run its course and die. The subsequent introduction of learning activities based on the same materials was never able to recapture the first fires of newness. There is a danger, of course, that the teacher's need to harness the motivation will stifle the child's urge to explore. When this happens, live mice can be as dull as the deadest textbook. Still, the teacher must take the risk. The effects of the risk can be minimized by the availability of options. If I interfere with a child's approach to compasses and turn him off, I may be able to let him turn himself back on again with a map or a magnet or some combination which will lead him back toward a compass.

An analogy always creeps into my mind when I think of group time or free time. I can't help comparing the teacher to the man at the circus who spins plates on a long table. He will spin the first five or seven in rapid succession. Then he will have to run back and give the first two an added push. Then he will rush down and start numbers eight, nine and ten. Then back to numbers three and four for their added push. Then on to eleven and twelve, and so on until he has a row of fifteen or twenty plates all spinning at once. He works fast for five minutes. Teachers work as fast as they can or want to, but for a whole year. The spinner of plates starts with identical, inert, balanced plates. The teacher starts with a diversity of kids, some balanced at different points than others and some unbalanced. Some will start themselves spinning; some will need to be started; some will spin in the wrong direction; some will spin on the bench but not on the table; some will spin only in the morning. But the reason the analogy won't stay out of my mind is the memory of that nervous back and forth action, a little push here, a little push there, a glorious moment of standing by to watch them all going at once. That's the teacher during group time. That glorious moment was when George and I confronted each other in the hall with nothing to do.

If kids, like plates, would all "spin" for a predictable length of time, the human race would not be as interesting but group time would be a lot easier to schedule. As it is, there's no way of knowing when a child is going to be finished and happy, or bored and unwilling to finish, or in need of another push. The teacher in group time needs to have his options ready because he can never get group time down to the simple pattern of the plate spinner. There will be times when he can sit down to read administrative bulletins, but there will be other times when ten kids will need him at once. It's at those latter times when he needs the materials that we never produced, materials that will let a child begin and continue to work independently. If the materials are not there the teacher must be either a magician or a disciplinarian. Most teachers are not magicians.

This sampling of one team's experience during the course of a year in a classroom that was only partly a learning center (there were more conventional times of the day than those described above) gives meaning to the phrase "creative teaching," but similar growth was happening throughout the network. The special first-grade classroom of learning center teacher Lovie Glenn, regarded by many as the supreme achievement of the form, even became the subject of a feature film which depicted the increasing autonomy and creativity of the children during most of a school year. A tour de force of public relations, the film was completed in the winter of 1968–69 and shown to a growing body of admirers and potential converts throughout the country. The teachers in the learning centers proved, perhaps more than any other group of teachers in the city, that excellent teaching could be an important art form.

But the learning centers staff also had to be masters of human relations. To those who were sympathetic with the network's goals, the merits of the entire program were obvious. As far as the tradition-oriented teachers—who greatly outnumbered the creative ones—were concerned, however, there was room for debate.

Checkpoints
Along the Network Route

Jackson School, 12th and Federal Streets, South Philadelphia

The Jackson School is housed in one of the much older buildings —the wooden-floor, fieldstone vintage—of the school system, but it is nevertheless completely up to date in terms of power struggles. To begin with, there are several "older" teachers in the school, one of whom is nearing, in this winter of 1967–68, her fiftieth year of teaching. The principal, Rocco Gigante, who came here in October after two years as an administrative assistant in one of the system's "youth development centers" (disciplinary schools), demurs when confronted with a request to visit her classroom or those of her other senior colleagues; it is, he suggests, simply Not Done. At any rate, there is a solid vein of traditionalism among the faculty, more vividly self-perpetuating here than in most schools (with 450 students, Jackson is relatively small).

Until October 1967, Jackson's principal was a progressive-minded man named Lionel Lauer, and it was because of his receptiveness to change that the school became one of the arms of the learning center network in the first place. But Mr. Lauer has moved up; he is now assistant to the district superintendent of District 3. This might have created insurmountable problems for the learning center, only in its second year at Jackson, were it not for the fact that the District 3 office happens to be located in the Jackson building. Mr. Lauer is around a great deal; even though supporting the learning center is no longer part of his job, he remains vitally interested. During the 1967–68 school year— and with shifts in staff, during the 1968–69 school year as well— the outpost at Jackson includes one learning center teacher; a teaching team linked to the learning center by a roving staff member from headquarters; another burgeoning team; a science lab; and a number of interested observers among the faculty. Jackson is also the setting, in 1967–68, of the after-school do-it-yourself workshop run by Don Rasmussen and later expanded into the Philadelphia Teacher Center.

There is, in short, relatively unusual support for new teaching styles at this particular school. Even the principal has become a consistent admirer. This is due partly to the fact that, while one of the best learning centers in the city is quietly evolving in a third-floor classroom, a fanfare of publicity has arisen over the team room across the hall, which has been virtually adopted by headquarters. Everybody in Philadelphia who is interested in innovation has been talking about it all winter; John Holt has visited it and praised. Mr. Lauer believes that it is "the best example of team teaching in the city." It is a grand feather in Lore Rasmussen's already resplendent cap.

In her mid-thirties, Marcia Kirby, one half of the team, is a dynamic teacher on her way up. The daughter of a social worker, and herself the product of an experimental elementary school, Mrs. Kirby explains that she had wanted to be a teacher since she was four—"I used to get teachers' editions of textbooks and teach my dolls." She teaches, she says, much in the same way that her mother raised her—"When I was fifteen, she said 'Try cigarettes if you want to.' I was rarely told to do anything; I was allowed to make up my mind." After eight years in various other Philadelphia schools, Mrs. Kirby began teaching at Jackson when Mr. Lauer appointed her, the first full-time black teacher in the school, as part of a drive to introduce new vitality into the faculty.

Marcia Kirby emphasizes that she has always been a rebel, that even in other schools she has taught in, "my kids did everything." There is indeed an unusual amount of freedom in the team room, though the structure has changed during the year: The room began as two separate areas, one for group activity, the other more or less free, and evolved into various small sections—for study, for science experiments, for reading lab materials, for math; there is even a miniature store where kids sell such small items as candy and pretzels to their classmates. But Marcia Kirby's is very much the dominant voice; she is an unquestioned authority, and kids respond instantly to her admonitions when she sees that they are getting out of hand. She is actually a good deal stronger, both as a personality and as a controlling influence in the classroom, than the majority of teachers, but the vital difference is that she would rather cultivate independent minds than servile spirits.

Dominick Casara provides an interesting counterpoint to what Mrs. Kirby describes as her occasional "meanness and toughness." He is quiet, relatively inexperienced (prior to coming to Jackson, he taught for two years in a Catholic high school), and much more inclined to work with one child at a time. "He has developed within himself," observes Mrs. Kirby in the tones of a proud master teacher, "without learning all the nasty tricks." She admits, too, that under his influence she has "mellowed some."

But Marcia Kirby remains a fighter and a dissident voice within the faculty. One of the teachers has complained that the team room is turning out Rap Browns and Stokely Carmichaels. Mrs. Kirby's answer: "We're teaching them to question!" The most incendiary issue, mainly because it affects the rest of the school in a way that the activities within an individual classroom cannot, is the question of whether Mrs. Kirby's students must line up when they move through the halls. Lining up is one of the foundations of order in most elementary schools throughout the country—children scarcely make a move out of their classrooms without forming a neat line—but here at Jackson (and at other network schools as well) this sacred tradition is being questioned. "Mrs. Kirby says lining up is for babies," one of the students from the team room tells the principal. Later the principal explains: "Her kids don't line up. Staff reaction has been very negative to this. We had a meeting about lining up—I was willing to make it a school policy that kids could go up to class early, but the staff rejected it."

The 1967–68 school year at the Jackson School has been a series of crescendos with Marcia Kirby playing tympani. But even in the midst of battle, most public school teachers have a thoroughly disarming way of retaining "professional dignity." The superficial order has hardly ever varied; even a few hellions running through the halls cannot really disturb hundred-year-old traditions. Marcia Kirby has scarcely dented this genteel minia- ture of the system.

Finally, in the spring of 1968, Mrs. Kirby and Mr. Casara learn that they will continue working together in a newly formed laboratory school in a separate building—a cooperative mini- school with a faculty of six teachers, sponsored by the Learning Centers Project. Mrs. Kirby is especially happy that she will now have the freedom to do what she wants without the constraints of the conventional school environment; the new school will be a genuine community.

By the fall of that year, the normal learning center approach, with its emphasis on friendliness and cooperation, has restored the outward signs of peace to Jackson. The confrontation is over; Marcia is gone. A new team is moving rapidly ahead, with the help of a visiting teacher from headquarters and K-rations of interesting equipment. "The staff thought that Mr. Lauer and I were playing favorites," the principal comments when asked about the absence of Mrs. Kirby and Mr. Casara. "She didn't meet her kids on line. They've all been saying that now Jackson's quieter. Marcia just couldn't accept the fact that you can't go in and change everything right away."

"Marcia polarized the place," observes the learning-centers roving staff member. "It probably won't happen now."

Patterson School, 70th Street and Buist Avenue Southwest Philadelphia

No matter how much a school system strives for uniformity, some schools will come out far richer in every way than others. Almost always in Philadelphia, this means that the particular school with advantages is either in an area of severe poverty or that it is blessed with an especially lively principal. (A lively community can be just as influential, of course, but usually a lively community ends up with a lively principal anyway.) Patterson's principal is James Knopf, a youthful man with a quick sense of humor. Partly because of Mr. Knopf's openness to experimentation, Patterson trails a string of innovative honors: The school is a center for intern teachers from Temple University; it was the first school in a planned K-4-4-4 cluster; it is one of the school system's "magnets," specializing in individualized instruction; and, of course, it features an active branch of the learning centers network. Mr. Knopf actually seems friendly to the network representatives, and when he drops in to say hello to them, he could almost be a fellow traveler.

Both learning center teachers, Anita LoSasso and Alan Banbury, are youthful and energetic; both hail from Colorado. Anita is a specialist in biology, Alan's training is in math. Like most of the network teachers—Marcia Kirby is an exception—Alan and Anita share a quiet affability, openness, and humor that render their potential threat to established practices at the very worst a folksy, friendly, happy kind of revolution. Their object is apparently to neutralize the usual confrontations so thoroughly that the establishment will not only want to be overthrown, but will enjoy it.

Alan Banbury's teaching at Patterson takes place principally in the learning center itself, where he is host to a fairly steady procession of visitors from the second grade. This has already inspired a few second-grade teachers to try some of the learning center techniques in their own classrooms, and occasionally Alan will visit these rooms to conduct brief lessons in such complexities as, for example, the use of Cuisenaire rods. Anita's job consists almost entirely of ministering to a relatively older group of teachers in the first grade. She will visit their classes, for example, and conduct occasional "freeing-up" lessons on a regularly scheduled basis. But one of the greatest achievements of the network at Patterson is the "staff development" seminar which Alan and Anita have been conducting on Monday afternoons for a group of fifteen or so regulars.

"Staff development" is another cliché of school reform that probably began as a good idea. Most teachers are highly approving of staff development workshops—meaningless or not—simply because they are paid to attend them, usually at a rate of six or seven dollars an hour. In Philadelphia, a large number of staff development programs have been geared recently toward changing attitudes; the success of many of them is highly debatable, if the teachers' own reactions are any criterion. ("It was so boring," says one. "We just sat around and looked at each other.") But like the learning centers themselves, and like the increasingly popular Philadelphia Teacher Center, the Patterson workshop is set up to offer direct experiences with new materials; lectures are rare, equipment plentiful. (Two other network schools have similar workshops.)

On a fairly typical day the teachers spend the first forty-five minutes or so working with pegboards in an attempt to solve various problems of set theory. The group of first-grade teachers is chortling happily at one table; most of the other teachers in the room are younger women. A few are experimenting with a battery-operated bell, which has yet to ring. Even though several teachers express confusion about set theory, the room is filled with the quiet noise of self-motivated activity, the ideal noise that every learning center teacher strives for.

Finally Alan asks everyone to stop for a while to watch a film about a class conducted under the auspices of England's Nuffield Foundation Mathematics Project. The film's title is *I Do—I Understand*—taken from a Chinese proverb popular with learning center teachers and prominently displayed on the door to the learning center at the Jackson school: "I hear and I forget— I see and I remember—I do and I understand." The subject of the film is a series of experiments done by students in an English school.

"In a classroom," says the voice of the narrator, "we tend to think that if there's quiet, there's concentration, but this isn't true at all. . . . Language plays an essential part in mathematics. Children learn more from each other, working out problems, than they could ever do listening to a teacher." The teacher is too often like a sergeant major, the voice tells us, as the camera examines the contents of a lab-classroom; the more personal a teacher can get in his teaching, the more personal he can get with the child. "The whole of math teaching is in a mess because the syllabus hasn't changed in three hundred years," the voice says. "What we're looking for is a change in the whole approach, the whole attitude towards mathematics. . . ." Then the film proceeds to show a classful of unnaturally cooperative, but apparently happy English children measuring, weighing, guessing, working with spheres and scales, and inventing mathematical games in the schoolyard.

When the film is over, several teachers say that they would like to see it again. Alan demonstrates, in response to a teacher's question, a home-made trundle wheel for measuring long distances in yards, similar to one used in the film. Another teacher expresses doubt about the absence of a conventional authority figure in the filmed classroom. "*Blow* their minds as far as authority is concerned," Alan says. "I'm all for that." At the table where the first-grade teachers are sitting, there is a slightly nervous giggle.

Waring School, 18th and Green Streets, North Philadelphia

Joyce Warden, the pretty young learning center teacher, has been moved up from her apprentice's post to replace a departing colleague who still teaches in the school but is no longer officially connected with the network. She is among the network's more articulate theorists of change. While some learning center teachers prefer to wait—rather like merchandise that may hopefully attract a curious shopper—Joyce Warden is more inclined, in her own delicate way, to proselytize. This is due in part to the fact that the network has not caught on quite so readily at Waring as at some other schools, for a number of reasons. One is the fact that Waring is the home school for the 90 or so children who are bused daily to the Drexel School in South Philadelphia, where Marcia Kirby, Dominick Casara, and several other teachers are having certain problems in attaining a state of harmony and community. The vibrations from Drexel are not entirely good; several parents in this very poor black and Puerto Rican neighborhood have withdrawn their children from the program. The school is more uptight than it would ordinarily be where the learning center approach is concerned.

Technically, each learning center teacher, like auxiliary reading teachers, music teachers, physical education teachers, and others not assigned to an all-day classroom, is included in the category of "supportive services"—usually each child will visit the learning center for only a few hours each week. Alienation and isolation are endemic to the structure of the typical urban school, and Waring is no exception. In February 1969, however, the principal has initiated a faculty meeting for the specific purpose of presenting exactly what kinds of supportive services are available. The meeting has been a crucial moment for Joyce Warden.

"The program had had difficulties in previous years," Mrs. Warden says in recalling the meeting. "There were feuds about lining up—to me that's one of those petty classroom organization things I'm not interested in; if I were going to stir up a big fight at my school, that would be the *last* thing." At any rate, her purpose, during the five-minute period allotted to her at the meeting, was to establish a new climate and reputation for the program. "I had a copy of the Learning Center philosophy in front of me," she recalls. "It's an old statement, but it says that a learning center is a room equipped with certain things and explains why they're there. I said, 'This is the philosophy of the learning center, but the sad part of innovation is that there ought to be a lot more dialogue—I've had a delightful time down in the learning center, but I don't think any of you know it. No one has a corner on the right way to teach children; I'm filled with materials, equipment, and supplies—come down and see me.'" One kindergarten teacher asked what has become the most predictable question skeptics raise: Had the program been evaluated? Mrs. Warden answered that it had, that she hadn't read the evaluations, and that in her opinion the learning center couldn't be compared to a regular classroom at all. There were no more questions.

Though the school's principal complimented her on the talk, Mrs. Warden says, "I've had opposition from teachers—it's kind of like a prejudice, as if I were a black person, I suppose. Some teachers don't want to share the kids with me." On the other hand, some teachers have wanted to "come down" to the learning center (it is located in the cellar of the crowded building) and find out about it during their children's scheduled visits. Or, Mrs. Warden says, teachers will sometimes continue projects when kids "bring things up" to the classroom.

Vivien Wyatt, a first-grade teacher at Waring who appears to be in her mid-thirties but is actually fifty-one, was a learning center teacher for two years; in the fall of 1968 she decided the time had come for her to innovate on her own. "I left the learning center to be more free," she explains, with a smile at the irony. "In the learning center I could have each class once a week or a little more often than that. Even if I had them once a day I couldn't continue something with a child—I wanted to see the kid within the next hour or in the afternoon; I wanted to be there while he was waking up." Moreover, Mrs. Wyatt believes that she has more influence in the school as a regular teacher: "I'm not set above them; I'm not beneath them. Joyce doesn't have problems with this. It hurt me when teachers couldn't accept what I was doing even when I explained it over and over and over again. I wasn't inexperienced; I had fourteen years of Quaker preschool experience. But the other teachers saw it as a playroom. This way they're on a par. They come in and say 'Hey, look at what you're doing!' Joyce is better at what needs to be done than I am."

But Mrs. Wyatt has even more persuasive reasons for her move out of the official network. "Lore Rasmussen is a prima donna," she continues. "A very necessary prima donna. I'm fifty-one years old; I'm not Lore's little satellite. I don't want to be in the learning center where I'm expected to make a splash. I want to be in my own classroom and do my own quiet little innovating—and shut the door if I fail. While I was teaching in Friends schools, I became a Quaker. I like people to come in and watch and learn what they *can*. This is the Quaker way. We say if you don't want to copy it, we would like to be friends with you anyway."

By the winter of 1969, with its continual budget crisis and tighter finances imposed by cuts in federal funds, no innovative program in Philadelphia could be confident about its future. More important, "the system" had won the first round in the great battle for change—the clashes of 1967–68—so easily that innovation no longer seemed as much of a threat to the establishment as it had when Mark Shedd spoke all the frightening words Rick deLone had written for him upon his arrival in Philadelphia. The distinction between the old and new regimes had begun to blur; once again, everybody at 21st Street was the establishment. Things could never be the same, of course; quiet little power struggles within the top administration had replaced the big noisy ones of the confrontation days. And the Learning Centers Project, unwarlike as it was, had to be involved.

"My guess," observed Milton Goldberg, Lore Rasmussen's colleague of more peaceful days, "is that if the project were to go on *just* the way it is now, it would fizzle out." This guess demonstrated an instinct for the vicissitudes of power. The Learning Centers Project had to remain powerful or withdraw from the fray; for—as Vivien Wyatt, the refugee from battle at the Waring school, had observed—no matter how much the network was involved in the cause of individual freedom, ultimately, because it *was* a network, it had to continue along its course of gentle seduction.

"The crises of last year are over," Lore Rasmussen observed in February 1969, referring as much to the need of many network teachers for her personal support as to the political problems of individual schools. "The learning centers are running by themselves, and lots of principals are replicating them—in many schools we're becoming classroom models. We've had high priority of all the Title I projects. We have many supporters at 21st Street." Mrs. Rasmussen also had numerous ideas for expansion, mainly within schools whose principals wanted learning centers of their own.

Nonetheless, even for the Learning Centers Project, one of the great boasts of Philadelphia's innovators, the future was terribly uncertain. "All the people working with us are not enough to change the whole school system," Mrs. Rasmussen readily admitted. "The forces we're working against are societal forces."

But societal forces, a barrier to libertarian education on a wide scale, were not the immediate cause of uncertainty. The real problem was simply that nobody knew any longer who made the

big decisions at 21st Street. The Philadelphia public school system had scarcely begun to decentralize; a decision about the
future of the learning centers would have to come from the top—
and the top was shrouded in smoke. "I feel as if I've been building a mobile," Mrs. Rasmussen reflected. "But I don't know where
the hook on the ceiling is. You can build a mobile that goes on
and on in infinite space, downwards and outwards. But I don't
feel that sense of being related to a solid idea."

The time had come, it was clear, for somebody in power to go
to bat for the learning centers; and the crucial moment would
soon pass. It was possible that a decision at the top could expand
the network into something very like a model of the British infant
schools, which had not come to dominate English primary education, but which offered a solid, broad-based alternative to traditional institutions. It was possible that such an expanded network could in turn be a model for school systems across the
nation. But that such a move could actually succeed in a city at
war was most unlikely—if not downright miraculous.

There would always be resistance to the learning centers, even
if they were allowed to grow. There would always be teachers
who opposed them, in all sorts of subtle ways, because of the
freedom they allowed. Parents too, especially upward-striving
parents who saw "the system" as their salvation, could not be
counted on for their whole-hearted support. The results of
nationally standardized reading and math tests had shown again,
even in the fourth year of the reform regime, that Philadelphia's
school children were still far below the national averages. "I can't
guarantee that this will raise the Iowa test scores," observed
Lore Rasmussen at this crucial time. "In a learning center you
not only learn to read; you learn what you *want* to read." Until
some research-and-development genius could come up with an
appropriate evaluative "instrument," in short (considering the
growth of the "r and d" field, this would eventually happen),
the Learning Center philosophy had to be taken basically on
faith. Indeed, the early evaluations of the program done by the
Franklin Institute had singled out Lore Rasmussen's leadership
and the network teachers' messianic zeal as important factors in
the program's success.

It was not a time when real faith came easily to urban warriors, however. Perhaps faith would return to fashion, someday when the war was over. For the moment, most people, caught up in the great trap that history had set for them, would demand that steps toward freedom and equality be strictly measurable.

Snapshot: *At Lovie's*

I am visiting the classroom of Lovie Glenn, one of the Learning Center teachers at the Pastorius School, in Germantown. According to many people I've spoken to, Lovie is among the best teachers in the city. She is even the subject of a feature film prepared by a Boston educational consultant firm.

Lovie is a young black woman with a delicate, appealing smile and an air of unself-conscious wisdom; I have only been in the room for a few minutes, but I can see that she has established a relationship of supreme trust with her "special" class of first-graders—special because none of them has ever been to school before.

I have taken a seat near the group to watch them go through the roll by reading each other's names, but just before they begin, several children come to see who and what I am. Their eyes are wide open, and they're smiling. Suddenly I am startled to realize that, without the slightest fear, they are running their hands all over my face to see what my beard is all about. "Are you Santa Claus?" asks a girl. "No, I'm not Santa Claus," I answer. "His beard is usually white." The girl hesitates for an instant, but she trusts me too. "*Is* there a Santa Claus?"

It is clear to me by now that one of the main lessons of Lovie Glenn's classroom is honesty. "There *was* a Santa Claus a long time ago," I answer. "A real live Santa Claus. People loved him so much that when he died, he lived on in their memories, and they think of him as if he were still alive." She seems satisfied with the answer, and then turns to Lovie, who is seated on the floor surrounded by children.

A Poet Drops Out

PAUL FINEMAN (as I'll call him, for reasons to be explained) had been swept in by the new wave, but his was not a story of dramatic confrontations or showdowns. He was a gentle poet; he had no real taste for drama. He told his students on the first day of the seminar—it was supposed to be a course in the teaching of creative writing—that he would leave at the end of the year to found an "intentional community" on a farm somewhere; he didn't know where yet, he and his "lady" would just look around for a place. They had a group of friends who wanted to join them; they'd been planning it for more than a year. They would write poetry, weave, make pottery, and farm the land.

Not until long after he was gone did I learn that he'd stayed only as a favor to a friend at 21st Street—the curriculum specialist in affective development—and that he'd wanted to get away for more than a year. At first I romanticized him, saw him as an enemy of the system, wanting to remain within it, struggling bravely to teach *his* way, to let the students fly, against the impossible odds of the ancient machinery and the robot people. He was one of the few real poets I've known, but he would have been the last to foster any illusions about himself. His disgust with systems in general had been growing over a number of years; he didn't need experience in the Philadelphia schools to learn how awful they could be.

No, Paul Fineman must have been discouraged by other systems first—the systems of his own childhood and youth, the systems that, like all systems, inevitably work at inhibiting poetry —for poetry is one of their principal enemies. I know he felt this even though we never discussed it in any detail. We didn't need to—when I first talked with him in the administration building at 21st Street, he looked at me somewhat desperately and said, "I've got to get out of here." He searched my eyes to see if I understood, then glanced apprehensively at the walls of the hallway where we were standing, as if oppression lurked within the grain of the woodwork. That was about all we needed to say about systems.

But finally, as he had planned, he left Philadelphia. In the minds of his students he would linger as a fascinating memory, almost like a figure from a dream. He must have changed their lives in some way, he may even have begun to change the system—but who could define the change? We can all recognize a bad teacher; we can describe the stupidities and mock the mannerisms; we can deplore the waste of time when students are imprisoned in the classroom. Paul Fineman had a profound effect on his students, but his main contribution may have been nothing more—or less—than a capacity for magic.

I was in the office of Paul's friend at the Board of Education when I first saw him. Paul generally avoided 21st Street, but he had some business that had to be taken care of and, while there, dropped by to say hello. Norman and I stopped talking when he opened the door. He was wearing a dark, vested suit—he wore the same suit on almost every occasion that I saw him—and a messy-looking shirt and tie. His long, dark hair was halfway between outright hippie and merely fashionably straight—but, like his appearance in general, unkempt. Somehow the round rimless glasses didn't give the slightest air of affectation. He looked as if he might have been wearing them all his life.

It was impossible to tell how old he was. Sometimes I later observed, he seemed thirty-five or forty, but with eons of suffering behind the eyes; at other times he was almost a boy. His straight, rather aristocratic nose and full mustache were the only parts of his face that didn't change regularly. He could be strikingly handsome—as if the whole face fell into harmony with the nose. But then the face would go awry, and he would look like a tired old man. His body—he was of medium build and height—could be youthful and athletic or slack and lifeless. As I got to know him, I kept trying to figure out what he really looked like; but he never stayed the same long enough for me to know.

On this occasion he was only in the office for a minute or so, and he was obviously troubled. It seemed that there had been some confusion about whether whites would be allowed to take part in the proceedings at Resurrection City in Washington, later that month; word had gotten around that black leaders were against whites having anything to do with their cause. I gathered that both he and Norman were planning to be involved in the Washington demonstration in some way.

"Who was *that*?" I asked as soon as he had left the room.

"Oh, you ought to talk with him," Norman answered, then paused, seemingly at a loss for adequate praise. And finally: "He's a beautiful guy. A really beautiful guy."

By coincidence I met Paul in the hall outside Norman's office about ten minutes later, and we had our first conversation—the one in which he was in such a hurry to get out of the building. He did have time to mention, though, that he'd had to contend with all sorts of obstacles in his work and that he'd be leaving the system shortly. Nevertheless, I wanted to hear about what he'd been doing; I figured that the failures of the new regime could be as revealing as the successes. We agreed that I'd phone him in a week, then get together for a talk at his home.

"Fineman and Company"—the identification under the doorbell connoted dozens of bodies in an unconscious heap. I hadn't quite recovered from the immediate impression of general messiness ("I think people were offended by his *appearance*," one of his students later told me), and, for the moment, that was the main cue I was going by. It was reinforced by an inmate-ish girl in pajamas who appeared briefly at a downstairs door, then vanished when Paul called to me from the second floor landing. He was dressed in khaki shorts, sandals, and a blue denim work shirt. We shook hands heartily, like old friends.

The room was small and dark, sparsely furnished, with a bedroom to the rear and a narrow kitchen to the right—no bodies, just a couple of cats. With Bach organ music playing on the phonograph, it was a world of soft gray light and absolute peace. Paul gave me a glass of Greek wine, and I settled down on an old chair pillow on the floor. He sat on one of two sycamore stumps —exotic sculptures with whirling grain and speckled bark. I sipped the wine and looked around.

There were Japanese prints and fabrics woven by his lady on the walls, books on shelves, and odd, arresting found objects on tables. Windchimes hung from the kitchen ceiling, near the living room doorway. A silkscreen on the wall opposite caught my attention, and I went to examine it. Paul explained that a friend of his had done it as a poster for the Angry Arts week a year earlier. Alongside the stilted-looking lettering of the announcement, which dominated the poster, was one of Paul's poems. I read it with difficulty—it was about war—and grunted noncommittally. I hadn't been able to grasp all of it in the half-light, but I wasn't sure I liked what I'd seen.

Yet, the room established the palpable importance of poetry in the life of its owner. I began to see flashes of unexpected beauty in what had seemed at first a random and careless decor. The atmosphere was slowing me down; somehow my awareness of everything had become more intense.

While this was happening, over a course of minutes, Paul asked me about my book. I started to tell him from the beginning, but he interrupted me before I'd even got to what the book was about. Apparently I'd said enough to satisfy him. He was ready to tell me about himself. He was ready to talk.

His voice, like his appearance, shifted through a spectrum of moods as easily as sea reflecting sun. There was often a scratchy, reedy quality—an old hen's noises, softened by a lifetime of indignant surprise. At other times the voice was deep, rich, and virile. Or, without any warning, it would cease altogether. I could never get used to these choked pauses, during which his eyes seemed to fill with tears and the tension of the jaw suggested a monumental effort at control. Often I had the feeling that he was about to shatter, almost literally, into thousands of pieces, that he was holding himself together by sheer force of will. But he was capable of such compelling strength that I would then wonder how I had ever doubted it.

He talked, at any rate, with his perpetual sea change of voices, for two and a half hours, and I listened in a state of growing rapture. I had never heard anyone talk so beautifully. As I listened, I sensed that my responsiveness was encouraging him to attain even greater heights. My notebook lay on the table next to the bottle of wine, but I couldn't force myself to reach for it. I was afraid to break the mood. More than that, I felt that it would be a violation of something sacred to sit there taking notes. When we finally left the house together, I had to blink my eyes in order to readjust myself to the world outside.

Because of my reluctance to insist on the usual amenities of an interview, much of Paul's life, particularly the source of his poetry, remains a mystery to me. When I later asked him if he understood how he "got that way," he feigned ignorance. He was born in Newark, New Jersey, in 1932, he told me, the only child of a furniture salesman for Montgomery Ward. There were no writers in the family, no poets. His father was Jewish. And Paul had spent most of his youth in a small town in West Virginia. This alone gave me pause—a Jewish family on Main Street didn't fit any of my urban stereotypes.

The Finemans lived briefly in Philadelphia, though Paul always preferred West Virginia, and for a while he was an undergraduate at the University of Pennsylvania. But he didn't like Penn; he wanted to write poetry. Finally he got in touch with the leader of a small coterie of literary critics and poets who held forth at a Midwestern college and published an influential quarterly. His new mentor invited Paul to visit the college. There he audited courses and wrote poetry, then finally enrolled as a full-time student. He also began visiting Ezra Pound in the mental hospital outside Washington where Pound had been virtually a prisoner of the state for many years. But Paul became disenchanted with Pound; he was too cerebral, Paul said, and didn't really have a feeling for the rhythm of language.

After college, Paul joined the Mississippi freedom fighters. For more than a year, he traveled in the Deep South, working on voter registration drives and other civil rights campaigns. He'd seen a black child stoned by an angry mob as she tried to go to school. His own life had been threatened on several occasions. He'd met great people, he said, but an atmosphere of earthly hell prevailed.

Then he came back to Philadelphia, where for many years he wrote poetry (he had published a volume of poems, though I never saw it) and taught English as a substitute in the public school system. He subbed about three days a week and wrote the rest of the time, and it was in the Philadelphia schools that he began to develop his "course."

The main idea of the course, he told me, was that people cannot write until they can compose, that the real key to writing is the generation of ideas and stories—in short, creativity. This may seem obvious, but Paul's basic approach to generating stories was anything but simple; he believed that students first had to be free. Daydreaming was an important element in this freedom; echoes of Zen Buddhism pervaded his approach.

Fortunately, I don't need to rely on our conversations for a glimpse of what Paul did as a teacher. He was working on essentially the same things throughout his teaching career, first with the kids as a substitute (he insisted that subbing could be a profitable experience, both for teacher and kids, once the usual disciplinary hurdles were surmounted), then in the seminar for teachers in 1967–68. I talked with several of the seminar students, and I learned enough from my talks with them to put together a reasonably complete picture of what he'd done.

The seminar itself was almost an accident. In the spring of 1967, Paul had given up teaching and writing to work full-time, for more than a month, on Philadelphia's Angry Arts week. The main purpose of this project was to assemble a community of artists, writers, and poets whose collective solidarity, with a minimum of doctrine, would constitute an affirmation of creative life and a protest against the war. I later met a number of people who participated, and most agreed that the Angry Arts week was one of the best things that ever happened to the Philadelphia artistic community, and that the project should have continued indefinitely (though, like a good party, it died). It was through the Angry Arts week that Paul met Norman Newberg, who had recently become the affective-curriculum man for the Philadelphia public schools. Norm and his wife were well known around Philadelphia as a team for poetry readings.

Paul had gone to the central administration with a proposal for a staff development seminar several times in previous years, but he'd been discouraged. "We're paying committees $10,000 to write curriculum," one official told him. "We don't need this." He'd pretty much given up on the idea long ago. But Newberg said he ought to try again, that there was a new superintendent, there were good people around. Norm introduced him to Rick deLone, whom Paul liked immediately when he went for an interview at 21st Street. They talked for half an hour; deLone said "Let's try it," and one of the most unlikely adventures in institutional education was on its way.

Paul insisted on "completely ordinary" people, not specially chosen turned-on types; he wanted young, old, black, white, conservative, permissive. He wanted to see if his ideas could work in the totally real world—he already knew that they worked in the world of the Angry Arts commune. Thus, Paul's students came to him almost at random. Everyone who answered the standard form letter, circulated among fifth- and sixth-grade teachers in District 2, was admitted. At the beginning, there were twenty-five enrollees.

But the real world took its toll even before the seminar's first meeting. Unable to help all his people at once, deLone lost track of Paul Fineman and assumed that things were going according to plan. They weren't. Exactly why they weren't was one of those bureaucratic mysteries, but whatever the reasons, the wheels of 21st Street were grinding exceedingly slow. For one thing, the seminar was never formally approved. Paul's students had to make time for the seminar during the school day; because of this, many of them dropped out before they even knew what the seminar was about. The others managed somehow to slip away from school for a couple of hours; one told me that she sneaked a parent from the neighborhood into her classes to take over while she was gone.

In addition to this crippling obstacle, the seminar was plagued throughout the year by inefficient management at 21st Street. Important materials were delivered, after long delays, in the wrong sequence, thus obscuring the design of the course. But everybody at 21st Street was "cooperating"; they all thought Paul was tremendously talented. It was just that nobody really helped him. Proposals and requests seemed suspended in time and space; urgent phone calls fell into a void. And there were never any villains or saboteurs—just a lot of nice, smiling people who had so many other things to look after.

I think that most of us who could accept Paul at all tended to think of him as some kind of saint. But this certainly wasn't his own view of himself. Although his students couldn't remember any instance of his criticizing the recalcitrant administration when I asked if he had, I know that he often talked about the administration as if he were involved in guerrilla warfare. "We have to think of ourselves as burglars chuckling in the cellar of 21st Street," he told his students when I visited his seminar one day. "We're trying to rob them of everything they think is important. We're cracking the safe, breaking down the walls, and going off into the night." If Paul Fineman was a saint, he wasn't the waxy, hairless type.

But at least his enemies had been kept at a distance, and on a Wednesday afternoon in October, in a classroom of an elementary school in South Philadelphia, Paul met his student teachers for the first time. He began the class by writing on the board part of a quotation from one of Emily Dickinson's letters: "Nature is a haunted house; art is . . ." Anyone who could finish the sentence, he told the class, ought to leave—that person didn't need to take the course. The complete quotation (which sounded like the key to all human understanding when he intoned it to me): "Nature is a haunted house; art is a house . . . that wants to be haunted."

"He made us relax," one of his students said, during a group discussion that I taped in the spring of 1968. "And that's one of the first steps to creativity, being relaxed. We went through a series of . . . things. We got up and moved around and closed our eyes and rubbed our arms and hands."

"But first," said another, "we had the *wu wei*. [The term refers to a Zen concept meaning, roughly, "no thought."] We pulled down the shades and closed our eyes. Clear your mind of everything, nothing on your mind at all. And the children reacted very

well. My children just became *limp*." (The modus operandi of
the seminar, in short, was for Paul to tell the teachers what to do,
then for the teachers to repeat the lesson with their own fifth-
and sixth-grade classes.)

"I watched my partner try *wu wei* in class," one member of a
teaching team said, "without much success. Then Fineman came
in a couple of weeks later and also tried it. Fineman had no connection with the class whatsoever; it was the first time the children had seen him—yet he had no problem at all with *wu wei*.
I sat there on the radiator looking at him and found myself
becoming as involved as the kids were. Having to put your head
down on the desk, with the lights out and the shades down—
going into yourself and coming back out again. It was . . . almost
hypnotic, and I think it was due to a large extent to the involvement that Fineman had with his own thing, *wu wei*, and the
teacher has to feel this depth of involvement himself."

"After the relaxation," one teacher continued, "came the concentration. He gave us exercises in watching the candle—to focus
our concentration after we'd relaxed. And we went on from
there."

"The idea," elaborated another, "was to make the candle in
your brain as real as the candle out there and then to blow out
the candle in your brain so that your brain would be empty and
receptive to vibrations from the universe."

"Did you do that, John?" asked one teacher rather skeptically.
"Could you see the candle? I couldn't see it."

"*I* could," offered an elderly woman. "Perhaps I'm more gul-
lible, but I did, and . . . I don't know whether the children were
just teasing me or not. . . ."

The "candle" and other, similarly mystical elements of the
course seem to have constituted the real watershed of attitudes
among Paul's students. I later heard, for example, that after Paul
had explained the candle, one student leaped up and shouted,
"I can't do that! I can't have my kids file into class in a line, sit
quietly at their desks, close their eyes, and blow their minds!"

My own prejudice, which may have elicited some of these
responses during the discussion, was that the course was so
uniquely Paul's, so much the product of everything he was, that

few students, if any, could imitate him with even remote accuracy. But it was equally clear that Paul had provided his students with some clever techniques which they could use without the addition of any special magic.

"I myself," one of the teachers said, "was not equipped with the proper techniques to bring out my students' creative ability. Mr. Fineman gave me techniques that brought out things that I had no idea the children knew . . . and it really shocked me. It wasn't that it wasn't in them; I just didn't have the techniques to get it out of them."

One of these techniques was the presentation of three unrelated pictures from which the kids were asked to form a complete story. "Heretofore," the teacher continued, "I had been giving children isolated pictures and they would write a story based on one of them. But here you had the three, and they seemed to have absolutely no connection with each other, and the way the children could create stories from the three pictures that were altogether different from each other—there was no copying of ideas. . . ."

"I was interested in the phrases he gave us," said another. "We had 'an airplane on fire' and 'a girl laughing' and 'wet candy.' These three phrases aren't related at all, and yet the children made up very interesting stories from them."

But even the "techniques" of the course were a precise reflection of Paul's personality, not just a series of gimmicks. He made up booklets of stories—"hero tales," fables, and myths—that, like everything else he did, aimed at the development of a primitive, universal sensibility and a capacity for wonder. One regular class activity was the creation of "code stories"—actual drawings which represented the principal elements of a myth or tale. Kids were encouraged to talk their own stories into tape recorders without any thought of writing them down. And technical details were the hobgoblin of little-minded teachers; Paul insisted that his students refrain from citicizing the kids' work, even from praising it—nothing the kids created, he said, was *wrong*. "I'm an old-fashioned teacher," said one of the group, "and even to refrain from smiling or nodding my head or making some gesture that the story was outstanding was a little difficult. But I found it worked, because children who felt insecure and felt that their writing wasn't very good lost that after a while. And I began to get good things from them."

"I did correct them," said another. "I think you have to establish some guidelines. Even the sentence. I wanted them to do *something* with that sentence, begin it with a capital letter. So I wasn't too flexible about some things."

"I've been talking as if my children were behaving so beautifully that they weren't being taught," continued the first, with an undertone of guilt. "In between the creative writing classes I taught grammar. Punctuation, paragraphs—we used Roberts's *Linguistics*."

Clearly the seminar students I spoke with had not rushed to embrace the kind of freedom that Paul represented. Although they were unanimous in their praise of him, most of them preserved a modicum of caution. Paul's achievement, at best, was a strong beginning. He had the ability to lead people into awareness, and he had opened a door to a vastly different world.

"I don't think anyone could give the feeling that we received from Mr. Fineman," one of his students commented toward the end of our conversation, after remarking that there ought to be more courses in creative writing. "Mr. Fineman has something within him that we *felt* when we followed through with the course. He really has something to offer, not just a technique of teaching writing."

"Mr. Fineman was a philosopher," said another. "Way down deep. Some of our sessions would leave the humdrum of classroom work and that sort of thing, and he would philosophize on different things and it was just like . . . just sitting under a very very talented, *learned* person. And because of this ability and the knowledge that came through when he gave us these dissertations, it made me feel very inadequate. It was his knowledge and his philosophy of life that gave him such depth, that I know *I* don't have and I wouldn't dare try to follow."

Yet I believe that they wanted very much to follow, to try. This was certainly true on the one occasion when I saw them together. I'd met Paul after the official conclusion of the course, but he invited me to join the group for their final meeting—a sort of farewell party. There were ten teachers in the room that day (attrition had reduced the original number of enrollees to twelve regulars). Paul's lady—a warm-looking, dark-haired girl —and I were the only guests. One of the teachers had baked a cake; somebody else had brought a gallon of wine—sneaked it into the building in a brown paper bag. We sat there in a semi-circle, eating cake and sipping wine, feeling awkward, not knowing what to say. We chatted idly, but it was almost enough just to be there together sipping wine in a public school classroom. Paul read several of his poems; we greeted them with a profound, puzzled silence. But finally, the meeting had to end. "I wish you didn't have to go," one of the teachers almost wept. "I feel so *inadequate*. I'll never be able to do what you do." Paul had one of his choking pauses, and his eyes seemed to fill with tears. "I'm very *hurt*," he whispered. "You have to be able to carry on yourselves."

I'd gotten to know Paul rather quickly, but that final seminar was only our third meeting. I needed to see him, to talk with him, again. I still had questions—particularly about what I still, in my ignorance, believed to be his year-long battle with the system. But there were other, more subtle questions. Basically, I was skeptical about him; he seemed too good to be human, and I wanted to get to the mystery of him, pigeonhole him in my well-ordered view of the world, figure him out—not so much for my book as for myself.

One of the teachers in the seminar, a young man who was among Paul's greatest admirers, owned a farm in northeast Pennsylvania, near Scranton, and lent it to Paul and his lady for the first half of the summer. They had departed for the farm early in June, returning only occasionally to Philadelphia. Their plan was to look for a farm of their own, then to settle there with the friends who would form their intentional community. They had no telephone, but I managed to reach Paul one day when he was in Philadelphia and invite myself up for a weekend. Paul consented to the invitation gladly, and his lady drew me an elaborate map showing the way. She included a picture of a house, two whimsical people, and two cats.

To reach the farm, I drove through ancient Appalachian hills; the Susquehanna wound through the hills in broad rushes, and everything was a rich green. It was right; it was where Paul belonged—away from the city, away from power struggles, systems, death forces, enemies. I told him so when we had a chance to talk, and he said, "I was never there. I've been here all the time."

I had brought my tape recorder, hoping that somehow a beautiful conversation would happen again and I would be ready to get every word of it. But, as I told Paul when we left, I never seriously considered using it. Somehow he'd managed to convey, without ever saying it, that he was willing to let me write about him, but only up to a point—that there was a certain invisible threshold past which we would cease being friends and would be, instead, mere users of each other. This excessive delicacy annoyed me somewhat, I must admit, even though I thought I ought to respect it.

Indeed, it was the delicate side of Paul's nature that I saw most that weekend. Trekking among the hills, we picked wild flowers together; we examined the intricacies of stones by the roadside; we discussed the miraculous life cycles of various plants and animals. We so immersed ourselves in the tiny wonders of Nature that finally I had to take a long walk up a hillside to get away from it all.

Before I left, though, I did have a chance to talk with Paul and to ask him what I hoped were penetrating questions about his past. By that time I'd conjured up a fantasy of a sickly little boy, a social outcast, a sissy, always reading and chasing butterflies while the other kids played ball. No wonder he hadn't been able to "make it" in "the system"! And finally, after fumbling for a way of asking that wouldn't be too embarrassing, I managed to get him to talk about it. "I was a star athlete in high school," he said. "Played football, baseball, and basketball." He laughed with easy confidence. "You're probably looking at the only poet who ever tried out for the Pittsburgh Pirates."

He settled finally in West Virginia—without his lady, however. They separated after a sudden, violent argument the Sunday of that weekend when I last saw him. The friends who witnessed the breakup tell me that it had something to do with trust—but

I won't try to fathom it. He writes beautiful letter-poems from West Virginia; I'd like to include one here, but I can't, of course. Besides, there is probably no better way to conclude my reminiscence than to offer something that one of his students wrote. It tells a lot about him, because of all the kids' writing he had available that afternoon of our first long conversation, he chose to read this one. He read it magnificently; he emphasized each syllable, lingered on the pauses, sounded the deep notes of sadness and the high tunes of laughter. He read all the "mistakes" exactly as they were written. It was as if he and the fifth-grade girl named Alicia had written it together; it seemed that her voice was part of his as he read it:

BENTY

Benty was a big boy. He is 15 years of age. He was a verry intelligent boy. Benty was eager to learn. He is a lonesome fellow. He loves to talk very much. Benty would always walk around stalking. He was a very bad fellow. Benty was afraid of everything.

Benty doesn't have a family. He is a orphan. His mother died just a few days after he was born. His father died in a plane chrash. Benty lives in a little cave not far from the jungle. Benty's homesick. He doesn't have any food in the little cave anywhere. How can Benty stand it, living without anyfood. Benty doesn't know. If only he had a mother and a father to care for him.

One day Benty was very mad so he decided to go for a walk. Benty was mad at his ownself. Benty keep on walking until he came to the jungle. He got lost, Benty was afaird. Benty layed down beside the tree. He was hungry, but there wasn't anyfood around anywhere. Benty layed down, it was dark out here in the jungle.

The next morning when Benty woke up he couldn't understand where he was. He was very afraid now. Benty looked up high in the sky. On the very top branch of the tree was some fruit. It looked very delicious to him. How could Benty get up to the top of the branch, he really didn't know. Benty wished there was a ladder somewhere.

Out in the jungle Benty saw a native who said, "How do you do, my friend."

Benty was afaird, then he came to himself that someone was talking to him. "It is my pleasure to meet you! I am very glad to make your acquaintance."

"It is my pleasure to have you come to this jungle" said the native.

"What is you name?" said Benty.

"Oh, my name is Mr. Blackson," said the native. "We have beautiful women in the jungle here," said Mr. Blackson.

"Oh may I go to see them," said Benty.

"Why yes you may go," said Mr. Blackson.

"Oh boy!" said Benty.

When Benty got to the place where these girls were he was very glad to see the girls. Benty sat down to think it over, about the girls. He was thinking over going away to hide somewhere. At first Benty was thinking over, going away and getting married. But he didn't think it would work out so good. So he just keep on thinking it over wheather he was going to get married or not.

While Benty was thinking this over he saw two girls coming toward him. He thought they were very beautiful. He couldn't decide wheather he should say anything or not. Then one girl skope up.

"What is your name, my name is Marshall," she said. "I hope you like my name, I know you have a beautiful name."

"Oh yes I do like your name it is a beautiful name, my name is Benty," he said.

Then the other girl said, "My name is Reathell. We girls live here in the jungle, we hope you will come live with us."

"Oh I will," said Benty. So Benty, Reathell and Marshall lived happily all their lives.

Paul Fineman:
New Vision

PAUL FINEMAN left Philadelphia early in the summer of 1968, and the last time I saw him was when I visited his farm near Scranton. But we had become friends, I thought. Moreover, he knew that eventually I would write a chapter about his work in the school system. We carried on a heavy correspondence as he quested slowly southward, making occasional stops of a week or two when he came across a prospective farm or community somewhere along the way.

It was an eloquent correspondence—the product of two professional verbalizers delighting in what they could do with words and having no reservations about showing off. My letters, usually two or more pages of solid type, generally dealt with Philadelphia and my book, but I never failed to let Paul know how much his friendship and his whole way of life were tugging at me. I hardly questioned my belief that he had found a kind of rare inner peace that I ought to want and would want if I could only rid myself of all my competitive hangups and latent aggression. Perhaps, I told him, I would visit the community someday and surrender myself to it, chuck the rat-race. Trying to be as honest with him as he had been with me, I never failed to remind him of my doubts: I felt that in his wisdom he had gone far beyond me, that I ought to want to follow and would be a better person if I could, but that obviously I was far from ready.

His letters reflected what I assumed to be the very kind of

half-crazed inspiration—the poetic genius—that I found so intimidating. Written on lined yellow paper in an agonized scrawl, marred by a dark frenzy of crossings-out, they usually talked about the purity of Nature, the quest for peace, and his plans for the community. Occasionally, they would move spontaneously into free verse.

The only intrusion of hard reality on our poetry-fest was a series of brief notes I received late in the fall, in which Paul said that he was in desperate need of money—could I inquire at 21st Street about the possibility of a consultant job which would permit him to remain in West Virginia? Eventually, in fact, Rick deLone and some of his network people did manage to get Paul back into the school system's employ.

But our correspondence began to lag. I finished the chapter in October, stuck it away in a drawer (for "seasoning," I told myself), and tried not to think about it. For some reason that I wasn't fully aware of, I didn't want Paul to see it. In addition, I always had some hollow excuse for not visiting him in West Virginia—without knowing why, I didn't really want to go. A couple of times Paul even made it to Philadelphia for brief visits, but, for no very good reason, I missed him. Finally, in January, still unaware of why I felt so uncomfortable about our friendship and the chapter, but assuming that it was simply my inability to be as transcendental as I wanted to be, I reread what I'd written for what seemed the fiftieth time, typed it up neat, and sent it off.

I was in Philadelphia on a Monday when the vibrations reached me. A friend with whom I was in close touch mentioned to me that Norm Newberg had phoned her that day with an urgent message for me from Paul Fineman. I was to phone Paul immediately. I could almost hear his voice shaking in the background as she told me about it. My first thought was that something horrible had happened to him and that he needed my help because he had no one to turn to. It must be extremely serious, I thought, for him to call me this way. And I realized, with a twinge of guilt, that Paul must feel much closer to me than I to him—he was definitely not one of the people I would have called if I'd been in trouble.

Checking first with Newberg, I discovered to my surprise that Paul's urgent business was not some hypothetical peril, but the

chapter, which he'd received that morning. Newberg didn't know
the details, just that Paul was upset. But he took the opportunity
to ask me, with what sounded like profound suspicion, when he
was going to see what I'd written about *him*. The implication was
that if I had misrepresented the work of a single idealistic poet,
God only knew how I would mess up the affective curriculum
project. Delayed by an interview that afternoon, but scarcely
eager to talk with Paul anyway, I finally put through a call to
West Virginia at about eight o'clock that evening.

The gist of the conversation was that Paul found the chapter a
complete distortion of himself and his course, that it was "loaded
with factual errors," that it included information that would hurt
a number of his friends and possibly get him into trouble with
some business associates, and that he wanted all mention of him
removed from the book. He and the other members of the community had read the chapter aloud and discussed it in detail;
they were all profoundly disturbed. The reason he'd called, in
fact, was that they wanted me to come to West Virginia immediately to discuss it with them. For most of the conversation my
principal feeling was that I had betrayed a treasured friend and
that I was an incompetent journalist.

But finally, toward the end of our talk, I began to recover from
the self-righteous battering I was getting. I could understand his
being sensitive to certain things in the chapter, I said—I had
emphasized some of my doubts about him, after all, so that the
chapter wouldn't give an impression of blind adulation. But he
ought to try to see it from my point of view. I had put a great
deal of thought and emotion into that chapter. I had not just
tossed it off; nor had I in any way meant to insult him. The
chapter was intended as a tribute, and I had tried to make the
point that I considered him much closer to self-fulfillment and
true freedom than myself.

I had tried to make him into some kind of *saint*, he told me.
I'd completely misunderstood him. And furthermore, he'd expected the chapter to be principally about his course, not himself.

He may have thought *he'd* been misunderstood, I said, shouting, by now, into the telephone; but I, as a writer—and he certainly ought to understand *that* part of my reaction—deeply
resented his lack of appreciation for my work. I would have to

think about what he'd said—I hadn't intended to hurt his friends at 21st Street, and I would make some changes. But I'd be very reluctant to withdraw the chapter completely.

Before the end of the conversation I had already made up my mind. I would change his name, alter certain details of his life, and protect his friends—but otherwise keep the chapter in the book almost exactly as I'd written it. Gradually, however—as I turned the conversation over in my mind, as I discussed the episode with other people who knew him—I came to realize that the chapter was not quite as valid as I had originally thought. To some extent, in fact, the chapter was a lie, just as our supremely trusting friendship and a good deal of Paul's teaching had been a lie. The exact nature of this lie had profound implications for education, and my experience with Paul Fineman could not be considered accurately rendered unless I included this whole new perspective.

What were the lies we told and, with so much intensity, allowed to flourish for so many months?

My own lie, I could now see with perfect clarity, was refusing to admit that I never really believed in Paul Fineman's skillfully calculated facade. I must have known from the beginning that he was not the open, trusting friend of all that he wanted me to think he was, but I could not admit this either to him or to myself. And despite evidence to the contrary, I let myself believe that he was a great teacher, when in fact he was nothing more than a great *talker*.

In hypnotizing his students—briefly he had hypnotized me too; I was as susceptible to words as any of them, perhaps more so than most—he did the very opposite of great teaching, though far too many teachers would consider him ideal. Hypnosis—the word that came up so frequently when people talked about Paul's effect on them—was simply a gentle form of intellectual oppression. When a teacher "hypnotizes," he usurps his students' minds. By compelling them, through his personal magnetism or charisma to fasten their attention on *him*, he deprives them of the opportunity to think and question. Because Paul Fineman was eloquent and because he knew so much, few of his students were strong enough or critical enough to resist; many positively reveled in their submission to his influence. There were moments, I am sure, when Paul was responsible for the awakening of awareness and intelligence that great teaching inspires. But the feelings of inadequacy he created in so many of his students— including me, for a while—probably balanced the good he had done.

I was as angry with Paul, after the telephone call, for having told his lie as I was with myself for having told mine. Eventually, though, I began to understand the kind of need that motivated him—it was a need for adulation, a need to protect himself from real involvement, a need that showed itself from the beginning in subtle, nonverbal ways, so that I felt always warned not to ask questions, but to listen, just listen. . . . There was considerably less self-awareness in his lie, I guessed, than in mine. If he had not hated the chapter so—it forced him to look at the reality behind what he seemed to be—I might have felt compassion for him.

I would probably never have been attracted to the great teaching of Paul Fineman, of course, had I not at one time considered such teaching the perfect model for my own. In spite of himself, he had helped me to learn.

Snapshot: *Discipline*

Among the most "radical" structural innovations in the Philadelphia schools were the various tutoring programs in which older kids worked with younger ones, usually in the basic skills that they themselves were only beginning to master. This kind of tutoring had several advantages: It broke up large classes into small groups; it removed any threat the teacher might present in giving or withholding approval; both tutor and student learned in the process. But in essence, it was merely a return to the practices of the one-room schoolhouse, and the reason for doing it was similar—there were not enough adult teachers to reach every student individually.

A reading teacher at an elementary school in Germantown tried this approach with fifth-graders as tutors and third-graders as tutorees, and the following exchange of correspondence, from two boys who spent most of their time together fighting, was one result of her efforts.

Dear Mark, I like you to but if you be bad I get mean went *people* get bad I bet them up and try to kill them I am sorry Mark please be good for me before you said you will be good but you was bad I told your mother on the letter but you did not bring it back if you like me tell me I will tell you to.

Your friend Robert

To Robert
I will be good for you.
I like you very much.
You are very good to me.
You are good and very kind.
Your are smartey.

love Mark

The Affective Curriculum:
Programmed Sensitivity

WHEN PHILADELPHIA HIGH SCHOOL TEACHERS talked about how they had become involved in the affective curriculum, they usually referred to a feeling of dissatisfaction with what they had been doing in their classrooms before. The traditional curriculum, they said, had begun to be as stultifying—and "irrelevant"—to them as it was to their students. What was the point of teaching rules of grammar or dates of ancient wars, anyway? How could isolated bits of information, however orderly in their presentation, help people to cope with a world going mad? Most of the affective curriculum teachers had had enough of the system and its values; they were ready for new answers. And they were not waiting for those answers to come from on high—with few exceptions, they were rebels and innovators. But the reform era in Philadelphia was a time of unusual alliances; people at the top levels of the school system were also looking for alternatives.

The affective curriculum developed so gradually, so logically, so organically that there really was no clear beginning, middle, or end to its growth. The very nature of this curriculum made it a high-risk program that had to be taken, like the equally radical Learning Centers Project, largely on faith. Ultimately, of course, it would pass through some process of evaluation; but the success or failure of an affective curriculum, dealing principally with emotions and values, would always be difficult to measure. Even the initiated sometimes had trouble understanding what it was all about. It was, at any rate, the very antithesis of the neat packages that curriculum offices usually prepare; more than anything else, it resembled a religious movement.

If there were rivalries for leadership within the cult, they were obscured by general unanimity and good will. For a long time, however, the shadow cast by John C. ("Terry") Borton seemed a bit larger than anyone else's. Borton was the movement's prime mover and theorist; even after he left Philadelphia in the fall of 1967, he continued to exert a strong influence.

On the surface, Terry Borton's story was not much different from that of any middle-class liberal who had reached young adulthood in the 1960's. Born in Washington, D.C., and raised in Virginia, Borton had gone to public schools, majored in English at Amherst, and, after graduation, continued work in English at Berkeley. There he quickly became involved in civil rights activities, organizing fund-raising drives for freedom rides and a tutorial project. In 1963 he joined Berkeley's graduate internship teaching program and began his teaching career at Richmond High School, a relatively poor school in a nearby industrial city. Within a year, at the age of twenty-six, Borton became cochairman of Richmond's English department—the result, he explains, of a "coup." And at about this time he published his first article— on "teaching the culturally deprived"—in the education supplement of the *Saturday Review*. This was the end of Borton's nice-liberal-boy-next-door phase; a man of tremendous ambition and drive, Borton was going places.

The particular place Borton went to in the summer of 1964 happened to be Philadelphia. At first his purpose was to take graduate courses at Temple University, but he soon became friendly with Alex MacColl, then the assistant headmaster of Philadelphia's Friends Select School, and began dropping in for sessions of a drama workshop run by a young teacher who had been hired by the Friends Neighborhood Guild—the social service arm of Philadelphia's Quakers—of which MacColl later became director. Borton had been planning to write articles about experimental projects to begin with, but he found the workshop particularly exciting. "Ghetto kids were putting on productions of Shakespeare and using the text," he recalls. "Here were kids who could handle anything the world had to offer." Borton stopped attending classes at Temple and spent the rest of the summer watching and participating in the program. By the end of the summer he and MacColl had developed a proposal for a new workshop, to be held the following summer at Friends Select, in which the main purpose would be to "find ways to bring people into communication and to make a desegregated school truly integrated"—a continuation of what Borton had been doing in California.

Friends Summer Workshop
Friends Select School—Summer 1965

My title in the program was assistant director. Mainly I was assistant *to* the director, Terry's assistant. . . . Terry planned the whole thing, wrote the syllabus, and Alex did a lot of the work of recruitment, lining up of staff, and so on. Terry had one person, Ann Hornbecker, to do the drama. Alex got Paul Keene to do the art section; Terry was going to do the literature, and then Alex recruited the assistants for each of the three people, and I was Terry's assistant. . . .

I helped with the recruiting in the sense that everybody who came to the workshop came to Friends Select on a weekend and talked to one or two of us for evaluation. We were very conscious that we get a wide distribution in terms of economic, racial, and religious background, and we got a fantastic mix. . . .

The main thing we wanted to do at the beginning was get the kids out into the city doing things. The very first session the kids ever had we divided them up and told them to go out into the city and see what was going on around it. We'd shown them some films that had been done at the Annenberg School [of Communications] that dealt with Philadelphia. We hoped it would give them some different perspectives on the city; and we'd collected a sort of collage of different people's viewpoints of Philadelphia. Then we said Well, what do you think Philadelphia is? Take the afternoon off, go off in pairs, and find out. Take some wall rubbings if you want, talk to people, travel someplace. We'd invested about twenty-five dollars in bus tokens, and as long as the kids were using them for workshop purposes they could go anywhere they wanted. . . .

The kids did some pretty amazing things. There's a compass right in the center of City Hall, which is a walkway—you can walk through the building—and a bunch of kids, about five of them, sat down on the compass, facing out, looking up, and whenever anybody would stop they'd say What do you think Philadelphia is? This was a mind-blowing experience for us, because we didn't expect it from these kids. Some kids got a rubbing from the second floor exterior wall of the Free Library. . . .

The focal point for the entire summer was really the drama— partly because Ann was really good at it. . . . By the end of the six weeks kids were beginning to . . . well, for some of the kids it was very similar to a religious experience in the sense that you come up to something which is just so full of mystery that you find it very difficult to express it to anybody else. We found that kids were acting out in this improvisational theater some of their own deep-seated things. . . .

One time, for instance, this one particular exercise was to teach somebody to do something, but without using any particular language, using gobbledygook, nonsense syllables. People would pair up and do this for the rest, always very conscious of the audience— the audience was always a part of what was going on. One kid got up—this was in the literature room and there was a photograph of James Joyce, I think it was, on the wall—and this guy taught this girl who happened to be Jewish to salute it with a Nazi salute. And it was very strange because the girl just got completely tight—all through gobbledygook, he told her how to do it, shouted at her, held her arm up, started pushing her around—and some of the kids who were watching got very uptight. She wasn't cooperating with the situation and this started up a whole chain of events.

Part of the whole context of the workshop was that one of the groups had not been functioning as well as the others and everybody knew it and it was a source of concern to everybody, and upstairs in the art room these kids got together—they were the "bad" group and they were jealous of the "good" group—and decided they would come down and disrupt the good group. They came down and they marched into this group where the gobbledygook thing was going on; they thought that just by marching in, they would show the good group that they couldn't function well all the time either. And in this confrontation situation a fight broke out.

It gives you an idea of how wrapped up in their roles the kids could get. . . .

. . . Literature was a big bull session, but Terry was always doing things to confuse the kids, to pull them, to draw them out, to question some of the assumptions they made about things. For instance, one time, at the beginning of the second week perhaps, they walked into the literature room and the chairs were in a circle as they always had been but this time the chairs were facing out, quite clearly by arrangement. The students came in—this was before they'd really caught on; they didn't really know each other that well anyway—and they sat in those chairs and they didn't say anything, waiting for Terry to show up. The time came and Terry didn't show up and they remained silent and didn't do anything; they sat in the chairs facing out. Then Terry came storming into the room, pissed as hell, and said What the dickens do you have these chairs like this for? Why don't you turn around and talk to each other? What are you—rocks? stones? He said Keep them that way, and then he gave everybody numbers. . . .

A lot of this was really shaking up the kids psychologically. In our desire to somehow create an involvement, a central core, . . . to connect all this fantastically different experience, we had to develop a curriculum that was not the sort of school curriculum you'd normally get. And what we came upon was a thing that first of all nobody had any background in—this drama thing, the improvisations. Nobody was quite prepared for the way Terry did his literature thing. The art was the only thing that the kids could really touch base on—it was very high quality, but it was straightforward.

Obviously there was no generalized reaction—it varied from kid to kid. There were a couple of kids that we just missed completely. . . . You never really know; I know this from just working with people on a two-hour basis. Years later I'll meet someone who will tell me that because I turned him on to social concerns he got beaten up by the cops in Chicago—I turned on one of the big Progressive Labor militants. . . .

I know the program was a jolt for a lot of the kids. Whenever the kids come back, they talk about the program, they talk about the kids there, they talk about how college is just a bunch of shit and they know it. . . . I met one guy who comes from an orthodox Jewish family, a very close family, his father's been dead for a long time, he's now a freshman at the University of Chicago, he's just turned eighteen. When I saw him—I saw him just before Christmas, in mid-December—he told me he's now wrestling with the problem of whether he should register for the draft, which is a hell of a thing for a kid from an orthodox Jewish family—his mother has been helping to sell bonds for Israel and so on. I hadn't seen him for a while, but where we met was out in Lewisburg, Pennsylvania, where there's a prison where a lot of c.o.'s are being kept right now. A bunch of us had gone out there to visit them, and this guy showed up and I said What are you doing out here? I never expected to see you in something like this. And he said Well, I'd heard about it, and I'm on your mailing list; I heard about it and I wanted to come out. I don't know why. There's nothing in my background, there's nothing I've ever learned that should make me want to do it, but there's something chewing at me, like I shouldn't register for that draft. . . .

I said What is it? He says I don't know, but every time I think
about it I come right back to that workshop.
—Excerpts from taped interview with Bob Eaton,
staff member of Friends Summer Workshop,
who later became a full-time worker
for the Quaker antiwar movement
and was skipper of the ketch that sailed
to Vietnam on a mission of peace in 1967

Terry Borton had a strong sense of theatricality; he was one of
those teachers who can mesmerize a class with a story, and he
conveyed the impression that he saw more in everything than
most people. Yet, in contrast to his dedication to honesty and
openness, he had an air of subtle aloofness that made him even
more intriguing. Perhaps the strongest part of Borton's appeal,
however, was his involvement in a perpetual, enigmatic, almost
self-consuming quest. For several years the developing affective
curriculum mirrored this quest, and, as with all quests, the road
was not always smooth.

"I never felt that Terry could do for himself," observes Alex
MacColl, Borton's friend and colleague of many years, "what he
wanted to do for other people, or let other people do to him. I
never saw Terry in a situation where he was involved in a process
that would be self-revealing. Terry's either removed from the
situation or he's in control of it." But MacColl was fascinated by
Borton in spite of these reservations. Borton had a tendency,
MacColl says, to "grab ideas, throw them into the hopper, and
run off with them—you could see Terry's ideas constantly bombarded with new ideas. He nearly drove people crazy at Penn
Charter [Penn Charter School, where Borton spent his third
summer in Philadelphia] with changing ideas. *My* most significant contribution to the program is that I was a constant critic."

Borton was largely responsible, at any rate, for the constantly
shifting and evolving nature of the program. A basic commitment
to humanism, self-knowledge, and honest communication was
the foundation of his thinking, but in the growing turmoil en-
gendered by America's social conflicts, a commitment to humanistic values was not enough. Humanism had become an
almost fashionable attitude by the 1960's; one had to have a
specific program to survive the competition. Never intending to
lead a movement entirely on his own, Borton welcomed real

dialogue, even to the extent of sending out prepublication copies of his articles so that he could consider the opinions of his friends before revising them. He often seemed to lean over backwards, in fact, in order to remain open-minded.

Norman Newberg, who became Borton's principal collaborator within the Philadelphia public school system, had managed to surmount the usual hurdles that American society places in the path of the creative, particularly when they become a part of its educational institutions, and in the summer of 1965, drawn through various acquaintances in the Philadelphia artistic community, Newberg received an invitation to join Terry Borton in his experiments at the Friends Summer Workshop. Newberg and Borton had so much in common that a long-term partnership was an almost inevitable consequence of their meeting. Like most of their colleagues-in-change, they were united in their opposition to the conventional curriculum of the schools in which they had worked, but Newberg, at the age of thirty-two—when he first met Borton—had had a good deal more antiestablishment experience.

For several years, Newberg had been a free-lance director, working with unconventional theater companies in Philadelphia, putting on various productions of the one-time avant-garde— Pirandello, Camus, Ionesco—acting, and studying. In between directorial stints or college degrees, he had done some teaching— English at Rutgers University, in New Jersey, creative dramatics in a variety of independent workshops—and he had even taught briefly in the public school system of his native Philadelphia. While working in the Philadelphia schools, however, Newberg realized "the complete futility of teaching slow kids in the manner of traditional education." He believed that a whole new curriculum had to be found—"a curriculum," to use the phrase that later became a hallmark of the Newberg-Borton collaboration, "of concerns."

It was not simply a matter of the "slow kids," of course—a fact which began to emerge, and finally to seem patently obvious, as the movement toward a more relevant curriculum gathered momentum. "Faster" kids were simply more willing to put up with the traditional curriculum, the advocates of affective education claimed, because it was founded on their predominantly white, middle-class values, and because it happened to be the accepted instrument for advancement in American society. As Mario D. Fantini and Gerald Weinstein, two leading educational theorists whom Borton had worked with, observed in a book on educational change, *all* students were "disadvantaged" under the traditional system.

Newberg and Borton's interest in the full range of human potential, particularly in the unity of mind and body, was a logical outgrowth of what each had been doing separately for years—their underlying principles and commitments never changed—and gradually, during the crucial period when their part of the movement began to get under way in Philadelphia, it came to reflect an increasingly widespread interest in group dynamics, sensitivity training, general systems theory, and even cognitive development. The roots of this were evident in the drama and literature courses of the Friends Summer Workshop, but the difference was that, with a little help from their friends, Newberg and Borton were beginning to find a theoretical framework for the kind of learning experiences they had previously pursued largely through intuition.

The new theories of achieving human potential were partly a response to the practical problems of mass mental health needs—hence the emphasis on group interaction and small groups as basic therapeutic units. Moreover, the time-consuming and expensive forms of traditional Freudian therapy that had been the mainstay of mental health programs for decades could no longer meet the needs of a frighteningly overcrowded world. And the Freudian emphasis on predominantly intellectual, analytic processes was no longer as fashionable as it had been. Newberg and Borton simply recognized that the latest answers to the problems of twentieth-century life currently gaining favor in the world outside the schools—the Esalens, the sensitivity training laboratories, the communities devoted to self-awareness —could be useful inside the schools as well.

Although the affective curriculum dealt directly with people's "self-concepts" and stressed emotional growth, Newberg and Borton constantly reminded observers that their program was not an attempt to introduce group therapy to the public schools.

It was not even *like* group therapy, they insisted; group therapy was a concept so threatening, so suggestive of Big Brother mind control, that they strove to avoid it—even though their own teacher trainees (and several of the program's opponents, including Board member William Ross) tended to make the comparison quite readily.

Whatever one called the program, it was essentially an assault on rigidity and repression. Different words might disguise it somewhat, but in seeking substantial change on a system-wide basis, it posed a profound threat to the basic behavior patterns of people and institutions everywhere. The program had flourished on its own little island at Friends Select, but after Rick deLone's crucial visit during the summer of 1965, a direct confrontation with the school system seemed to have been destined from the start.

DeLone had visited the program to write an article about it for the *Evening Bulletin*, but, convinced that he had discovered the best possible answer to the problems of the schools, he lost no time in becoming Borton's leading power broker. His first move was to obtain enough federal support for the program— through his friends at the Board of Education—to establish a summer school, in 1966, that drew students and faculty from public, private, and parochial schools throughout the city. This led to a second summer as well; by the fall of 1967, the Philadelphia Cooperative Schools Summer Program enjoyed a city-wide reputation as a turned-on refuge from routine education. And, completing the beachhead operation during the school year that separated the two summers, deLone managed to get an important job for Terry Borton in the Board's curriculum office.

Borton's main goal at 21st Street was to interest his colleagues in what he was doing. His colleagues were all too eager to listen, he soon discovered, as long as listening was all they had to do. Dozens of top-level school officials "talked change" with Borton for most of a year. But in June the affective curriculum was still an interesting oddity as far as the school system was concerned.

The program itself, nonetheless, continued to mature. By this time the affective curriculum had become a highly sophisticated process with a strong theoretical base borrowed in large part from the writings of Fantini, Weinstein, and Jerome Bruner, a

Harvard educator who was among the most original thinkers in the field. No longer a mere process of turning-on and an uninformed probing of psyches, the program had evolved into three principal courses—Communications, Urban Affairs, and Drama —in which students were guided in exploring problems of knowledge and identity. In 1966 the courses centered on a progression of probing questions about identity, the self, and personal concerns; the 1967 summer courses introduced a variation on the basic theme that developed a series of metaphors—one of the most popular, for instance, was the "zoo" unit, in which students explored the question "What's *human* about human beings?"

The most controversial innovation of the 1967 summer program, however, was the Teacher-Student Project—the first concerted effort at disseminating the ideas of the Cooperative Schools program within the Philadelphia public school system. For Borton had decided, after his frustrating year in the Board's curriculum office, that simply baiting a hook was insufficient to the job at hand—the only answer was to work directly with a group of teachers and to develop the program within a specific school.

The Teacher-Student Project involved forty people, half of them students and half teachers from a Germantown junior high school whose principal, somewhat more liberal than most, had agreed to cooperate. Borton himself was the director of the project, and, with the help of a team of T-group leaders from Temple University, he exposed his "co-learners" to six weeks of intense involvement in a wide variety of experiences, including the courses in Urban Affairs and Communications and what became a series of grueling "encounter" sessions. He hoped that when the twenty teachers returned to their school they would continue to use some of the ideas they had picked up during the summer.

But this first confrontation between the affective curriculum and the public school system vividly illustrated how radical the new project really was. Although there had been tremendous excitement and emotional involvement, Borton later admitted that the Teacher-Student Project was not a success. Writing in an article whose main subject was the pitfalls of a system that merely talked change, he observed that when the teachers returned to their school, they used the new freedom of communication among themselves and the principal (provided in a staff development follow-up program) not—as intended—to implement the workshop's techniques, but "to concentrate on school organization, personnel problems, and student discipline."

Teen-agers, especially the diverse group that the directors of the Cooperative Schools had chosen from a long list of applicants for three summers, had the flexibility to respond to new ideas. Teachers and administrators, with their long-standing commitments to the basic assumptions of the system, were not so ready to change even if they wanted to. Borton's experience with his glibly cooperative colleagues and the failure of the Teacher-Student Project were good indications of what "institutional rigidity" really meant. But the campaign was still in its early stages.

"Peg Spencer is having a hard time at Franklin. She's fighting a lonely battle."

—Gratz High School English teacher
involved in fall, 1967, field-testing
of the Cooperative Schools Communications course

One day the assignment for the class was to rearrange the room and make a different kind of environment out of it. They were piling up chairs into sculpture and making a lot of noise. In five minutes there were two vice principals up there. Later they told the department head that I had to cover the door because I was disruptive. One day two teachers from the English department were standing in the doorway saying "That woman is crazy. She's just crazy." And there was a vocal group of outsiders, black militants—around this time kids were coming in with leaflets every day. The thrust from the community for change was mainly for more spelling, grammar, and vocabulary; the only non-conservative demand was for black literature. Here I was with this permissive course at the same time that the community was making demands for a three-hour intensive English course. My kids wanted to know when they were going to do English. . . .

—Margaret Spencer, Interview

It was the fall of 1967, the official debut of the Shedd administration. From the Cooperative Schools Program of the previous summer, six talented young teachers had been recruited to field-test the Communications course; in addition to Benjamin Franklin High School, the field-testing was going on in two other schools, Edison and Gratz, with teams of two and three, respectively. But the fall of 1967, with its watershed of November 17— after which nothing could be quite the same in the Philadelphia school system again—was not a time for putting new programs smoothly into effect. Terry Borton had left for Harvard at the end of the summer and was visiting Philadelphia only as a paid consultant to the Office of Affective Development; Norman Newberg had taken over Borton's job full-time. But Newberg's talents were needed for more immediate purposes than supporting a network of radical teachers. Newberg had more experience with group dynamics and sensitivity training than any other administrative official, and contrary to all his plans, he found himself involved in a new stage of affective curriculum that occupied most of his time through the winter. The convenient, though somewhat awesome, label for this phase of Newberg's job was "crisis intervention."

Newberg had been an advocate of sensitivity-training T-groups among school personnel long before November 17, but the student demonstration had so rocked Philadelphia's warring factions that nothing short of a major effort would keep the lid on. The Shedd administration's answer was the series of "retreats" which assembled school administrators, teachers, and leading black militants to talk honestly and work out their problems face to face.

"It's a way to disarm the opponents," Newberg explained, several months after the retreats had been abruptly terminated. "Before you can have dialogue, you have to have confrontation and expression of rage. In most racial confrontation, neither side wants to play the game—we don't have rituals for the expression of anger. I'm searching for a way to get school people to recognize the difference between angry feelings and violent acts. As long as people are still using words and sounds, there's still hope." But for most school people (read "whites") the language and the feelings had been too strong to bear. The retreats had caused such an uproar in Philadelphia that even a few members of the City Council had denounced them.

Actually the retreats were not so different from what Newberg and Borton had been doing in their classrooms all along: They got a group of people together and forced them to be honest with each other. The main difference between the retreats and, say, a class in the Cooperative Schools Program was the level of hostility and factionalism which the participants brought to the group. ("In the retreats one of the things I did," Newberg said, "was give the black community a full opportunity to vent its rage while still providing support for the white community. Retreats break down roles. . . .") But while there were basic similarities between the retreats and the classes in affective development, the retreats had never been more than devices for blowing off steam; they were not truly educative. Newberg had tried to enlighten the participants, but the rigidity of their attitudes had been too much to contend with.

There had been a good deal of "spin-off" from the retreats, defenders of Shedd's policies were quick to point out—techniques of sensitivity training were being used throughout the school system; a majority of the principals who had participated in the retreats favored more experimentation. But Newberg's proposal for a special high school in communications in which sensitivity training would be a key aspect of the curriculum got lost in the fray, and the retreats were never resumed, even though there had been talk of a new series during the 1968–69 school year. When the school system succumbed to a violent week of racial confrontation in October 1968, the loss of momentum within the Shedd administration produced a bitter contrast with the aftermath of the November 17 demonstration. The real heroes of the 1968 disturbances were Police Commissioner Rizzo—whom even the liberals praised for his good judgment and restraint—and the chairman of the Philadelphia Commission on Human Relations. Shedd and Dilworth stood conspicuously aloof, and in comparison with the previous year, attempts at dialogue between the school administration and the various black and white warriors in the community were negligible.

The proponents of affective development had simply learned the same painful lesson that most radicals were heir to when they attempted to institute basic changes in the school system with any speed: Confrontation was too impractical and risky a tactic to use. Somehow the system could resist confrontation in exact proportion to its strength and directness. If change was to come at all on a wide scale, it would have to come slowly.

Newberg continued to act as a consultant for a number of different projects in group dynamics throughout the winter of 1967–68, but in the spring of that year he and Borton began planning for an extensive program that would be the first non-threatening test of their ideas since the relatively insignificant field-testing of the Communications course, which had been lost in the fray. Both Newberg and Borton had wanted to take time for research, reading, and writing during the summer of 1968, but an atmosphere of rush, of now-or-never, had infected the entire Shedd team. The winter was over, and revolution had ceased to be a happy game.

The 1968 summer project was a new departure in that it was set up to work within the limits of a fairly conventional teaching situation. Paul Fineman, Newberg's poet protégé, had had similar motives when he tried out his "course" with a group of randomly selected teachers (as opposed to a hand-picked group of self-styled rebels) on a much smaller scale. The object in both cases was to see how far new ideas could go in changing the methods and attitudes of teachers who were not already dedicated to educational reform. For the first time, Newberg and Borton would be fighting the system on its own territory.

In addition to this basic difference, the 1968 summer program introduced a highly sophisticated theory of "process teaching" that Borton had turned on to while working with Fantini and Weinstein and that he had spent most of his year at Harvard developing. Students in the project, Borton explained in a guide to the summer program, would learn processes "with which to gain greater conscious control over themselves, their interpersonal relations, and their environment." Basically the summer program would consist of courses in communications and urban affairs, as outlined in a book entitled *Education for Student Concerns* that Newberg and Borton had hastily completed during the spring. The book featured a lengthy introduction to the theory of process teaching ("process as content," Borton called it) and twenty lesson plans, carefully defining each progressive step, for each of the courses. All that the teachers had to do was follow the lesson plans, loosen up, and swing.

My main reason for joining was that friends pressured me to do it. I was distrustful of some things in the program. It takes me a while to adjust to new things—the whole Shedd "revolution," for example. There's a certain amount of feeling of threat, insecurity, what-not, especially with something that's so completely different as this. But one reason that I decided to go ahead was that I was dissatisfied with what I was doing.

My initial reaction to Norman Newberg was not particularly positive either. I first met him at an introductory meeting in April, but I'd seen him at the school. He'd come into my classroom to conduct a lesson. When I got there the room was a mess and I blew my top. I said What the hell are you people doing; get this junk off my desk and get out of here.

I resisted the training sessions too. I was more involved in what I was doing at the time, some writing I was working on. The training sessions were an immersion in sensitivity training. At the first session we played the cumulative name game. I remember saying to myself My god, they're paying people $8.25 an hour and they're sitting here playing games. . . .

After about an hour of this I began to realize that I was just going to have to let my hair down and go along with it. I told Newberg that I might not be able to go to all the sessions, though—I was doing a teacher's guide for a textbook at the time. But I managed to get to all but half of one session.

I decided to go along with it because I had made a commitment. I still wasn't sure what this was or why it was happening, but it became clear that they were teaching us what we were going to do with the kids. We were being thrown into the "immersion" situation but we weren't being told what was happening to us. I think I really did resent that. . . .

The first two weeks of the summer session were sheer hell. We were trying to get into the material, but the whole trumpet concept is difficult to understand. [The "trumpet" was a complex theoretical paradigm that Borton adapted from his work with Fantini and Weinstein as a guiding principle for the affective curriculum process. Essentially, it was a description of three stages of awareness: immersion (sensing), transforming, and acting (on the awareness gained through the process).] As a result of the program I became interested in some of the Weinstein and Fantini stuff. I devoted part of a graduate course at Penn to Weinstein and Fantini's book *Towards a Contact Curriculum.*

We were having these afternoon skull sessions, and about the middle of the second week, one afternoon when Hank [Kopple, the supervisor of the Urban Affairs course] and Norm weren't there and the Urban Affairs and Communications people were together, those of us who were beginning to be a little upset opened up on Terry and really gave it to him. We told him we hadn't been prepared enough, that a lot of it seemed like gingerbread. Terry was pretty upset. We were having difficulty adjusting to the program, and we felt we hadn't been prepared for the adjustment. It started with a girl from the English department, then another English teacher, a man—both dropped out of the program later. Then I jumped in from the Urban Affairs side and really gave it to him with both barrels. What happened at this point was that a lot of us felt that we had almost been sent out as sacrificial lambs. Here we were face to face with a new program. We had four hours' worth of kids every day; there was a lot of it we didn't understand. You can read all the theory in the world, but there's a large gap between theory and practice.

Terry was troubled. He just sat there and took it in, almost as if he was up on the cross and we were hammering in the nails. Terry does seem to have a certain vulnerability because he's so damned good. . . .

I was upset myself. I'd had a negative experience with a kid earlier in the week. I like to use what I call the Alan King approach. I go through a whole patter. I try to utilize any kind of charisma I can create. I keep the kids in the kind of direction I want them to go in. But in the affective curriculum you can't do this any more, and as I said to my wife, Goddamn it, they took away my stage. I demand certain things from the kids and I *get* them—I don't have discipline problems. And I was having trouble adjusting to the relatively loose atmosphere of the program.

—Interview with Jerald Rosenthal,
Urban Affairs teacher in 1968
Affective Education Research Project

Discontented or not, all but two of the twenty volunteers stayed with the Affective Education Research Project until the end of the summer session. Some of them had been searching for an alternative and were ripe for the new approach; others tried to open themselves up to it by fighting their own resistance. And after his initial hostility, Jerald Rosenthal was emerging as one of the most ardent converts. While the work of the program teachers was uneven, it was good enough to convince Newberg and Borton that their chances for making it were better than they had ever been—the system, it seemed, could change.

Observations in
Benjamin Franklin High School Affective Education
Research Project
Classes, August 8, 1968

Class in Urban Affairs:

Yesterday this predominantly black class went on a field-trip neighborhood tour of predominantly white and Italian South Philadelphia. Though they had been brought to South Philadelphia by bus, several boys in the group got into a fight with a group of white boys during one of the neighborhood walks. The Franklin students had gotten back into the bus, and the bus was about to leave the neighborhood, when the white boys attacked the vehicle and smashed all the windows with baseball bats.

Today the class is involved in a discussion of the incident. Though there are over thirty students in the room, the level of involvement is extraordinarily high. The main focus of the discussion is on the details of yesterday's incident, on exactly what happened—who did what and why. At one point, Hank Kopple, the Urban Affairs supervisor who has been alerted to visit the class today, uses the technique of role-playing—portraying a white kid while one of the students plays a black kid—to clarify a point about attitudes. The class is remarkably together.

"Most people would come in and say this was a noisy and disruptive class," observes one of the teachers at the end of the period. "I was a more traditional teacher until I got into this program, but I'll never go back to the old way."

Class in Communications:

The class has just completed an exercise in which two students carry on a conversation, but constantly move their chairs away from each other as they continue talking, then discuss the effect of the spatial separation. No real excitement here. The best teachers have bad days, of course; this teacher is not only among the best, in Newberg's opinion, but he is already on his way to becoming a team leader for a center that will train teachers in the Communications course.

"I'm going to divide you into groups," he tells the class, "and

I want you to talk about your concerns." The last word has a hollow sound—when one has had more than superficial contact with the program, such key words verge dangerously on being clichés. "We're going to divide into small groups," the teacher explains, "and each person should present at least one concern of theirs."

The class arranges itself into small groups of five or six. "I want to go to college," one boy says quietly, but earnestly, to his group. "I want to buy a car, I want to . . ."

Class in Communications:

The middle-aged black woman leading this class is visibly uncomfortable with the free atmosphere she has been instructed to encourage. The lesson for the day—familiar from the program's publicity films, and a long-standing component of the course—is to arrange the room so as to create a new environment. A group of delighted students is dancing about a ceiling-high sculpture made entirely of chairs. The teacher is terrified and constantly admonishes the kids to calm down, to be seated, to listen. It is a contest which the kids have easily won; there is simply no rapport here between teacher and students, the sculpture notwithstanding. In a "traditional" class the teacher's effectiveness would have been reduced long ago to mere police work.

A boy sitting quietly on the radiator observes that he really enjoys this class. He refers to it jokingly as "charm school," but he adds that it has changed his attitude toward school for the first time. "They let you think about things," he says. "They ask interesting questions." Meanwhile his classmates continue to tease the teacher into a state of abject helplessness.

One of the boys "accidentally" topples the sculpture, creating a thunderclap of falling chairs. The teacher, like any other teacher who has failed to bridge the communication gap, begins to shout. . . .

"I love to teach American history," observes one of the urban affairs teachers at Franklin, "but the kids don't like to learn it. They *care* about this. Today I'm asking for examples and definitions of 'chicken' and 'courage.' Yesterday we had a role-playing session in which a girl gang went up to North Philly after King's assassination to fight another gang and one girl backed out. Last week we had a role-playing session where I played George Wallace addressing a group of racists at the Spectrum. One kid was a black cop guarding the door; other kids were black militants. . . ."

Process teaching can be used in any field, advocates of the urban affairs course claim—even with such familiar high school history chestnuts as "1820 to the Civil War." So far, however, the course has focused on more immediately relevant questions.

> Don't avoid questions of vital importance, like race, sex, and power. This curriculum is designed to get kids in touch with these concerns—we're giving them cognitive skills for dealing with the affective domain. Our emphasis is on process; we don't want to turn kids on and leave them with no way to handle the experience. That's what we used to do; it wasn't enough. . . .
> —Paraphrase of a memo from Terry Borton
> to 1968 summer teachers

Communications class at Bartram:
The lesson for the day involves dreaming. Students have been asked to create with clay or crayons a graphic representation of a dream. For a half hour or so the class, clearly happy both with the activity and the teacher—a dark-haired young woman who seems to like them in an open, totally unpretentious way—have been working on their dream-pictures and talking quietly. When the discussion begins, the level of interest is high to the point of fascination. One boy has made a phallic–looking stick of clay and uses it to beat a clay face which, he explains, represents his girl friend. "Take that!" he shouts, beating the face with the stick. The class greets this with astonished laughter.

"What's your explanation of the dream?" the teacher asks.

"That's my girl friend," the boy says. "And I'm *mad* at her."

In contrast, another boy has made a precise and unimaginative statue of a man. He tells the class that he wasn't really interested in doing this at all, that he did the minimum to avoid getting involved in such a stupid activity. Several students observe that the statue is totally rigid and unbending, like the boy himself. Finally the discussion moves on, but the boy grows increasingly aggressive in criticizing the artistic quality of other people's work. He is almost shouting when the teacher calmly interrupts him to ask, "Who are you really mad at?" And in a flash of rage he turns accusingly to the member of the class who had been riding him hardest about his excessive "control," glaring at his enemy, speechless with anger.

After the session with Terry, we decided to throw in a few relatively more traditional techniques. For example, with every lesson I began by putting up on the board a brief explanation of what the lesson was about. A training session had suggested we would not have such things as copying notes any more. I was glad to get rid of it, but I felt we needed a stable anchorage. . . .

I was still skeptical, though, even after the skull session, but somewhere around the third week, we had distributed *Two Blocks Apart* [a book about a black boy and a Puerto Rican boy who live in different sections of Harlem] and the kids were actually reading the books quickly. They even did well on a quiz I gave them. After *Two Blocks Apart,* I expanded the reading list, and the kids read more. I would never have introduced books like this in a normal class. These aren't books you give kids in school. I teach American history and government; I teach a semester on sociology in which we use a standard text, a good text, edited by the department chairman. But after I gave the test, I began to see that the kids were really responding; they really were picking up things from the program.

Kids began talking in class who never talked before; others wrote who'd never written before. Why? We were dealing with things that had a more immediate relationship to them. "Urban Affairs" is a misleading title—we're not teaching city government and some of the crap that some of the texts have in them now—they're no more interested in that than they are in Ferdinand Magellan. This deals more with their neighborhoods, their schools, their lives. . . .

The whole question of process as content wasn't cleared up at the beginning, but when it finally became clear that we were teaching processes, the whole thing became clear. . . . Terry said We're not giving you gimmicks—this is a whole philosophy.

Something happened during the summer that had a lot to do with my change in attitude. Terry asked to talk with me privately about things one day. He said he liked what he'd seen happening with me, that I was doing a good job. After this encouragement, I turned around and said Would you like to see my teacher's guide that I've been trying out? I brought it in the next day. Gradually I began to turn to Terry and Norm and Hank for support—I identified with the people and the program. We had a shindig at Sue Lear's on the last day, and I went out of there, frankly, bombed and feeling bad because I wasn't going to see those people any more. It encouraged us to build up a feeling of camaraderie—I look on a great number of those people as friends. This is what it should be with the kids too. It brings about a sense of identification with something that's good. I have begun to believe that there is a certain amount of inherent goodness in the program. When I saw Terry last week [in mid-March 1969] I almost took his arm off I was so glad to see him. . . .

At the end of the summer I was told by several people that I had done an outstanding job. It flattered my ego, made me feel good. I thought Goddam it, I really did beat it; here was something I really had conquered. When they asked if I'd be willing to take it on during the school year I said yes immediately. . . .

I'm not an idealist in the conventional sense, if I am at all. I'm more of a materialist, I like nice things. I'm glad that I have a number of good suits in the closet, shirts in the drawer. And I don't drive a Volkswagen, I drive a middle-sized Pontiac. Norm observed this about me at a meeting once. Somebody like Hank Kopple is completely the opposite in this regard. Hank has always struck me as a very liberal guy, almost . . . arty; I'm more towards center politically, high-strung. A lot of the stuff coming from downtown seemed to be dominated by the free spirits and overage hippies; some of us saw them as threats. I've been able to overcome all this because I've felt so comfortable in the program in the last few months. . . .

—Interview with Jerald Rosenthal

I'm an English teacher, and after a while I discovered that there was no English content, that *process* is the content. Basically there are two groups of teachers, though—content people and kids people. The first like to teach literature, history, science, etc. The second kind likes kids and people. The second kind belongs in this course, but not the first kind. I'm the first kind.

The course cuts through taboos. There's a lesson on graffiti, for example. The teacher is directed to write things on the board that kids call out. I wouldn't do it; I refused to do it. I called in Norm and ask *him* to do it. . . .

If the stuff offends the teacher, he can't do it. I just can't *do* this stuff. If you take it out in the field and mandate it, you'll have people disregarding it. . . .

I've worked in Israel. I could excuse poor Yemenite kids, but I

don't like Negroes. I'm Victorian and prudish. I just don't like
these kids. I'm prejudiced, I admit it. Other people like them
better. . . .

—Communications teacher in 1968
summer program

By the winter of 1968–69 the affective curriculum was as well
entrenched in the Philadelphia public school system as any innovative program could be. Ten lead-teachers from the summer
were directing branches of the program involving a total of thirty
teachers in eight schools; Borton and Newberg had collaborated
on two anthologies—with such unusual features as Feiffer car-
toons and excerpts from Norman Mailer—to supplement the
courses in Communications and Urban Affairs; Borton, Newberg, and his wife, Joan Newberg, had made a record of far-out
poetry readings that included spontaneous bits of discussion
among students; Borton's own book, *Reach, Touch, and Teach,*
describing the adventures of his career, would soon be published;
the school system's printing office had published a book-length
version of *Education for Student Concerns* which interested observers throughout the system were reading with considerable
avidity, occasionally with sympathy—and, in short, the affective
curriculum was among the most carefully developed, sophisticated, and attractive of all the new programs.

The prospects for radical change were no better in Philadelphia by this time than they were anywhere else, however. The
school system would probably never be "together" again. A
weekend retreat for the leaders of innovative programs and key
administrators in the spring of 1969 proved conclusively that the
program leaders could expect no system-wide power to come
their way in the foreseeable future. The programs would have
to continue as glorified band-aids; at best they would grow
within the relative shelter of a friendly sub-district or school.

Newberg and Borton would always be able to "go anywhere
they wanted," and the teachers they would leave behind if their
movement lost momentum would probably survive as they had
before—in lonely, idealistic grandeur. Borton was closely allied,
in fact, with a powerful group of educators, media czars, and
leaders of human potential communes who amounted to a kind
of national headquarters for turning on. Even if it died in Phila-

delphia, the movement was likely to grow stronger on a national scale; humanism was too much a going thing in the dehumanized sixties to suffer death easily.

Was the affective curriculum actually the wave of the future? For the moment it had the appearance of a collaboration of truly dedicated humanists pursuing long-range goals of brotherhood, community, and self-awareness among all men. Perhaps someday, however, it might become simply another aspect of the power structure—part of a curriculum that would prescribe blowing one's mind eighteen hours a day with an orgasmic media mix and "relating" intensely in T-groups the rest of the time.

This grim twisting of humanistic ideals was certainly feasible. The ill-fated retreats could be seen, after all, as a harbinger of a time when the last battles for humanity would have been lost and the System would simply impose "humanization" sessions as a safeguard against suicidal, or murderous, despair. That future would be a time when the petty question of who controlled various parts of the world would have been solved and the only serious problem confronting world leaders would be sustaining the illusion that there could still be dignity in the phenomenon called mankind. Humanization rituals might well be the answer.

This kind of future was not impossible to imagine—Huxley and Orwell shattered the West when they first envisioned it. Terry Borton, Norman Newberg, and their colleagues meant well, of course, but they were living in a time when power over people's minds, even in the cause of mutual liberation, seemed more likely than ever to be the ultimate panacea.

Tim

TIM WAS the kind of kid that everybody wanted to save. He had an air of doom about him—the permanent slouch of a beggar, the evasive eyes of one who believes that he is an incurable failure. But he was good-looking, an almost delicately thin, blue-eyed blond boy of fourteen (when I first met him), above average height for his age and growing fast—two or three inches within the year that we continued to see each other. He dressed carefully too—his slacks, shirts, and jackets (windbreaker-type, in all but the warmest weather) were usually what the proprietor of a respectable men's haberdashery in the shadow of the neighborhood El might have called "color-coordinated."

Concerned adults with any perception could spot him right off as one who needed their attention. His need was clearly visible even through a habitual cloud of apathy, for he kept part of himself awake and alert, ready for action if anything worthwhile came along. It usually didn't, of course. Life, both at school and at home, bored him and scared him. It was possible that he'd tune out completely some day; with his sensitivity, he wouldn't be able to stand it.

Chances are that even if Tim had gone to a terrible school, some interested teacher would have become aware of him and tried to help him. There are always a few teachers like that in any school. But Tim was lucky. Conwell Middle Magnet School was considered by most people to be among the best in the city, and it was only a block away from Tim's home, a typical row-

house in the poor-white section of Northeast Philadelphia called
Kensington. Tim's five brothers and sisters, some of them now in
their thirties, had also gone to Conwell, but the school had
changed radically within the last few years. Although the principal had come there before the Shedd era, she was a super-
charged innovator with a reputation as a rebel even during the
old regime. Now, with the support of the new Board and the
commitment to change, she was, in her own words, "the queen
of the May at 21st Street."

Tim was having a big run of luck in the 1967–68 school year,
for, in addition to the special benefits of Conwell (there was a
huge waiting list of kids from all over the city whose parents
wanted them to go there), he was among fifteen "underachievers"
who were chosen to represent Conwell during the first session of
the Pennsylvania Advancement School. Whether Conwell and
the Advancement School were successful in what they were
attempting to do is of almost secondary importance beside the
fact that they exposed students to some of the most concentrated
and truly dedicated efforts at educational reform in the city. I
don't mean to suggest that such an elusive quality as dedication,
surely more than a matter of hours spent on the job, is the magic
ingredient for a good school, or that reformers invariably run
better schools than conservatives. But I'm certain that Tim came
in contact with a larger number of adults who were sincerely interested in his welfare than he would have under normal conditions.

Part of the reason for this was, of course, that he attracted
them. His psychic signals communicated that he was a victim of
the system all the reformers wanted to change; he had high
scores in his mental ability tests (he was, if the tests actually
meant anything, bright), but low achievement. To each new
reformer he was a native in a jungle only recently open to
missionaries.

At the Advancement School, where I first met Tim, he was
much less outstanding than he would have been in a more conventional setting—for during the month of my visit the Advancement School had turned all but the most frightened kids into
glowing dynamos of life and intelligence. The freedom of the

place allowed them to open up almost completely. This had its negative aspects, and one of them was that the less aggressive kids tended to get lost. Tim loved the Advancement School, but he spent a lot of his time fighting to be heard.

The first time I paid any attention to him was when he did most of the talking one afternoon at a typically chaotic team meeting. These "dialogues" between kids and staff usually consisted of the staff trying to convey some important message— rules, news of the following day, threats—and the kids industriously putting them on. Tim's strong adolescent Philadelphia voice (the accent is a lusty combination of the Bronx and the Deep South) was conspicuous that afternoon, but what struck me about him was his use of woods like "groovy," "cool," and "boss"—hipster talk that one rarely heard from this particular group of boys. After the meeting I called his attention to the discrepancy and asked if he spent much time with an older group. Yes, he said; the younger kids just wanted to get into fights and fool around, but the older kids had fun. What kind of fun? I asked. He was vague: Listen to music, dance, stand on the corner and look at the girls, stuff like that. . . . The conversation was brief, and I didn't give it much thought. I hadn't singled Tim out as extraordinary, and while I was curious about this aspect of his behavior, there were other kids I found more interesting.

It would be easy for me to say that Tim was clearly a more intelligent kid than most of his contemporaries—even a superior one. The test scores, such as they were, indicated this, and so did numerous adults I later talked with about him. In addition, he knew so many things that I would never have expected in a boy of his age and background. He seemed to have read a great deal; he was acquainted with a wide variety of books and stories (once he told me that he'd tried to read *War and Peace*). He knew things about politics and culture that he couldn't have seen on television. He really dug the Art Museum, he told me, and visited it often. And while some of this must have been an effort at ingratiating himself with an intellectual who'd befriended him, I know that he couldn't have invented it.

But I hestitate to call this intelligence. Even if he had had experiences and insights that were beyond his years, the main quality that made all us concerned adults rave about him, I think, was that he was so old for his age. He had so much in common with us, appealed to us on our own level so, that we tended to think of him as some kind of marvel. I say "we" with humility. The more I knew Tim, the more possessive I felt about him, regarding him as a bright young brother who needed my help.

But I got to know him slowly, more by accident than by conscious intent. One day at the Advancement School, for example, a teacher had set up a project in which kids were asked to build a model of their "dream house." I happened to visit the room soon after the project began; Tim had balked at getting involved, wouldn't even try to do a floor plan—in his case, apathy often seemed to be a palpable disease. I joked with him. I bet you *can't* do it, I said. He gave me a knowing look. Don't pull that psychology on me, he said; my school sent me to a psychiatrist, and they couldn't find out anything at all; I know all about psychiatry—the truth is, I'm lazy. (A moment later, another boy, who'd been working eagerly on his floor plan, stopped, thought a while, and finally said: "I know why you asked us to draw these things—you want to find out if we're nuts.")

Another time I stopped to say hello to him at the end of the school day, during the brief period when the boys were supposedly writing their journal entries (few of them actually complied). He was filling a page with clumsy block letters that read: THIS SCHOOL IS A J O SCHOOL. That doesn't mean 'Jay real,' does it? I asked, remembering Tim's own private expression of approval. Nah, he answered, without stopping. What does it mean? I asked. He went on writing. It isn't 'Jay' anything. . . . I mused. Jerk off, he said to the book.

One of the first schools I wanted to see after concluding a period of extensive observation at the Advancement School was Conwell. It wasn't so much that Tim and the other Conwell kids had encouraged me to visit the school by telling me how new and different it was, but rather that most of the administrators with whom I discussed innovative projects in the early days of my research told me Conwell was one of the best developed and most "exciting" of them all. Even highly critical observers insisted that it was among the best schools in the city. And most of them agreed that this was largely due to the efforts of Mildred Wilson.

A handsome woman in late middle age, with piercing blue eyes, Mrs. Wilson gave me the grand tour on the day of my visit—grand because it was so thoroughly exhaustive and rapid-paced that by the end of it my arm ached from the effort to get it all down in my notebook. Among other things, I learned that Conwell was a "magnet school." This program, one of the new Board's earliest innovations, involved the concentration of all or part of a designated school's activities on a specialty that would give it unique drawing power to attract students from all over the city. One purpose of the program was racial integration; another was the development of specific innovations on a level that the ordinary school budget wouldn't usually permit. Conwell's specialties were individualized instruction and team teaching. Eventually the school would provide computer-organized learning "packets" for each student, and although this aspect of the program was still being developed at the time of my visits, the carpeted team rooms were already in operation.

The learning laboratory—also carpeted and, in comparison with similar rooms at other schools, lavishly equipped—featured listening centers, sets of programmed texts, carrels, records, and a vast array of additional materials typical of the best "instructional materials centers" (educationese for new-fangled library). But the learning laboratory was more than piles of equipment. Anne Patterson, the wife of John Patterson (who had conceived the magnet schools program in the first place), was the permanent learning lab teacher; an attractive, lively woman with honey-colored hair and what was clearly a deep affection for the kids, she was, along with Mrs. Wilson, one of the school's prime movers. There was also a math lab, equipped with Madison Project math materials and several calculating machines.

In short, Conwell had so many good qualities—by no means unique, but nevertheless unusual for even the most up-to-date urban schools—that it certainly deserved its reputation. It had been extraordinarily long before the new Board, in its effort to come up with some lofty-sounding innovations, called it a magnet school and gave it more money (the main virtue of the innovation), and it was still growing when I saw it. Just as important as the educational hardware and—as they say in the trade—software, however, were the personality and philosophy of Mildred Wilson, which dominated the school. Mrs. Wilson had always "taught offbeat," she told me in her relaxed, slangy manner—"I'll use anything that ever came down the pike or anything that rolls out of a kid's mouth." She wasn't interested in I.Q.'s or behavior, she said, although Conwell was a well-disciplined school. The Conwell report card featured an evaluation and a graph, in addition to the usual grades. ("You've got to consider what windmills are worth tilting.") Her main purpose, she said, was to "develop young individuals who can help themselves." On parents' night, for example, she had addressed all the parents at the beginning of the evening over closed-circuit television, then turned the kids loose to lead their parents wherever they wanted.

At one point on the tour we passed a boy working on a poster in an upstairs hallway (the school was still being renovated) for a TV presentation he would make the following week. "He's a quote, unquote, incorrigible," Mrs. Wilson told me. "Supposed to throw fits. He's being given a lot of free opportunity; he's going on TV to explain his biology project. The other kids used to pick on him, but they've begun to respect what he can do. The family background makes your hair stand on end." Conwell had only six hundred students—hence, the unusually personal approach. "No school should be bigger than seven hundred," Mrs. Wilson said. "It is absolutely essential that every adult know every student."

We were just winding up the tour and returning to Mrs. Wilson's office when I looked up from my writing long enough to see Tim, accompanied by a disciplinarian-type man, probably a vice-principal, whom I had earlier seen "dealing" with an unruly student. They came out of an office as we walked by, went a few feet down the hall, and, with an air of grim purpose, entered another office. In a moment they were gone.

What was Tim doing here? I asked Mrs. Wilson. I knew him from the Advancement School—wasn't he supposed to be over there today?

Mrs. Wilson threw an admonitory glance to heaven. While

waiting for the bus to take him to 5th and Luzerne this morning, she explained, Tim had gotten into some pretty wild horseplay and thrown a rock at another boy, hitting him on the forehead and nearly putting out one of his eyes. As a result, she was suspending him for a few days. He'd been very apologetic afterwards and said it was an accident. But he had to learn. She'd made him clean up the blood from the sidewalk.

That was the Mr. Hyde in him, she said. They'd done everything in the world for that kid. He had an odd permanent swelling on his forehead; they thought there might be some brain damage, and they'd arranged for him to see a doctor. He'd spent quite a lot of time in the learning lab and done some outstanding work with Mrs. Patterson. A few years back, Tim had been in Mrs. Wilson's "acres of diamonds" group. But part of the problem was that teachers who'd been at the school "for a million years" clung to the bad reputation of Tim's brothers and sisters— "there was a certain amount of glee when he got into trouble."

I still remember Tim's face during the moment that we saw each other in the hall. It was an expression I soon came to recognize easily, a sort of neutral face. The mouth (almost cherubic) full open, a combination of a scream and a yawn, the eyes in constant flight. Sheer terror, but still the inevitable boredom and apathy. A mask: "It looks like they might kill me this time, really kill me; what a drag. . . ." The quick understanding, the helplessness.

But even then I wasn't hooked. Perhaps the obvious depth of his need kept me off, but for a number of reasons—among them the fact that I would no longer be seeing him almost every day, would no longer be visiting the Advancement School so often— I made no attempt to find out what was happening to him.

A few weeks after my visit to Conwell, one of the teachers at the Advancement School asked me if I'd participate in a learning experience that he was setting up for a group of ten or so boys. The main feature of the experience was a two-day visit to many different parts of New York, in order to compare them with similar parts of Philadelphia—the course was urban affairs, and the boys had already spent more than a month holding "classes" in the neighborhoods where they lived. But an equally important aspect of the trip would be staying overnight and

spending the evening with some people who actually lived in
New York. I lived more or less in both cities, but I had an apartment in New York where the boys could stay. My friend's idea
was that the boys should be able to see as much of the life of
their hosts as the hosts were willing to let them in on.

Tim was in the group, but he wasn't one of the two boys who
stayed at my place. Marty and Ron had such a good time,
though, that they wanted to come back again. I told them I'd be
glad to do it, but they'd have to pay their own way the next time.
They'd save up their money and pay for everything, they said,
train fare and everything. And Tim and Dave, two of their other
friends, also wanted to come.

It was several weeks before the boys and I settled on a convenient date and made our arrangements, but then, as the
agreed-upon weekend came closer and I'd had no reply to my
final letter of details and schedules from any of them, I gradually
discovered that the plan was even more impractical than I
would have thought. Ron's and Dave's parents had inexplicably
changed their minds, I discovered when I contacted each of the
boys, and wouldn't let them go. Marty had trouble raising the
money, but I offered to lend him some so that he could make the
trip. Tim was the only one who'd be able to come with no
problems at all. Finally even Marty copped out; he simply
failed to appear at Penn Station at the appointed time. There
was no phone at his house in Philadelphia, and I didn't find out
what had happened until the next day, after sending a telegram
with my phone number. It turned out that he hadn't had enough
money for the train after all, and he didn't know how to reach
me.

When Tim and I finally discovered that we were going to be
alone together for much of the time, apathy descended on him
like a suit of lead. I suggested fifty or a hundred different "activities," it seemed, and he insisted that he didn't care what we did
at all. The eyes in flight, the mouth half open, the slouch—it
didn't matter to him; nothing mattered. We assaulted the city
joylessly and worked hard to appreciate the company of a friend
of mine who joined us at intervals.

Our eyes met only a few times during the entire weekend,
and our conversation was fitful. I knew that he thought my

apartment was boss; he wanted to have one like it someday. I knew that he thought Negroes were getting too uppity, that people were giving them everything they wanted. We also disagreed about the war. He was thinking of being an architect, and had been seriously considering it since he'd spent the first New York visit, a month or so earlier, with an architect and his family in a converted brownstone on the Upper West Side. He liked driving around with me in my car and probably would have been content to do nothing else.

But something must have happened behind our masks. Soon I found myself planning a return visit to Conwell. The main reason was to spend a day at the school on my own, an unguided tour this time. But Tim was very much on my mind.

Shortly before this visit, I happened to be at the Advancement School one afternoon, and a teacher whom Tim had been rather close to showed me a letter that Tim had sent him. Penciled in a barely legible agony-scrawl, the letter said that things were okay, he couldn't really complain, nothing much was happening at Conwell, though he was spending a lot of time with "Patterson" in the learning lab, and that he was trying to get some help with his writing, which had been getting a lot better recently. The letter was obviously a bit of naïve showing-off; we estimated it to be somewhere around third-grade level.

I mentioned the weekend in New York. Yes, the teacher had heard about it a week or so afterwards, when Tim dropped in at the Advancement School to say hello. He'd told everybody that he'd had a jay real time. What a tremendous relief, I said—I hadn't. I was going on at length about our failure to communicate; I held the letter in my hand as I talked, and finally I stopped—I suddenly realized that despite his talk about such manifestations of high culture as *War and Peace* and the obvious evidence that he knew how to read, Tim had gotten all the way to the eighth grade in a state of semi-literacy.

Literacy in American society is the key that frees the mind; once a student has mastered this essential skill, he can never be a complete slave again. Without it, as long as the culture continues to perpetuate its forms and its values, he is a slave to those who run the society in which he lives.

The great leveling machine of the American schools sweeps

millions of citizens to dirt early in their lives, for the culture of poverty does not include the early development of "basic skills." How soon can a student admit that he has no place in the society and drop out? High school is the crucial time—usually, as in our big cities, the victims of poverty are shunted through the lower grades, but in high school their failure can no longer be denied. Thus, they are forced to admit that they will never make it. Unless they are people of extraordinary courage, they are lost, useless. Unless they have extraordinary awareness, they cannot seriously question whether there was any point in making it at all. All the freedom schools in all the ghettoes in the country are the merest wisp when compared with the gross national product.

I remember Joe, a handsome black boy at the Advancement School—bigger than most of the kids, outgoing, aggressive, a natural leader. But he'd perfected his own vaudeville routine by the eighth grade. It was a real joke in the school, the way Joe would roll his eyes like some Hollywood nigger and croon "*Ah* don' know" to almost anything we asked. He was a good athlete, though, and he could dance. "*Ah* don' know"—and then he'd break up in laughter, double over with it, it was so funny. He just didn't know *nothin'*. But Joe could still communicate with us concerned teacher types, still get across the last urgent message and plea. What about all the sullen boys who lurk outside Benjamin Franklin High School, at Broad and Green, at noontime, smoking and sneering at the passersby and mumbling into their collars? What do they know?

Tim was white-blond, and a racist too, but his situation was remarkably similar to theirs. He was, of course, fantastically lucky, compared with them. His greatest luck was being white. Moreover, he'd been raised (I soon learned) in a family of adults who let out their frustrations in witty attacks on each other; his whole childhood had been a process of such fast aging that he'd learned to become an eloquent beggar, to "relate" to adults. People were trying to save him—the dedicated ones from all over were throwing their energies into his cause because he seemed so close to salvation (so like them), because with him they at least had a chance. And finally, after seeing his letter, I joined them.

There was nothing particularly sudden or determined about

my joining, however. I was simply more interested in him, during my next visit to Conwell, than I was in the school. I talked with Mrs. Patterson at length about him. She told me he'd been doing well with programmed learning materials (no writing required), but he was rarely asked to go to a class. One of his main activities was showing visitors around the school—he was charming and outgoing with them. I suggested that he do this with me, and so we set off together for an English class with a teacher I'd met a couple of times outside the school, a class that Tim was scheduled to be in anyway.

At first, I thought he was showing off for my benefit, that he was determined to wreck the class with his witty gibes, his mockeries of the teacher, his shouted interjections, to show me how cool he could be. But clearly they were all used to this behavior; students and teacher alike greeted it with an obvious here-he-goes-again look. The teacher was ex-ceed-ing-ly patient; if I'd been in her place, I think I would have murdered him.

He sat next to me on the radiator, and a few times I tried to get him to shut up. He saw that I was annoyed with him, and he obviously knew that he was "misbehaving," disrupting. I think that he wanted to stop. But he couldn't. Again and again his husky jiving voice would ring out with some devastating comment; clearly he had no control over what he was doing. "I hate this," his mockery said, "and I wish to hell that I could be part of it."

At the end of the school day, he walked me to my car, and for the first time the walls were down. I think he'd been so glad to see me when I came in to the learning lab that morning (so I really did care about him; I wasn't going to ditch him, never see him again; I didn't think he was a complete jerk, even after spending a weekend with him) that he finally began to trust me.

School was a drag, he said, as he shuffled along the sidewalk, hands in pockets, looking down. Everybody was always giving you a rough time—at home, the cats on the corner, all the old people who wouldn't let you hang around the candy store; everybody was a drag. And he didn't have any idea of what he'd do in the summer—probably just hang around and swim up in Juniata Park sometimes with the other cats. And he'd just been

fired from his paper route, because they were laying cats off.
And, by the way, when would he catch me again?

I'll be in touch with you, I said. But you know how busy I am
when I come to Philadelphia; it's hard for me to get out here
very often. Suddenly I had an inspiration. Hey, I said, why
don't you write me a letter?

Quickly he looked away. Nah, he finally answered, I can't
spell.

The hell with spelling, I said.

I saw him standing in the middle of the street when I looked
into my rear-view mirror. He was slouching, watching my car
drive away.

It didn't occur to me until much later that when the teacher
at the Advancement School showed me his own letter from Tim,
one of my reactions was jealousy.

The next time I saw Tim, I went to Conwell specifically to
visit him. It was in June, shortly before the end of the school
term, and I phoned first to make sure that Tim had come to
school that day. Mrs. Wilson told me in a tone of complete
disgust that he would probably be in late again, that he just
wandered in any old time. She had decided, she said, that he
was getting too much attention. ("He needs the full attention
of an adult full time," Mrs. Patterson told me at one point.) She
extended the privilege, at any rate, of releasing Tim into my
care for an hour or so, and we walked out into the warm spring
day with a mutual feeling of relief.

Tim was haggard-looking and low that day. He had come in
late, of course, and he told me why: He and his mother had sat
up all night waiting for his fifteen-year-old sister to return home.
But maybe she'd run away; maybe she was in the hospital—they
didn't know. Not the *older* sister, the one who was married and
getting divorced, the one whose husband had moved back with
his parents immediately after the marriage—the *younger* one.
In fact, while we were walking, we saw the older sister across
Kensington Avenue; she was pretty, red-haired, lively-looking,
and when she saw us, she beckoned him over with a knowing,
suspicious look, as if to say, *Now* what are you up to? I had the
feeling that in her brief appraisal of what she saw, I was

probably a hippie narcotics dealer, Tim was into another of his exploits, and the whole thing was sort of cute in a disgraceful way.

And finally, as we talked over coffee and Coke (and cigarettes; Tim lit up the minute we were on the street), we got down to the subject which had been nagging me for weeks: What were Tim's plans? Assuming that he got *out* of Conwell, where could he go to high school? What was he going to do for the summer? What was going to happen to him?

As for high school, I could already guess the alternatives. Central, Philadelphia's prestigious middle-class haven for test-takers, was out, of course, and thus the road to success was already fairly well blocked. The neighborhood vocational high school, which I had visited and found to be a typically rigid civil service institution (with a few creative teachers, as usual), was a lesser evil; but Tim's grades probably weren't good enough to get him in—he wouldn't know until the end of the summer. He was hoping to go there, though I knew that if he did, it would only be a matter of weeks before he'd find the work impossible to keep up with, no matter how simple-minded it was. The last choice was the neighborhood dumping ground high school, where Tim would have as hard a time doing the work, if he tried, as anywhere else. It seemed that the brilliant little native in the jungle was about to be devoured by the beasts.

There would be no Mrs. Patterson. If overprotective, she had nonetheless reached and helped him, and she was the only one at Conwell to whom he felt close. There would be no well-intentioned buddies like the teachers at the Advancement School to sustain the flickering life in him long enough to teach him the skills he'd never learned. None of his brothers and sisters had ever finished high school—one of the brothers was in Vietnam; the other was working as a truck-loader and would probably owe the rest of his life to the union and the bank. Perhaps if the first concerned adult who took him under his or her wing had never noticed Tim at all, he would have been able to accept his future optimistically—he would be getting a share, after all, of the American dream. But now he knew that he was headed for hell; to that extent he'd had a good education.

Since he wouldn't know about the vocational high school until the end of the summer, the vacation itself presented a problem. But, again, apathy overwhelmed him. He just couldn't think of anything to do. After I'd hammered at him for a while, he finally admitted that one of the school volunteers who worked at Conwell, his "conference counselor," had taken an interest in him and that her husband was an important man in the redevelopment of Penn Center. There was a possibility, he admitted, that he could find a job through her, perhaps in an architect's office. I played a tired old game, daring him to call the school volunteer. I bet you won't, I said, trying to joke; I bet you're chicken. This time he just stared at me. Yeah, he said, but I don't want to get shot down.

I made a few attempts to interest some friends in Tim's summer, but some inertia that I was only half-aware of held me back. I always seemed to have too many other things to do. Finally it was the end of June, and I wrote Tim a brief letter saying that I hadn't finked out on him (guilty that I had), but I'd had no luck in finding him a job.

The summer passed quickly, and I made no further attempt to get in touch with him. If I saw him again at all, I'd decided, I'd just check out which school he'd gone to and feel bad about it. I never expected a letter from him; he must have concluded, I thought, that I was through with him altogether. When my phone rang one afternoon late in August and I heard Tim's voice, however, I suddenly realized that I wasn't through with him at all—rather, some sense of balance had told me that I was doing too much of the work, that before we went any further together, he'd have to give something. Even phoning me, I thought, took tremendous courage. We agreed to get together in Philadelphia the following week. And he'd heard about his high school; he'd be going to the dumping ground.

The night before I was to meet him, I told some friends the whole story. It was sad, I said, that he'd have to go to the dumping ground, perhaps even sadder because he'd been so thoroughly experimented with and cared for. Murray Suid, whom I had met through a program for media development he'd been running, got the message right away. He'd taught at a school in Massachusetts, he said, a liberal private boarding school, that might be willing to offer a kid like Tim a scholarship; he thought it was worth a try. Tim's phone call had restored the balance of initiative, I thought, and without too much consideration of the consequences, I said I'd mention the possibility.

But there was more to my decision than just mentioning possibilities. I'd seized on the phone call as a desperate signal for help, and very quickly I became entangled in a web of missionary deeds that nearly strangled both of us.

He wasn't at the appointed meeting place the following morning—we usually met in front of City Hall, which is in the exact center of Philadelphia—and when I phoned his house (I talked briefly with his grandmother), he was still asleep. I told him to get the hell down there. When he finally arrived, I lost no time in mentioning Murray's suggestion. There was nothing certain about it, I insisted. I knew nothing about the school. There was a good chance that he wouldn't be accepted and that he wouldn't receive a scholarship if he were accepted. But from the little I knew about it, I gathered that it was something like the Advancement School. Tim wanted to hear more, and we went to Murray's office to get the full story.

Murray was absolutely straightforward, but he avoided a hard sell. His main point was that Tim would have considerably more freedom there than at most schools and that he'd probably have more of an opportunity to work closely with the teachers. The next step, we all agreed, was for Tim to write a letter to the headmaster inquiring about an opening and mentioning Murray's name. Tim began to settle into his shell as we headed back toward City Hall. Write a letter, I said; write anything, it doesn't matter—just tell him who you are and ask if there's any chance of your getting in this year and maybe if you could visit the school to look it over. The letter didn't have to be elaborate or fancy—and besides I'd help him with it if he wanted.

He wanted me to help him with it, he said, but he hated writing letters. The spelling . . . Never mind the spelling, I said; just write anything. I won't do it *for* you, but I'll go over it with you and we can correct any errors together. We arranged to meet the following week, when he was due to start classes at the dumping ground. He said he'd bring a copy of the letter.

One night during that week, however, he called me at home. School was terrible, he said. He just wouldn't be able to take *that*

crap. Bad teachers? I asked. He hadn't met the teachers yet; it
was the other kids he objected to—always stopping you in the
hall and asking you for a quarter. Big kids. Okay, I said, write
the letter.

I waited for an hour—this time in front of the main branch
of the Free Library—until I decided that he wasn't going to
show up. When I called his home, he told me in a barely intelligible mumble that he'd gotten into trouble, that his parents
wouldn't give him any money to come downtown, that they were
real down on him. I could hear someone shouting in the background for him to get off the phone. Still hoping, I said I'd
meet him in Kensington the following morning before school.
Be there, I said, or I'll . . . don't make me threaten you, just be
there. He'd be there, he said, above the shouting.

"K and A," they call it—the crossing of Kensington and Alle-
gheny Avenues, the heart of lower-middle-class-white Kensington. A strip of neatly kept shops along Kensington; an El station
that dwarfs everything else, even the bank on one corner; a few
luncheonette-type restaurants. Seven-thirty in the morning, and
the city was waking up to its mind-numbing routine. This was
Tim's home ground all right, George Wallace territory; and here
I was trying to liberate the poor kid. What right had I to be
there?

He must have asked himself the same question, for once again
he was late. This time he got out of bed and met me in a
luncheonette near the El station within fifteen minutes. His
parents were giving him a rough time about the school, he said,
especially his father. He smoked nervously and drank a glass of
water. And guess what? He'd forgotten the letter.

If your father is dead against this, I said, I do have another
possibility; the Parkway High School is going to open this fall,
and you might be able to go there—*that* ought to be something
like the Advancement School, and you wouldn't have to leave
Philadelphia. (The Parkway Program, to use what later became
the official name, had just received a grant from the Ford
Foundation; when I'd interviewed the director about his plans
for the school, he told me that students would not be subject to
entrance examinations. The place promised to be wide open and

basically human.) Tim was interested—anything was worth a try. But, I warned him, you'll have to write them a letter too. It was just the spelling that bugged him, he said.

The following week, Tim was in front of City Hall when I got there, ahead of time. He seemed more relaxed and happy than he had in weeks. He'd bought a new pair of boss shoes, high with a buckle-strap. We both noticed how much he'd grown over the summer; he was as tall as I. And he was very casual when he told me that he'd finally decided that the boarding school was out. Yes, I quickly agreed, it would be going against the wishes of his parents too much, and after all they were his parents. More than that, he said, he'd decided he really didn't want to leave Philadelphia. He'd just gotten together with some new cats on a new corner—there were parties, drinking, girls. He didn't want to go up in the country where there wasn't anything to do; he liked Philadelphia. The speech didn't sound remotely true, but I congratulated him on his luck. At least, I added, he could still apply to Parkway High School; there was a good chance he'd get in. Oh yeah, he'd write the letter that week.

We had planned to rent a sailboat on the Schuylkill; but it was too late in the afternoon, so we just walked along the riverbank as the sun set, leaving a slight chill in the air. And we talked entirely about Negroes. Tim wanted me to understand *his* position; it wasn't that he didn't like Negroes (he "slipped" a couple of times and said "nigger"), it was just that they were going too far, asking for too much. Did he know why they were so discontented? I asked, coolly, rationally. Yeah, but like his sister went to apply for a job, and they said Sorry, we have to hire nig—Negroes; so what does *that* prove? And his brother had appeared on television, speaking against integration by busing as part of a group of parents from the Northeast who stormed a Board meeting in protest. While we were walking, we passed a black couple fishing from the bank, and his voice got louder as we neared them—"I don't care whether they're black white pink purple green. . . ." he said loudly, breaking into a wicked smile when he saw my expression of dismay. And finally, sick of hearing about it, I said Okay, you're a goddamned racist—so what?

I left him at a subway station. He was lively and smiling, with scarcely a trace of apathy. I'll call you soon, I said. He seemed infinitely wise as he walked away from me: You'd better, he shouted back.

When I asked the director of the Parkway Program if he'd received a letter from Tim, he said that he had, that it was brief and intelligible, not noticeably illiterate, but void of any needless information—it just said that Tim was interested in attending the school. But, he reminded me, this did not guarantee admission. There'd been so many applications that, in line with his wish to keep admissions free of bias, the names of the prospective students would be drawn completely at random from a hat.

VI. *Prospects*

AFTER MORE THAN TWO YEARS of Mark Shedd and three of the "new" Board, no sensible person could talk about revolution in the Philadelphia school system with a straight face, and "turning on" had gone the way of all slogans. The great revolution had failed to deliver, had suffered so many defeats that it seemed never to have been more than a wild, clever dream. Slow reform was all too often the best one could hope for.

Mark Shedd continued to survive, his reputation for liberalism intact. He was no messiah, and he didn't even resemble John Lindsay very much after the initial burst of charisma; yet, in the spring of 1969, he offered a public defense of *High School*—a film documentary about the type of education perpetuated at Philadelphia's all-white, predominantly middle-class Northeast High—that recalled his cool-young-tiger days. The film, which indicted the education establishment by observing its operations with a devastatingly naïve "objective" eye, was rapidly becoming a national storm center, but Shedd asserted that he had no doubt it was an accurate portrayal of what went on in most high schools throughout the country. Shedd could afford an occasional cavalier gesture of this kind, for he had turned out to be surprisingly adept at urban warfare—he still had power; he even received the blessing, in May 1969, of a new two-year contract. At worst, he had become merely mysterious and aloof (one observer compared him to Eugene McCarthy). The conspicuous, easily identifiable ones were the easiest to pick off during battle, and Shedd seemed to have learned this lesson well, if not quickly.

The Board and the central administration were still committed to change. There was still support at 21st Street for "new programs." Although a good deal of the youth movement within the central administration had died, beginning with the departure of Rick deLone and planning head Graham Finney, many of the projects that were daringly new in 1967 were almost, if not quite, entrenched by 1969. Shedd's administration had become, in fact, a reform establishment; rigidity and petty resistance could no longer threaten it. During Shedd's first two years a tone had been set for the Philadelphia schools that would probably enable the system to survive most of the battles to come: The system had indeed opened up; barring some cataclysm that might wipe out the liberal regime at 21st Street, it would remain open. Word came from "Washington" that the Philadelphia public schools were the most flexible and innovative in the country.

The changes encouraged and brought about by the Shedd administration were, and would probably continue to be, the kind that made the Philadelphia school system better—more lively, even more efficient—than it had been in the bad old days of bureaucratic rigidity. To this extent the phrase "turning on" still summed up the kind of change the central administration and its friends throughout the system wanted. School had always been a drag; now school would swing. And, hopefully, everybody would have an integral "role."

After a difficult beginning and subsequent adjustments to its new home, the Pennsylvania Advancement School, for example, had begun to develop several guaranteed turn-on courses that epitomized the new educational style, and, with an eye to its political future, the school was actively disseminating these courses in schools whose principals were friendly. One outstanding feature of the Advancement School package was a course in psychodrama that had become a major attraction for the visitors who flocked to the school in daily surges. Psychodrama students —stimulated by well-amplified music and surprising, delightful, often thought-provoking exercises and improvisational skits— underwent a process halfway between hip gym and group therapy that was unlike anything they would find in a conventional classroom. Wherever one looked in the Advancement School, kids were—to use the modish, but intensely significant words—"involved" with "meaningful" "experiences." The Advancement School realized the dreams of many progressives, but its emphasis on turning on brought it into line with the most current McLuhanisms as well. Probably more than any other single program in Philadelphia, it was a harbinger of things to come.

Other well-developed attempts at changing the nature of the school experience—the Learning Centers Project and the Affective Education Research Project, for example—were also getting results, and offered a powerful case for redefining classroom structure altogether. There was no guarantee that they would raise the levels of students' basic skills, but the system's extensive computer-assisted and individually prescribed instruction programs indicated that such needs could be satisfied in far more efficient ways than before. Ideally, students would receive instruction in the basics as early as possible from machines, and the time of most teachers in a thoroughly modern system would be free for genuine human development. In Philadelphia, this vision was on its way to fulfillment.

Big systems do not turn on as easily as teeny-boppers, however. The central administration had given Norman Newberg, Lore Rasmussen, and several other curriculum developers relative freedom to try out their programs within the context of experimental laboratories and conventional schools; but at system-wide power the officials of 21st Street had drawn the line. No matter how much "support" the innovators received in terms of enthusiastic approval, as long as they lacked concrete power, their programs could be no more than the band-aids Lore Rasmussen often warned against.

The best illustration of this was the Parkway Program, one of the most ballyhooed of the new projects—the "high school without walls" that opened in February 1969 and immediately proceeded to fight for its life. The basic concept of the program had radical implications for the structure of American schools; instead of institutionalizing learning within the confines of some factorylike building, the Parkway Program used the entire city as its classroom. Students in the pilot project took courses from a variety of teachers, ranging from a core of permanent faculty members to the staffs of various businesses and cultural institutions throughout downtown Philadelphia (the program was named with Benjamin Franklin Parkway, the grand boulevard lined with cultural institutions, in mind). There were courses in insurance, for example, at the Insurance Company of North America and in police science at the Police Department; several of the nearby colleges admitted Parkway students to formal classes; the Franklin Institute, a science center, also opened its doors to the program; and, if students had trouble choosing from the list of available courses, they were free to plan independent studies of their own. Once more, but this time with unusual feeling, educators were calling the Parkway Program the most exciting experiment in urban education to date.

But resistance was widespread. Paul D'Ortona, president of City Council, had publicly criticized the Parkway Program; Richardson Dilworth had not helped matters much when he quoted various slurs against the program in what he meant to be a defense of it; school system gossips conducted a quiet, unrelenting vendetta. More to the point, John Bremer, the program's director—a calm, soft-spoken, politically shrewd Englishman who had presided for a while over one of New York's decentralization experiments—had suffered so much discouragement at 21st Street that he had become an outspoken critic of the central administration. At one point, Bremer and Shedd proposed rival programs—the Parkway Program and a much more conventional idea—for a U.S. Office of Education grant aimed at encouraging anti-dropout measures, but with no real support from the central administration, Bremer lost the grant and seemed likely to have to fight for the program's survival on his own. For several months he ceased even pretending to polish apples at 21st Street and instead plied the newspapers, the electronic media, and national magazines with a bubbly brew of disarming publicity. He was, admirers of his technique often commented, building "his own power base."

Considering the extent of this kind of perpetual internecine warfare, it seemed that the network of programs for turning on the Philadelphia schools, however highly touted, would remain undernourished. As usual, there were few conspicuous villains. After the months of wild battle that culminated in the firing of the 381, 21st Street had succumbed to a paralysis of power. The innovative leaders could only admit, when pondering the future of their programs, that it was difficult to know exactly who controlled their destinies.

But the uncertainties of power in the central administration were only part of the great mess into which Philadelphia, like all the other cities of America, was sinking deeper every day. There were the budget crises—the unending battles in City Hall, in Harrisburg, in Washington. There were the "demands of the community," mainly demands for the development of basic skills, as contrasted with the humanistic education most middle-class radicals wanted—and this battle, which reflected some of the deepest conflicts of American society, promised to continue indefinitely. Everywhere one looked, there was a warring faction demanding something; the central school administration could hardly be blamed for its indecision about institutionalizing new programs on a system-wide basis.

Assuming that the programs could survive at all, their effect would have to be slow and cumulative. Fortunately, they were not isolated from the real world; they reflected the most progressive educational thought and practice of the day, and they made extensive use of modern technology. Even if they confronted the system too directly or if some unanticipated disaster befell them, the kind of school environment they advocated was too closely aligned with cultural changes in the society at large to disappear altogether. The Advancement School might be wiped out by a political tidal wave—but somewhere, perhaps at first in an isolated classroom, then perhaps among a team of teachers, techniques of Gestalt psychology and psychodrama would re-emerge, multimedia courses would evolve, and the turned-on curriculum would endure. The participating generation was going to take over no matter how severe or extensive the growing pains.

In general the most "radical" educators were not political revolutionaries, but an educational avant-garde. The Advancement School, the learning centers, the affective curriculum, and the thoroughly "creative" course devised by Paul Fineman (to cite the selected examples examined at length in this book) were innovative because they echoed the new, emerging culture—the youth culture, the turned-on culture, the "postliterate" culture—and they contributed to the continuing growth of this culture in the manner of all dynamic art forms. Although these programs inevitably had political overtones—they were steeped in social conscience—it was mainly the avant-garde's general sensitivity to the world around it, rather than an essentially political way of thinking, that produced this concern. Basically, turning on the system was not a matter of politics, but of assimilating new forms. The conflict of cultures and generations happened to be part of the panorama of urban warfare; but while generational conflict would doubtless shake up the country a good deal longer, it was something the system could survive.

The real political issue was a redistribution of power. Both the turned-on avant-garde and those more politically oriented talked glibly about "humanizing" the system, but they used this spellbinding slogan to mean quite different things. For the avant-garde, "human" education was "groovy" education, education attuned to modern styles, but in the sense with which many "community" people used the term, it meant bringing the system closer to the people by giving them more control. And although the battle for humanizing the Philadelphia school system by turning it on seemed to have been lost (at least in its initial phase), the battle for power over the schools was just beginning.

At this late point in the urban war, "systemic change" had begun to take precedence as the "in" panacea among establishment liberals and urban planners throughout the country. The idea was that merely tinkering with the system could not solve its problems, that somehow somebody had to come up with a plan for entirely restructuring the large systems that had so blatantly failed to serve urban America. Pilot programs, laboratory schools, Titles I and III, Head Start—these were all among the extensive, but quite inadequate compensatory measures that, according to the critics, would no longer do. Not all of the critics agreed, of course; factionalism among liberals and radicals was rampant. The fact remained, however, that the survival of urban establishments everywhere, and especially those of the school systems, would depend on their ability to come up with highly visible and effective plans for solving the crisis of the cities. And by 1969 the single idea that had accumulated the most steam throughout the country was "decentralization and community control." The liberal school administration in Philadelphia had pledged itself to this kind of basic systemic change from the beginning, but it had been so slow in taking action that the sincerity of the pledge was highly questionable.

Decentralization was quite distinct, of course, from community control—that much the educational establishment everywhere had learned from painful experience and an endless barrage of misused terms. In order to make big systems more efficient and more "responsive," as the jargon had it, "to the needs of the community," administrative decentralization made good sense and was well under way in Philadelphia after a slow start. Here the term simply meant oiling the bureaucratic machinery by allocating certain powers to district and field offices. The difficulty of obtaining supplies was notorious in Philadelphia, as in other large urban school systems; the Shedd administration had taken measures to simplify the process. Even long-term program planning for the various outlying districts had been put more into the hands of the district superintendents, who had been given additional staff and budgetary powers. They were still part of the system, however; in becoming more autonomous, the district offices were simply following a central-office directive. And certain district superintendents were more favored than others—five of the eight were generally regarded as Mark Shedd's "men." Just as central office had once decreed efficiency as the goal of the system, now it was attempting to make creativity official policy.

Chances were that in the very long run the emphasis on creativity would be felt in the city's classrooms. One district had undertaken a five-year improvement plan in which community participation was actively encouraged; another had used its increased budget for an extensive program of staff development. "This seems to be what they want," confided an assistant district superintendent in the spring of 1968, "at 21st Street." There was a good deal of room, of course, for human error, and for human recalcitrance—just as creative teachers had survived in the old days despite the waves of rigidity that emanated from the central office, so in the new era the unturned-on would also manage to defend their private interests.

Community control was related to decentralization in that it also dealt with a redistribution of power, but in the case of decentralization the power remained in essentially the same hands. The Board of Education would say to district administrators, in effect: We are giving you a little more power than we

used to give you in order to help you do a better job. Community
control, as distinct from community participation, meant taking
power out of the Board's hands entirely. And the most controversial aspects of this power were those over which the battle
that tore New York City to shreds in the fall of 1968 had arisen—
the hiring and firing of teachers and the management of school
budgets.

By mid-1969 the Philadelphia Board of Education still had no
significant policy regarding community involvement, and the
Board seemed to be bargaining for time in its effort to avoid a
confrontation. The sting of New York had been felt across the
nation; already during the cooling-off period following the New
York school strikes, the authorities in Philadelphia began to play
up community "participation" as the dominant theme in an effort
to soften the coming controversy. Nevertheless, the question of
real control was not about to fade away. Nor could Philadelphians be encouraged by the fact that their city had avoided
a debacle like New York's—disillusionment with the Board's
unfulfilled promises might ultimately produce something just as
bad.

Philadelphia activists had been waiting for two years to see
what the new administration, with all its rousing promises, would
do. There had, indeed, been so many concentrated efforts at the
top to restructure the system, in terms of involving the community, that Shedd looked as if he meant to be true to his word.
The Board's planning office had hired a prominent radical
activist as community coordinator in developing a plan for the
first Model School District in 1967, and negotiations had continued between militant community workers and school officials
for several months. But, in addition to the "distrust of the school
system in the community" so often cited as the main reason
behind the collapse of the project, middle-class residents of
Center City had raised a ruckus when they learned that their
schools would be included in the proposed district—thus adding
class warfare and racism to the fray.

The new ninth school district in the city's Overbrook section—
a racially mixed, middle-class neighborhood not far from the
Main Line—was encountering problems in the election of its
governing board, which a group of angry whites claimed did not

represent the entire community, and after its liberal young administrator had been in office for a year, the district still had no legal existence (eventually, it was eliminated altogether for reasons of "economy"). During the winter of 1969 the Board embarked on another project for north-central Philadelphia in connection with the federally sponsored Model Cities Program, but this, too, failed to develop a workable collaboration. The 1969 Model Cities proposal included several recommendations for teacher training in connection with Temple University, but it never received the Board's endorsement. The worst fiasco among these "top-down" efforts at involving the community, however, was the Board's own commission to study the question of decentralization and community control.

This was the enterprise to which Graham Finney had turned his attention—instead of resigning completely—in the fall of 1968 and to which he had also enlisted the energies of Rick deLone. Operating on a $35,000 grant from the Board, the commission staff planned to do a full-scale study of decentralization and submit a proposal for action by the end of March. The commission consisted of sixty-eight representatives of the city's most important power blocs, including the teachers' union, the black community, big business, and the Board, but after two months of operation the commission's work had bogged down so badly that participants frequently failed even to show up for the sparsely scheduled meetings. No one seemed to know—or was willing to say—exactly what was delaying the commission's progress, but some insiders suggested that black leaders were "dragging their feet" in order to make time for building up their own plan. Certainly this theory was in line with the single failing that had plagued all the system's top-down efforts from the beginning: They could never be anything but pacification programs in the eyes of an oppressed community. When the commission's report fell due, Finney offered several different proposals for continuation of the group's task, but all of them amounted to slowly phasing it out. It seemed obvious by this time that if major changes occurred in the Philadelphia school system, they would not originate with the Board of Education.

There were no hard and fast rules for the decentralization game—the Ocean-Hill Brownsville District in New York, for example, was strictly a top-down operation, initiated by the Ford Foundation, until it managed to create community solidarity through the agonies of the strikes—but in Philadelphia, at least, the most promising efforts at shaking power loose from the Board were those that resulted from intense community organization. The Mantua-Powelton community, for example, while thoroughly embroiled in power struggles of its own, was more active politically than most, and even though the Minischool had not enjoyed a particularly successful first year, it seemed that community leaders would eventually win some kind of control over the proposed middle school simply because they were together enough to represent a serious threat. Similarly, Citizens for Progress, a West Philadelphia action group, had been granted a share of the decision-making at Sayre Junior High School because the group was too well organized to ignore. During the fall and spring of 1968–69, when the failure to make any real progress toward decentralization became increasingly difficult to explain away, school administrators often cited Sayre as one of the most successful experiments to date, almost as if they had thought of it themselves. Also fairly successful, despite a crippling degree of infighting, was a program in North Philadelphia through which students from Haverford, Swarthmore, and Bryn Mawr and students and teachers from various Friends schools participated in the operation of an elementary school. All these efforts had sprung more or less from the grass roots; all were supported by powerful community organizations.

The central school administration could point to more than a dozen efforts at encouraging community *participation* through a variety of approaches. By the spring of 1969, however, only one attempt at bringing the schools closer to the community had seriously threatened the balance of power in the school system as a whole. This was the long-term planning project devoted to the role of the community in the new Pickett Middle School, which was scheduled to open in the fall of 1970 in Germantown.

Supported by a wide variety of Germantown civic groups gathered under the umbrella of a comprehensive organization called the Germantown Community Council, the Pickett Ad Hoc Committee had formed in the fall of 1967 with the express purpose of developing a genuine community school. Many of the

Committee's leaders were occupied in what amounted to full-time careers of educational reform. They included Annette Temin—who had fought long and hard against the Anderson administration in what now seemed the old days of school activism—and Geisha Berkowitz, head of the Community Council's education committee and a prominent foe of the powerful old-guard Home and School Council. There were also heads of various sympathetic home and school associations (an affiliation with the Council did not enforce undying loyalty), several ministers, administrators of the local school district, teachers, and even occasional students in the group of fifty or so who pursued discussions and plans in semi-weekly meetings. But opponents were quick to point out that the group was almost entirely middle-class in background and that it lacked a broad base of community support. The school administration, at any rate, recognized the Pickett group as a potential leader in the move toward decentralization, especially because it began to attract attention at about the same time that the Model School District collapsed—a time when the Shedd team desperately needed "viable programs."

The outcome of the Ad Hoc Committee's efforts was probably more sad than tragic, though if tragedy is defined by a fall from a high place, a self-shattering realization of failure, the Committee certainly qualified. Divided into separate groups covering such facets of the proposed school's operations as staff, curriculum, and physical plant, the Pickett Committee, in its year and some months of existence, very nearly became a functioning school staff itself, so well informed were its members in the intricacies of innovative education, school management, and politics. There was probably no citizen group in the city better prepared to participate in the operation of a school.

But the question of guidelines remained open. "Guidelines" was one of the up-and-coming battle cries of urban school conflicts, and it would probably see heavy duty at the front in years to come. There had been *no* guidelines for the New York experiments, reporters close to the scene often observed—that was the cause of all the chaos. Without guidelines, "meaningful steps" toward decentralization could not be taken. Guidelines would have to be established, Mark Shedd finally told the Pickett Ad

Hoc Committee during a crucial meeting in May 1968, for the entire system. Shedd's meaning was clear: The committee could not possibly expect to be granted the kind of power it had sought from the beginning.

The May meeting was the turning point for the Pickett group, but the actual defeat came rather quietly early that summer. It was during the final preparation of the official proposal, in which the powers of the Pickett board were to be defined, that the Shedd administration heeded the warnings of the teachers' union, the principals' association, and even the Home and School Council. In private meetings at 21st Street during the month of July, representatives of the various groups gathered to discuss the proposal, and the result, for the Committee at least, was total humiliation. The Board's main concession to the Pickett board was the power to consult with the district superintendent in the evaluation of the principal. But even this prerogative was somewhat vaguely defined, and the absence of any mention of an actual veto suggested that the opinion of the community board would be largely advisory. Members of the Shedd team claimed that the Pickett board would be a major step toward decentralization, and their optimism was duly reported in the city's newspapers.

What had gone wrong? Why had the group's resolve weakened? Why had the committee not fought the obvious moves to castrate its proposals? The official head of the Pickett Committee, some apologetic colleagues pointed out, had once been a student of Reverend Henry Nichols, the vice-president of the Board of Education; there had been a certain reluctance to oppose, a certain timidity. Others said that they could not, in all conscience, provoke the kind of confrontation that had shattered the New York school system. Some observers also believed that the very fact that the Board had made the committee's job easier by providing a sympathetic, well-informed community coordinator had weakened its opposition. The twenty-five-year-old radical activist who had handled the job expressed tacit agreement with this view by resigning from the planning office at the end of August.

Whatever the reasons for the Pickett Committee's reluctance to fight for what every sympathetic observer believed it deserved, the castrated proposal was passed by the Board at its first September meeting with no serious opposition. Temporarily, at least, nobody's power had been transferred to anybody else.

For two months or so after the Pickett defeat, a small and constantly dwindling group of Germantown left-wingers who called themselves the Concerned Citizens and decried the new Pickett board as an outright fraud tried to stir up some action in the community for a much more extensive school take-over. The group's largest, best-attended meeting even featured Rhody McCoy, the mythic leader of Ocean-Hill Brownsville, who imparted subtle revolutionary cues. The Concerned Citizens began with the goal of organizing a community board that would have control not only over the new middle school but all its feeder schools as well. But after several weeks of diminishing enthusiasm, the effort succumbed to a bad case of opinionated debate.

Rhetoricians of the New Left might well have said that the Philadelphia Board of Education and the Shedd administration were insidiously undermining the community in order to maintain their own supremacy, but Shedd's actions seemed to be prompted more by timidity than by deviousness. If Shedd had given the Pickett board the power it wanted, he would have provoked a confrontation with the teachers and principals that could easily have ruined everything else he was striving for. The note of insincerity was merely the product of the subsequent publicity, in which the Board and administration attempted to pass off the Pickett committee as an important step, when it was actually another sop to the community's impatience, another measure for buying time.

In the long run, of course, such half-measures as the official Pickett board might prove some of the New Left rhetoric correct. It was possible that by throwing scraps of power to the community in frequent experimental gestures, the central powers could avoid the great battles that had rocked New York. It was possible, but highly unlikely. After the collapse of the decentralization commission, activists throughout the city began, in ever larger numbers, to organize their own movements toward control of the schools. Somebody would inevitably force a confrontation, and as community groups developed increasingly sophisticated approaches, the per capita pupil resources that the school system acquired through tax revenues promised to become a major issue. The big push among some of the best-informed groups would be founded, it seemed, on the contention that they had a legal right to educate their children as they pleased and that the city and state should allocate per capita funds to individuals or groups, rather than to such vested powers as a single public school system. Some activists expected that eventually the issue would be taken to court—and appealed to Washington, if necessary.

The question of per capita expenditures, perhaps more vividly than any other facet of community control of education, reflected the general tendency of twentieth-century post-industrial civilization: An exact allocation of per-pupil expenditure was the most do-your-own-thing alternative conceivable, the most consciously anarchic scheme that could exist within a governed system. And implicit in the entire movement, from community "participation" on the one hand to per-capita expenditure allocations on the other, was the basic assumption that somehow the quality of one's "education"—of one's life, in effect—was directly linked to having power over one's own destiny, that power was indeed the ultimate turn-on.

The mammoth, titanically authoritative Coleman Report, the most comprehensive survey of the nation's educational system ever carried out, had suggested this. The Office of Economic Opportunity had based its war against poverty on the assumption that it was so. Communities must have a voice in the institutions that run their lives, liberal intellectuals of the 1960's believed; there must be maximum feasible participation. The system was the enemy; only if everybody became his own boss could the sick society hope to achieve a semblance of health. From the most inventive minds, from a collective unconscious of the intellectual elite, had sprung the single idea that was tearing America to shreds, the idea that by the last third of the century had raged beyond anybody's control: Power to the individual; power to the community—and let the People fight for their future.

There was a chance, of course, that the nation would not survive the struggle for power that all the well-intentioned democrats from Harvard had unleashed. Perhaps America would someday make slavery official, instead of informal as it had been since 1865, and resolve all power struggles through governmental directive—that too was not inconceivable. But for the moment the nation's power elite was content to watch in chagrin as the intercommunity battles that it had initiated with all good intent accelerated into large-scale civil war. The price of participatory democracy, it seemed, could well be world-wide strife, but it took more courage and power than anybody had to buck the trend.

The schools were important; but in time the police, the fire departments, the hospitals, and every other public institution would come under attack in the great power grab that engulfed urban America. With the Philadelphia Federation of Teachers leading the opposition to community control at the American Federation of Teachers conference early in 1969, all of Philadelphia was girding itself for a holocaust.

To the extent that everything that happens in a person's life is part of his education, community control of schools was certainly a legitimate educational goal—feelings of power, as the Coleman Report had asserted, could be as salutary in the classroom as they were anywhere else. But "community control" could never be an adequate substitute for a desperately needed redistribution of wealth.

Poverty was only one facet of the nation's sickness, and it lacked the psychic strength of other, more subtle factors. Universal socialism, controlled by a benevolent oligarchy, would certainly by an efficient solution to world poverty, but to most left-wing activists it would mean bigger and more pernicious bureaucracies, more alienation and "dehumanization" than ever. The real yearning that lay beneath so much of the protest in America, the lust for participatory anarchy—most of it inspired by those who lacked nothing in material wealth—was more complex than the communist aspirations that motivated the activism of the 1930's; but the advocates of community control ignored the fact that complete individual freedom, based on maximum individual power, and complete social equality could not possibly coexist in a world choking to death from the sheer numbers of human beings. The more just the redistribution of wealth, the more freedom and power each individual would have to surrender to the state and the general good. Social justice was scarce, but individualism in an overcrowded era of mass electronic communication was even more precious.

Zbigniew Brzezinzski, a determinedly establishment-oriented historian, had horrified liberal intellectuals throughout the country with his essay on student revolutionaries, published in *The New Republic* of June 1, 1968, but his theme echoed through the media for months afterwards: Humanism, he maintained, was simply obsolete. The radicals who called for participatory democracy represented the "last gasp" of a dying order. Indeed, the vision of Orwell was so close that at times—on a sunny day on Park Avenue, perhaps, with the skyscrapers gleaming and the eyes of the harried passersby so empty—it was real enough to touch. The Orwellian future was at hand; the data banks were already filling up with information. And for a while "community control" seemed to be the magic gimmick that would stop it from happening.

But the Orwellian future could be a painless, happy time. Psychodrama and encounter sessions were fun, after all; someday the Pennsylvania Advancement School might well market mass-produced turn-on curricula to delight students everywhere. It might not be altogether horrible. One could envision an era when the means of production would have been mastered completely, and the social upheavals of the sixties, seventies, and eighties would have passed—hopefully, with a minimum of bloodshed and repression. The humanists and individuals would be taken care of somehow—perhaps on collective farms where they would be free to pursue their antiquated ideas in tribal isolation. George Leonard, the *Look* editor who was a buddy of Marshall McLuhan and Terry Borton, had envisioned the turned-on future in his book *Education and Ecstasy*, and though Leonard's had seemed an exaggerated vision, so had Orwell's when he published *Nineteen Eighty-four*.

The survival of the liberal administration of Mark Shedd, in the light of these broader patterns of social change, was of relatively small importance, of course. Richardson Dilworth, the beautiful prince, would eventually retire, no more able to predict with confidence that he had assured a healthy future for the school system than he could have been about the city—but at least he had tried. Eventually the legitimacy of the Philadelphia

Educational Home Rule Charter, the great progressive reform of 1965, would be tested by anti-establishment community groups seeking per capita allocation of funds. And God only knew what changes would occur in City Hall.

But these would all be the smaller battles, the skirmishes. Even the New York school strikes and the haggling over decentralization in Albany and the subsequent struggles for power in the nation's largest city would eventually fade into the over-all fabric of change. They were mere rumblings in relation to the larger questions: What would become of America in the twenty-first century? Could the human race survive? And if the human race could survive, could that elusive dream called humanity survive with it?

Trolley on Erie Avenue

IRREPRESSIBLY JAUNTY TODAY, with a happy scarf tossed over my shoulder, I board the trolley at the front, fumble for change, lean toward the driver to inquire about the route, then turn to the rear. I see a wide aisle extending about three-quarters the length of the car, single seats on one side, doubles on the other; then the rear exit door and, at the back, two rows of double seats and a full-width seat across the end. Without too much thought, I realize that the back is a more appealing place to be—physically more intimate and filled with kids. There is a palpable contrast between the adult word of moderation and politeness in the front of the trolley and the boisterousness of the rear.

Walking toward the kids, I see that they're all black. I wonder what school they're from, search my memory-map for the closest. My thoughts are tinged briefly with anger when I consider that they are probably in an all-black school. I am still hung up on the injustice of it.

Chaos, as I said, in the kids' domain. To my left, facing rear, a group of girls sit quietly, but they are goody-goodies. Behind them, boys climb over the seats, shouting obscenities—at each other, but somehow the obscenities shoot toward the front of the bus with the precision of arrows: "Give me that, you mutha-fucka!" "Sumbitch, leggo!" A few leaders have formed a ring; around it, a penumbra of hangers-on moving in and out, trying to get a look at whatever is going on inside.

I see that they have seen me. What, now, did I have in mind?

To start a discussion about how the black kids of Philadelphia can improve their self-concept and further social progress? To introduce myself and tell them I'm writing a book about the Philadelphia schools and I care about them? I stop at the exit door, looking at them all the time, and I think they see by my expression that I am on their side—they look me over carefully enough; they're only curious, that's to be expected. So I park myself by the door, leaning on a steel pole, watching them and enjoying their energy as they move among the seats like climbers on a jungle gym. I've made it clear that I'd rather be back here with them, but, by not going any further, I've let them know I respect their rights.

The surprise (I have been standing here for a couple of minutes, at least, before it happens) is a terribly long moment— all the thoughts occur within a few seconds, but each one remains separate and distinct. First, I realize that something strange has happened to my eyesight, that my eyes have almost literally fallen to the floor. I see floor, floor, rubber-tread material; I feel that I have no control over what my eyes are doing. With effort I focus them; I am looking at the goody-goody girls on my left. Their eyes are huge, popping white out of their dark faces, intent on me. Gaining more control, I manage to look toward the back; again, the kids are staring at me. My eyes move slowly down the row of seats on the right, then finally come to rest on the gleaming blade of a knife. A boy about my size is holding it pointed upwards and at me. Finally I look into his eyes. The back of the car is utterly still; all the kids are waiting to see what I will do.

The boy's eyes demand a response. "I have a solemn duty to challenge you," they say, "and attack you if you make the wrong move." I want to believe that this duty he has taken upon himself has nothing to do with me personally and involves little real emotion, that it is rather some kind of ritual, a necessary response of the now-sacred black world that I have invaded. Even the hatred in his eyes could be an illusion.

"Do you expect me to take that away from you?" I could say. But how could I say it without making it a challenge? "Now what do you want to do *that* for?"—another possibility instantly rejected. These thoughts are taking precious seconds; I don't think he has moved at all—we've been standing in equipoise, a frozen tableau, seconds ticking. The ritual will force him to move if I don't do something.

I cannot handle it with words, I decide. (What is on my face? Something about my expression holds him off, at least.) Finally, I turn slowly away from him to face the exit door, lean again on the steel pole, and take out my *Bulletin* to read. I only pretend to read, of course, as I wait for the awkward rending of my coat and the sting of pain—where? in the back? in the ticklish small of the back? in the neck? (that would be more intelligent).

Within a minute the noise and activity resume.

I crane my neck downwards to check the street signs, wonder where the kids will be getting off—my own destination is the Board Street subway. I envision the follow-ups, the confrontation on the sidewalk, the pursuit, the corralling in the subway. Then someone vacates a single seat at about the middle of the trolley; if I take it, this might be an admission of more fear than they suspect, and once they know I'm *that* afraid, we'll lose the balance. Anything, though, to get out of range. I sort of mosey, amble to the seat, as if I don't really give a shit. It works. And when we finally reach Broad Street, stepping down from the trolley, I make sure to look directly at anyone who happens to get in the way of my steady-straight vision. I make it to the subway.

I'm probably more afraid than I need to be—hours before the fear actually leaves me. Why don't they have cops down here? I think as I wait on the subway platform. Yes, even those cops who beat the kids with their clubs during the November 17 demonstration. The subway is indescribably bleak, dim, and sooty, an almost melodramatic setting for fear. The platforms are crowded with kids, many of them white. I am still being purposefully casual, reading my *Bulletin*. Where did my friends from the trolley go, anyway? I could not risk looking as we got off the car.

A black kid with short hair—sixth or seventh grade—comes up to me. "Hi," he says in a soft voice, a fragile whisper, almost as if he were imitating a queer.

"Hello." My mouth is tight. "Are you from the Advancement School?" It is the only school I've been at regularly enough to be recognized. I think I hear him whisper yes. "Uh . . . well uh what team are you on?"

He smiles intensely. "Six."

There are four teams at the Advancement School, and I immediately conclude that this scene is being watched by vigilantes stationed behind the thick pillars, that I have almost had it. I search for a place to run to.

"Can you give me a quarter for carfare?" Again that frail whisper. But the smile on his lips gives him away; it's insidious, scheming. Perhaps they won't mug me; maybe they just want to see me give away all my money—I picture a procession of beggars, all smiling gently, mockingly.

"I don't have any money to give you," I answer.

The smile remains as he turns away.

A few minutes later I see from the protection of my newspaper that he is approaching everyone on the platform with his shy smile and that they lean forward in order to hear his request.